François Rabelais

The inestimable life of the great Gargantua, father of Pantagruel

François Rabelais

The inestimable life of the great Gargantua, father of Pantagruel

ISBN/EAN: 9783337665159

Printed in Europe, USA, Canada, Australia, Japan

Cover: Foto ©ninafisch / pixelio.de

More available books at **www.hansebooks.com**

THE WORKS OF
FRANÇOIS RABELAIS

TRANSLATED BY SIR THOMAS URQUHART
AND PETER MOTTEUX, WITH THE
NOTES OF DUCHAT, OZELL, AND
OTHERS; INTRODUCTION
AND REVISION BY
ALFRED WALLIS

BOOK I.

FRANÇOIS RABELAIS.

INTRODUCTION

THERE is happily no necessity, at the close of this century of progress and enlightenment, to preface a new edition of the Works of Doctor François Rabelais (calling himself anagrammatically Monsieur Alcofribas Nasier) with an apology for printing it. If such an apology were needed, the statement that the translation used in these volumes has been, in one form or another, before the English-reading public for upwards of two centuries would be deemed by most people (it is known to have influenced the decision of one of our most eminent judges in favour of *Rabelais* considered as an English classic) a sufficient defence against possible attacks from the professional puritan. It is equally unnecessary to enlarge upon the aims and objects with which this most remarkable man composed his romances, seeing that the subject has already been exhaustively treated in the prefixes to the present edition.

The French have, indeed, raised their favourite author to a pinnacle of fame, which would surprise no one more completely than the object of their veneration himself, who was a humourist of the first rank, to whom the oppression of monkish abuses from which the people of his time were just emerging was not so much the object of righteous indignation as an irresistible incentive to hearty laughter. He was the link between the writers of romance and those of simple merriment. Great part of his book is a burlesque romance into which he has introduced a vein of buffoonery that is quite in accordance with the spirit of his age; and, notwithstanding Coleridge's belief in the depth and subtlety of the Gargantuan and Pantagruelian conceptions, we ought not to lose sight of the author's express declaration to the effect that he wrote them for the recreation of persons languishing in sickness, or under the pressure of grief and anxiety, and that his merry prescriptions had succeeded with many patients. 'Que plusieurs gens, langoureux, malades, ou autrement fachez et desolez, avoient à la lecture d'icelles, trompè leur ennui temps joyeusement passé, et reçue allegresse et consolation nouvelle.' And he adds, 'Seulement avois égard et intention pour escrit donner ce peu de soulagement que pouvois ès affligez et malades absens.' The religious disputes which then agitated Europe were, as Dr Ferriar says, subjects of ridicule too tempting to be withstood; this, with his abuse of the monks, excited such a clamour against him that Francis I., being informed that his book was full of heresies, expressed a strong desire to hear it read, and, as the story says, the king 'found no passage therein which could be mistrusted.'

It is true that Rabelais has been held up by
several writers at home and abroad as the founder
of French scepticism; but the late Mr Buckle,
a competent critic, after close examination of his
writings, could find nothing to justify such an
opinion. He certainly treats the clergy with
great disrespect, and takes every opportunity of
covering them with ridicule, but his attacks are
made rather upon personal vices than upon the
narrow and intolerant spirit to which those vices
were chiefly to be ascribed.[1] Readers are often
inclined, however, to regard with veneration that
which they do not understand, and to suppose
depth and gravity in a work in proportion to its
darkness, and it is probable that Rabelais is
indebted to the obscurity of his language for a
large share of his reputation as a social and
religious reformer. But Coleridge boldly ac-
credits him with the highest objects in a passage
that is well worth quoting in this connection :—
    'Beyond a doubt Rabelais was among the
deepest, as well as boldest, thinkers of his age
His buffoonery was not merely Brutus' rough
stick which contained a rod of gold; it was
necessary as an amulet against the monks and
legates. Never was there a more plausible, and
seldom, I am persuaded, a less appropriate line,
than the thousand times quoted

    Rabelais laughing in his easy-chair

of Mr Pope. The caricature of his filth and

[1] See a striking passage in the *History of Civilisation in
England*, Vol. II., chap. I.   Longmans, 1878, 3 vol.

zanyism shows how fully he both knew and
felt the danger in which he stood. I could
write a treatise in praise of the moral elevation
of Rabelais' work, which would make the
Church stare and the Conventicle groan, and
yet would be truth and nothing but truth. I
class Rabelais with the greatest creative minds of
the world—Shakspeare, Dante, Cervantes, etc.'[2]

It is not easy to determine the precise date of
the first translation of Rabelais into English.
Certain entries in the Registers of the Stationers'
Company indicate a period between 1592 and
1594; but not even the fragment of a sixteenth
century edition has survived to our own day.
It is certain that Shakspeare and Ben Jonson,
amongst the Elizabethan dramatists, were cognis-
ant of the name and attributes of the famous
giant Gargantua; but whether from actual
knowledge or merely from hearsay cannot now
be determined. The entries are thus quoted by
Mr W. C. Hazlitt[3] :—

Gargantua his prophesie. Licensed to John Wolf, 6th April
1592.
A booke entituled Gargantua. Licensed to someone, name
not given, 1592, and entry cancelled.
The Historie of Gargantua. Licensed conditionally to John
Danter, 4th Dec. 1595.

Of these three entries, the first and second
refer in all probability to one and the same
work, perhaps founded upon the ' Prophetical

[2] *Coleridge's Literary Remains.* I., pp. 138-9.
[3] *Collections and Notes,* ii., 508.

Riddle' fabled by Rabelais to have been discovered engraven upon a copper plate in digging
out the foundations of the Abbey of Theleme,
and attributed by him to Merlin de Saint Gelais.
The third, *The Historie of Gargantua*, is remarkable as having been licensed 'conditionally' to
John Danter the printer, who in 1597 put forth
the *editio princeps* of *Romeo and Juliet*. We
have said that no evidence exists that either or
any of the works so licensed were ever printed,
yet Shakspeare (*As You Like It*, iii., 2) makes
Celia say (in response to Rosalind's demand,
'Answer me in one word') 'You must
borrow me Gargantua's mouth first; 'tis a
word too great for any mouth of this age's
size.' This comedy is supposed to have first
appeared in 1599 or 1600. Ben Jonson, whose
Every Man in His Humour was printed in 1596,
has also a reference therein to Gargantua, and
similar instances might be extracted from other
dramatic works of about the same period.
There is also a bit of gibberish in *Twelfth Night*
(Act ii., sc. 3). 'When thou spokest of
Pigrogromitus, of the Vapians passing the
equinoctial of Queubus'—which a recent
commentator, Mr W. F. Smith, thinks may
have been 'possibly borrowed' from the speech
of Kissbreech before Pantagruel; it certainly
has a Rabelaisian flavour. Some French authors
have asserted the existence of a giant called
'Gargantua' in a romance which gave Rabelais
his first ideas upon the subject; but we
cannot discuss the point here. Speculation in

this direction is somewhat restricted, and as the researches of the late Mr J. O. Halliwell-Phillipp failed to bring to light even a fragment of an Elizabethan *Rabelais*, we may well despair of future success. Our author in his English dress must needs have had to encounter far more than the ordinary hazards that await books in general during their pilgrimage. Dibdin, it will be remembered by my bibliographical readers, accounts for the great rarity of the black-letter editions of Stubbes' *Anatomie of Abuses* (1583, etc.) by supposing that 'for the credit of the age and of a virgin reign . . . every virtuous dame threw the copy of his book which came into her possession behind the fire.'[4] Rabelais could scarcely expect better treatment than Stubbes at the hands of an Elizabethan matron.

But between the humorous and extravagant licentiousness of Rabelais, and the scarcely less objectionable puritanical indecencies of Philip Stubbes, there are many gradations which do not now concern us, although we fancy that the old 'anatomist's' opinion upon the works of Master Doctor Rabelais would have furnished a piquant addition to his chapter upon books, 'inuented and excogitat by *Belzebub*, written by *Lucifer*, licensed by *Pluto*, printed by *Cerberus*, and set a broche to sale by the infernal Furies themselves, to the poysning of the whole world.'[5]

So far as we are able to ascertain, the first

---

[4] *Bibliomania*, 1811, p. 367 (Note).
[5] *Anatomie of Abuses*, 1583. Sig. P. vij, *verso*.

translation of any portion of the writings of
Rabelais was made by Robert Hayman, who
appears to have been Governor of the Planta-
tions 'at Harbor-Grace, in Britaniola, anciently
called Newfound-Land.' His *Quodlibets*, printed
at 'London by Elizabeth All-de for Roger
Michell, dwelling in Pauls Church-yard at the
signe of the Bulls-Head, 1628,' quarto, contained 'two Epistles of that excellently wittie
Doctor Francis Rablais. Translated out of his
French at large.' Copies of this rare book are
in the British Museum and Bodleian Libraries,
and one was marked twelve guineas in the
Bibliotheca Anglo-Poetica. These excerpts are
'A rayling epistle, written . . . by F. Rabalais'
(*sic*), and 'Another epistle of . . . F. Rabelais
in praise of a grave Matrone,' translations
similar no doubt to those which are given at
the end of the present collection, and which
serve to show that some attempt at bringing
'the witty doctor' before English readers took
place prior to Sir Thomas Urquhart's venture,
made fifteen years later. This translation,
which is given entire in the succeeding volumes,
was not completed by the versatile Scot, who
died before arriving at the conclusion of his
task, and whose pen was taken up by Peter
Motteux, the translator of *Don Quixote* and
other works.

Sir Thomas Urquhart of Cromartie, Knight,
who was, in the opinion of his contemporaries, a
remarkable man, is alluded to by Motteux in his
preface to *Rabelais* as 'a learned physician,' an

error which may have arisen out of his author-
ship of certain mathematical works, etc.
(Motteux using the word 'physician' in the
sense of *physicist*), for there appears to be no
other foundation for the statement. Amongst
his other performances, he wrote 'A Peculiar
Promptuary of Time . . . showing the Pedigree of the Name of Urquhart in the
House of Cromartie since the Creation to 1652.'
8vo, London, 1652. From this strange book
we learn that he was knighted at Whitehall
by Charles I. in 1645, accompanied Charles II.
from Scotland, and was taken prisoner at the
battle of Worcester and sent to London, where,
having been enlarged upon his parole, he employed himself in literary work. He had been
a considerable traveller, and was well-skilled in
the languages of most of the polished countries
of Europe ; his *Epigrams* prove him something of
a wit, and his firm belief in himself, as evinced
in his *Discovery of a most Exquisite Jewel*, 1652, is
particularly characteristic. This latter book contains in every page the evidence of Urquhart's
obligations to Rabelais, as quotations would amply
show, but we must content ourselves with referring our readers to an excellent article in the
Retrospective Review,[6] wherein the *Discovery* is
examined. At present, we are more particularly
concerned with his translation of *Rabelais*, which
is accounted by the best judges to be the most
perfect version of any author whatever, equalled

[6] *Ret. Rev.*, Vol. VI., pp. 177-206.

only by Charles Cotton's admirable rendering of Montaigne's *Essays*, which much resembles it in the force and vigour with which, notwithstanding the obscurity, singularity, and difficulty of the original, the author's spirit has been transfused into a foreign language. Urquhart's *Rabelais* was first published by Richard Boddeley with a title dated 1653, to which, after Urquhart's death, *circa* 1660, was prefixed a general title dated 1664; in 1694, the translation made by Motteux to conclude the work appeared, and in 1708 the complete translation was published, with a preface by Motteux. From this beginning may be said to have sprung all the English editions with and without notes, illustrated and plain, that have since found their places in our libraries. One of the most careful of recent translators admits that his work has been done 'with Urquhart lying open and compared paragraph by paragraph,' adding that 'it was curious to note how the translations of a paragraph would prove almost identical word for word till a closer examination of the text showed that there could hardly be any variation in a faithful version.'[7]

Of Peter Motteux it may be enough to say that he was a Frenchman, who, commencing as a merchant in London, subsequently took up literature as his professed vocation. He stands to Sir Thomas Urquhart in much the same relation as Charles Cotton to Izaak Walton in the compilation of *The Compleat Angler*, 1676.

[7] *Rabelais* . . . by W. F. Smith, 1893, Vol. I., ix.

The influence of Rabelais upon English literature in the eighteenth century has been greater than many persons would willingly admit. Burton had studied him, as the *Anatomy of Melancholy* amply testifies; Sterne has imitated him, and *Tristram Shandy* owes much of its piquancy to passages which, as Dr Ferriar has shown, were incorporated from Rabelais and other French writers of the same school. A shoal of minor humourists, poets and essayists have pillaged right and left from the stores of sterling wit and humour which Rabelais intermingled even with the grossest parts of his book, and English novelists have availed themselves of all sorts of plots and episodes from the same prolific source. 'But for thee, Master Françoys, thou art not well liked in this island of ours . . . yet thou hast thy friends, that meet and drink to thee and wish thee well wheresoever thou has found thy *grand peut-être!*'[8]

It only remains to be added that the notes and references which encumbered the former editions of this version have been revised and considerably abridged, other illustrations having been added in some cases where the obscurity of the text seems to have been augmented by the efforts of the commentators to enlighten it. The interminable references to Pliny and other authors upon natural history are also curtailed, and much of Mr Motteux's prefatory matter, now obsolete, has been omitted. It is hoped

[8] Andrew Lang. *Letters to Dead Authors*, London, 1886, p. 74.

that this condensation, whilst leaving the text precisely as it is to be found in the earlier editions of Urquhart and Motteux, will satisfy readers who have hitherto complained, and with justice, of the tendency to overload the original with useless references and far-fetched speculations. The pictorial illustrations are reproductions in photogravure of those engraved for the Amsterdam edition of 1741 in three volumes quarto, and known as Picart's edition.

ALFRED WALLIS.

CONTENTS

VOL. I. xvii *b*

Contents

Contents

LIST OF PLATES

THE
Life of Rabelais

Francis Rabelais was born about the year 1483, at Chinon, a very ancient little town, situate near the place where the river Vienne loses itself into the Loire, in the province of Touraine, in France. His father, Thomas Rabelais, was an apothecary of that town, and possessed an estate called La Devinière ; [1] near which place, having first sent his son Francis to be educated by the monks of the abbey of Seuillé, and finding that he did not improve, he removed him to the university of Angers, where he studied some time at a convent called La Baumette, but without any considerable success. There he became acquainted with Messieurs du Bellay, one of whom was afterwards cardinal : and it is said that Rabelais, having committed some misdemeanour, was there very severely used.

A famous author writes,[2] that he was bred up in a convent of Franciscan friars, in the Lower Poictou, and was received into their order. Which convent can be no other than that of Fontenay-le-Comte,[3] in the said province, where he proved a

[1] Particular. de la Vie et Mœurs de Rabelais, imprim. devant ses Œuvres.
[2] Scævol. Samarthanus, lib. i. Elog. Clar. Vir.
[3] Thresor. Chronolog. de St Romuald, 3d part.

great proficient in learning; insomuch that, of the friars, some envied him, some through ignorance thought him a conjuror, and, in short, all hated and misused him, because he studied Greek, the beauties of which tongue they could not relish; its novelty making them esteem it not only barbarous, but anti-christian. This we partly observe by a letter which Budæus,[4] the most learned man of his age in that tongue, wrote to a friend of Rabelais, wherein he highly praises him, particularly for his excellent knowledge in that tongue, and exclaims against the stupidity and ingratitude of those friars.

Thus Rabelais, hating the ignorance and baseness of the Cordeliers, was desirous enough to leave them, being but too much prompted to it by several persons of eminent quality, who were extremely delighted with his learning and facetious conversation.

A monk relates,[5] that he was put *in pace*, that is, between four walls, with bread and water, in the said convent, for some unlucky action; and was re-deemed out of it by the learned Andrew Tiraqueau, then lieutenant-general (that is, chief judge) of the bailiwick of Fontenay-le-Comte; and, by tradition, it is said in that town that, on a day when the country people used to resort to the convent church to address their prayers, and pay their offerings to the image of St Francis, which stood in a place somewhat dark near the porch, Rabelais, to ridicule their superstition, privately removed the saint's image, and placed himself in its room, having first disguised himself: but at last, too much pleased with the awkward worship which was paid him, he could not forbear laughing, and made some motion; which being observed by his gaping staring worshippers,

---

4 Budæus Græc. Epist.   5 P. de St Romuald. Feuillant.

they cried out, 'A miracle! my good lord St Francis
moves!' Upon which an old crafty knave of a
friar, who knew stone and the virtue of St Francis
too well to expect this should be true, drawing near,
scared our sham-saint out of his hole; and, having
caused him to be seized, the rest of the fraternity,
with their knotty cords on his bare back, soon made
him know he was not made of stone, and to wish
he had been as hard as the image, or turned into
the very image of which he lately was the representation.

At last, by the intercession of friends, of which
Geoffrey d'Estissac, Bishop of Maillezais,[6] is said to
have been one, he obtained Pope Clement VII.'s
permission to leave the beggarly fellowship of St
Francis, for the wealthy and more easy order of St
Benedict, and was entertained in that bishop's
chapter, that is, the Abbey of Maillezais. But his
mercurial temper prevailing after he had lived some
time there, he also left it; and, laying down the
regular habit, to take that which is worn by secular
priests, he rambled up and down awhile, till at last
he fixed at Montpellier, took all his degrees as a
physician in that university, and practised physic
with reputation. And by his epistle before the
translation of the Aphorisms of Hippocrates, and
some works of Galen, which he published and dedicated to the Bishop of Maillezais in 1532, he tells
him that he publicly read physic in that university
to a numerous auditory.

It is vulgarly said, that Rabelais having published
some medical tract, which did not sell, told the
disappointed bookseller that since people did not
know how to value a good book, they would un-

[6] The bishop's see is now removed to Rochelle.

3

doubtedly like a bad one, and that accordingly he would write something that would make him large amends; upon which he composed his Gargantua and Pantagruel, by which the bookseller got an estate. But the same story has been told of our Sir Walter Raleigh and his selfish stationer; and it is a fact that the above-mentioned translation, which was printed by the famous Gryphius of Lyons, at first, in 1532, was reprinted many times before Rabelais began to write his Gargantua.

We do not know how he came to leave Montpellier, though probably he was sent by its university to solicit for them at court, and then was invited to stay at Paris, of which John du Bellay, his friend, afterwards cardinal, was not only bishop, but governor; at least, it is certain he attended him in his embassy to Pope Paul III., though I believe that the chief occasion of his going to Rome was to put a stop to the ecclesiastical censures fulminated against him for leaving his convent; and it is thought the Bishop of Maillezais abetted that desertion, and encouraged him in his studies at Montpellier, which perhaps made Rabelais afterwards dedicate to him, and own then, that he owed all things to him.

It is likely our doctor had then a prospect of the benefices with which he soon afterwards was gratified by that cardinal; and for that reason was glad to be eased of the censures under which he lay, which made him incapable of enjoying anything. The Bishop of Montpellier himself was a Protestant, and might have kept always his bishopric, had he written as mystically as Rabelais. The Cardinal Chatillon also was not only a Protestant, but married, as well as John de Montluc, Bishop of Valence; yet, as well as many others, in those times, who were against the errors of the Church of Rome in

their hearts, they had benefices in it, and favoured
• the Reformation, perhaps more than those who openly
professed it.   So Rabelais seems to me to have passed
into Italy only in the quality of a penitent monk,
being first obliged to submit to his abbot, and the
orders of the convent which he had left many years;
else, had he been then physician to Cardinal du
Bellay,[7] then ambassador to the Pope, he would
not have recommended himself to the alms of his
superior, the Bishop of Maillezais, as he does in
his letters to that prelate; to whom he writes, that
the last money which he had remitted to him was
almost gone; 'though,' says he, 'I have put none
of it to an ill use.'[8]   Neither would he have added,
that he used constantly to eat either with Cardinal
du Bellay, or the Bishop of Mascon, who had succeeded him in the embassy (doubtless upon the
other's promotion to the rank of cardinal), but that
much money was spent in dispatches, clothes, and
chamber-rent; which shows also, that though he,
as a friend, did eat with one of those two, yet he
paid for his lodging elsewhere.   By these letters,
which Messieurs de St Marthe, gentlemen famous
for learning, have not disdained to publish with
their learned and curious observations, of ten times
their length, we see that Rabelais held also a private
correspondence in characters with the Bishop of
Maillezais, to whom they are directed, and that
the bishop was far from being bigotted to Popery.
We also know by them, that Rabelais obtained his
absolution of Pope Paul III. the 17th of January,
1536, whereby he had leave given him to return
to Maillezais, and to practise physic, either at Rome

[7] Epist. de Rabel. Pag. 5, p. 49.
[8] Et si n'en ay rien despendu en meschanceté.   Ibid., Pag. 49.

5

or elsewhere ; that is, without any gain and only by charity. We also find that he had gained the esteem of Cardinal de Genutiis, accounted the ornament of the college, and Cardinal Simonetta, eminent for virtue, and other worthy prelates, besides Cardinal du Bellay, and the Bishop of Mascon, who procured him his bulls gratis, and had even offered him to make use of their king's name had it been needful.[9]

It is said that the cardinal, having brought him with the rest of his retinue to Pope Paul III., that they might beg some favour of his holiness, Rabelais, being bid to make his demand, only begged that his holiness would be pleased to excommunicate him. So strange a request having caused much surprise, he was ordered to say why he made it. Then addressing himself to that Pope, who was doubtless a great man, and had nothing of the moroseness of many others : 'May it please your holiness,' said he, 'I am a Frenchman, of a little town called Chinon, whose inhabitants are thought somewhat too subject to be thrown into a sort of unpleasant bonfires ; and, indeed, a good number of honest men, and, amongst the rest, some of my relations, have been fairly burned there already. Now, would your holiness but excommunicate me, I should be sure never to burn. My reason is, that, passing through the Tarantese, where the cold was very great, in the way to this city, with my Lord Cardinal du Bellay, having reached a little hut, where an old woman lived, we prayed her to make a fire to warm us; but she burned all the straw of her bed to kindle a faggot, yet could not make it burn; so that at last, after many imprecations, she cried, " Without doubt,

<hr>

[9] Sadoletus Ital. Sacr. T. 3.

this faggot was excommunicated by the Pope's own
mouth, since it will not burn." In short, we were
obliged to go on without warming ourselves. Now,
if it pleased your holiness but to excommunicate me
thus, I might go safely to my country.' By this he
not only, in a jesting manner, exposed the Roman
clergy's persecuting temper, but seemed to allude to
the inefficacy of the former Pope's excommunications
in England, and chiefly in Germany, where they
only served to warn our Henry VIII., and, on the
other side, the Lutherans, to secure themselves
against the attempts of their enemies.

He, that would not spare the Pope to his face,
was doubtless not less liberal of his biting jokes to
others; insomuch that he was obliged to leave
Rome without much preparation; not thinking himself safe among the Italians, who, of all men, forgive
raillery the least, when they are the subject of it.

So being come so far as Lyons, on his way to
Paris, very indifferently accoutred, and no money
to proceed, whether he had been robbed, or had
spent all his stock, he, who had a peculiar love for
ease and good eating, and no less zeal for good drinking, found himself in dismal circumstances. So he
had recourse to a stratagem which might have been
of dangerous consequence to one less known than
Rabelais.

Being lodged at the Tower and Angel, a famous
inn in that city, he took some of the ashes in the
chimney, and having wrapped them up in several
little papers, on one of them he writ 'Poison to kill
the King;' in another, 'Poison to kill the Queen;'
in a third, 'Poison to kill the Duke of Orleans;'
and having on the Change met a young merchant,
told him, that being skilled in physiognomy, he
plainly saw that he had a great desire to get an

estate easily; therefore, if he would come to his inn, he would put him in a way to gain a hundred thousand crowns. The greedy merchant was very ready. So, when he had treated our doctor, he came to the main point; that is, how to get the hundred thousand crowns. Then Rabelais, after the other bottle or two, pretending a great deal of caution, at last showed him the papers of powder, and proposed to him to make use of them according to their super-scriptions, which the other promised, and they appointed to meet the next day, to take measures about it ; but the too credulous, though honest trader, immediately ran to a judge, who having heard the information, presently sent to secure Rabelais, the Dauphin having been poisoned some time before: so the doctor, with his powder, was seized, and being examined by the judge, gave no answer to the accusation, save that he told the young merchant that he had never thought him fit to keep a secret, and only desired them to secure what was in the papers, and send him to the King, for he had strange things to say to him.

Accordingly he was carefully sent to Paris, and handsomely treated by the way on free cost, as are all the King's prisoners; and being come to Paris, was immediately brought before the King, who knowing him, asked him what he had done to be brought in that condition, and where he had left the Cardinal du Bellay. Upon this the judge made his report, showed the bills with the powder, and the informations which he had drawn. Rabelais, on his side, told his case, took some of all the powders before the King ; which being found to be only harmless wood ashes, pleaded for the prisoner so effectually, that the business ended in mirth, and the poor judge was only laughed at for his pains.

The jests of Rabelais were sometimes more productive of good, than the deep earnest of others.
Of which the university of Montpellier furnishes
us with an instance : none being admitted to the
degree of doctor of physic there, who has not first
put on the gown and cap of Dr Rabelais, which are
preserved in the castle of Morac in that city.[10]
The cause of this uncommon veneration for the
memory of that learned man is said to be this :

Some scholars having occasioned an extraordinary
disorder in that city, Anthony Duprat, Cardinal,
archbishop of Sens, then Lord Chancellor of France,
upon complaint made of it, caused the university to
be deprived of part of its privileges. Upon this,
none was thought fitter to be sent to Paris to solicit
their restitution than our doctor, who by his wit,
learning, and eloquence, as also by the friends which
they had purchased him at court, seemed capable to
obtain anything. When he came to Paris about
it, the difficulty lay in gaining audience of the
chancellor, who was so incensed, that he refused to
hear anything in behalf of the university of Montpellier. So Rabelais, having vainly tried to be
admitted, at last put on his red gown and doctor's
cap (some say a green gown and a long grey beard)
and thus accoutred, came to the chancellor's palace,
on St Austin's Quay; but the porter and some other
servants mistook him for a madman : so Rabelais
having, in a peremptory tone, been asked there who
he was, let his impertinent querist know, that he
was the gentleman who usually had the honour to
flay bull-calves ; and that, if he had a mind to be
first flayed, he had best make haste and strip immediately. Then being asked some other questions, he

[10] Voyage de l'Europe, T. I.

answered in Latin, which the other understanding not, one of the chancellor's officers that could speak that tongue was brought, who addressing himself to our doctor in Latin, was answered by him in Greek, which the other understanding as little as the first did Latin, a third was fetched who could speak Greek; but he no sooner spoke in that language to Rabelais, but was answered by him in Hebrew; and one, who understood Hebrew, being with much difficulty procured, Rabelais spoke to him in Syriac: thus having exhausted all the learning of the family, the chancellor, who was told, that there was a merry fool at his gate who had outdone every one, not only in languages, but in smartness of repartees, ordered him to be brought in. It was a little before dinner. Then Rabelais, shifting the farcical scene into one more serious, addressed himself to the chancellor with much respect, and having first made his excuse for his forced buffoonery, in a most eloquent and learned speech, so effectually pleaded the cause of his university, that the chancellor, at once ravished and persuaded, not only promised the restitution of the abolished privileges, but made the doctor sit down at table with him, as a particular mark of his esteem.

Much about that time, hearing with what facility, for the sake of a small sum of money, the faculty of Orange (some say Orleans) admitted ignorant pretenders, as doctors of physic, not only without examining, but even without seeing them, Rabelais sent the usual fees, and had one received doctor there unseen, by the name of Doctor Johannes Caballus, and let the wise professors and the world know afterwards, what a worthy member they had admitted into their body, since that very doctor was his horse Jack; or, as some say, his mule: for if there are various lections, there may well be also various traditions of the same passage.

Rabelais being at Paris, and more careful of himself than of his mule, had trusted it to the care of the printer's men, desiring them at least not to let it want water. But he having perhaps forgot to make them drink, they also easily, though uncharitably, forgot the poor brute. At three days' end the creature having drunk as little water as his master, a young unlucky boy took a fancy to get on its back, even like the miller's daughter, without a saddle ; another truant scholar begged to get behind him, so did a third, and eke a fourth. Thus these four being mounted like Aymond's four sons a-horseback on a mule, without bridle or halter, the real and living emblem of folly, the grave animal walked leisurely down St James's Street, till it came near a church, towards which it moved, drawn by the magnetic virtue of the water, which it smelt at a considerable distance, in the holy water-pot, which is always near the porch. And in vain our four riders kicked and called ; in spite of them the headstrong thirsty beast made up to the holy element; and though the church was almost full of people, it being Sunday and sermon-time, notwithstanding all opposition, the bold monster dipped its saucy snout in the sanctified cistern. The people that were near it were not a little amazed at the impudence of that sacrilegious animal, deservedly cursed with sterility, though it were but for this one crime ; many took him for a spectrum that bore some souls, formerly heretical, but now penitent, that came to seek the sweet refrigeratory of the saints, out of the more than hellish flames of purgatory. So the unconcerned mule took a swingeing draught of holy liquor, yet did not like it so well, there being always salt in it,

as to take a second dose; but having somewhat
allayed its raging thirst, modestly withdrew, with
her two brace of youngsters. However, the thing
did not end thus: for the brute was seized, and
Rabelais, being thought none of the greatest admirers
of the Romish fopperies, was shrewdly suspected of
having laid the design of that scandalous adventure.
Nor was the rude four-legged Johannes Caballus
released out of the pound, till its master had dearly
paid for its drink.

As he ridiculed the superstition of priests, he
also was extremely free in his reflections on the
monks, and truly he knew them too well to love
and esteem them; he is said not to have been able
to refrain his satirical temper, even while he was
reading public service; and instead of *Qui mœchantur
cum illâ,* as the Vulgate has it, to have said aloud *Qui
monachantur cum illâ.*

It is also said, that as he was kneeling once at
church, before the statue of King Charles VIII., a
monk came and said to him, that doubtless he mistook that king's statue for that of some saint ; but
Rabelais immediately replied, ' I am not so much a
monk (blockhead, I mean) as thou thinkest me; nor
yet so blind as not to know that I kneel before the
representation of King Charles VIII., for whose soul
I was praying, because he brought the pox out of
Naples into this kingdom, by which means I and
other physicians have been considerable gainers.'

Several physicians being once assembled to consult
about an hypochondriac humour, which confined
Cardinal du Bellay to his bed; they at last resolved
that an aperitive (opening) decoction should be prepared, to be frequently taken with some syrup by
the patient. Now Rabelais, who was his physician,
perhaps not being of their opinion, while the rest of

Life of Rabelais

our learned doctors were still discoursing in their
scientific jargon, to deserve the large fee, caused a
fire to be made in the yard, and on it to be set a
kettle full of water, into which he had put as many
keys as he could get: and while he was very busy
in stirring them about with a stick, the doctors,
coming down, saw him, and asked what he was
doing? 'Following your directions,' replied he.
'How, in the name of Galen?' cried one of them.
'You are for something that may be very aperitive,'
returned Rabelais, 'and by Hippocrates, I think you
will own that nothing can be more aperitive than
keys, unless you would have me to send to the
arsenal for some pieces of cannon.' This odd fancy
being immediately related to the sick cardinal, set
him into such a fit of laughing, that it helped more
to cure him than the prescription; and what made
the jest the more pertinent was, that keys are made
of iron and steel, which with water are the chief
ingredients in chalybeate medicines.

Hearing that the grave John Calvin, somewhat
prejudiced against him for his biting jokes, had
played on his name by the way of anagram; saying
'Rabelæsius—Rabie læsus,' Anglicè 'madman;' he,
with an admirable presence of mind, immediately
returned the compliment in the same kind, saying,
'Calvin—Jan Cul,' Anglicè 'Jack Arse,' adding that
there was anagram for anagram, and that a studied
trifle only deserved to be paid back with one worse,
extempore.

Thus while, like Democritus, he made himself
merry with the impertinences of mankind, nothing
was able to allay his mirth, unless it were the
thought of a reckoning, at the time that he paid it;
then, indeed, he was thought somewhat serious,
though probably it was partly that those who were

13

to receive it, might not impose on him and the company, and because he generally found his purse not overfull. However, the time of paying a shot in a tavern among good fellows, or Pantagruelists, is still called, in France, le quart d'heure de Rabelais ; that is, Rabelais's quarter of an hour (when a man is uneasy or melancholy).

Yet his enemies, the monks, and some others, tell us, that he seemed much less concerned when he paid the grand shot of life, than when he discharged a small tavern reckoning; for they say that he faced death with an unconcerned and careless countenance; and, in short, that he died just as he had lived. They relate the thing thus:—

Rabelais being very sick, Cardinal du Bellay sent his page to him, to have an account of his condition; his answer was, ' Tell my lord in what circumstances thou findest me; I am just going to leap into the dark. He is up in the cock-loft, bid him keep where he is. As for thee, thou'lt always be a fool: let down the curtain, the farce is done.'[11] A little before this he called for his domino (so some in France call a sort of hood which certain ecclesiastics wear), saying, ' Put me on my domino, for I am cold : besides, I will die in it, for Beati qui in Domino moriuntur.' An author,[12] who styles Rabelais a man of excellent learning, writes, that he being importuned by some to sign a will, whereby they had made him bestow on them legacies that exceeded his ability, he, to be no more disturbed, complied at last with their desires; but when they came to ask

[11] Je m'en vay chercher un grand peut-estre. Il est au nid de la pie. Which, verbatim Englished, is, I am going to seek, or look for, a great *may-be* (doubt or uncertainty). He is in the pye's nest, etc.
[12] Thov. His. de Jean Clopinel.

14

him where they should find a fund answerable to what he gave ; 'As for that,' replied he, 'you must do like the spaniel, look about and search ;' then, adds that author, having said, 'Draw the curtain, the farce is over,' he died.   Likewise a monk [13] not only tells us that he ended his life with that jest, but that he left a paper sealed up, wherein were found three articles as his last will, 'I owe much, I have nothing, I give the rest to the poor.'

The last story, or that before it, must undoubtedly be false; and perhaps both are so, as well as the message by the page; though Friegius [14] relates also, that Rabelais said, when he was dying, 'Draw the curtain,' etc.   But if he said so, many great men have said much the same.   Thus Augustus,[15] near his death, asked his friends whether he had not very well acted the farce of life ?   And Demonax, one of the best philosophers, when he saw that he could not, by reason of his great age, live any longer, without being a burthen to others as well as to himself, said to those that were near him, what the herald used to say when the public games were ended, 'You may withdraw, the show is over,' and, refusing to eat, kept his usual gaiety to the last, and set himself at ease.[16]

It was by a person, who, with those three advantages, was also a great statesman, and a very good Latin poet, John, Cardinal du Bellay, Bishop of Paris, who knew Rabelais from his youth, that he was taken from the profession of physic, to be employed by that prelate in his most secret negotiations; it was he that knew him best, yet he

[13] P. de St. Romuald Rel. Feuillant.
[14] Comment. in Orat. Cic. tom. 1.
[15] Nunquid vitæ mimum commode peregisset.
[16] Lucian.

15

thought him not unworthy of being one of the prebendaries of a famous chapter in a metropolis, and curate of Meudon in his diocese.

It was, some say, in that pleasant retreat, that he composed his Gargantua and Pantagruel.

The freedom which Rabelais has used in this work could not but raise it many enemies: which caused him to give an account in his dedicatory epistle of the fourth book, to Odet, Cardinal of Chatillon, his friend, of the motive that induced him to write the three former books. There he tells him, that though his lordship knew how much he was daily importuned to continue it by several great persons who alleged that many who languished through grief or sickness, reading it, had received extraordinary ease and comfort, yet the calumnies of a sort of uncharitable men, who said it was full of heresies, though they could not show any there, without perverting the sense, had so far conquered his patience, that he had resolved to write no more on that subject. But that his lordship having told him that King Francis had found the reports of his enemies to be unjust, as well as King Henry II. then reigning—who, therefore, had granted to that cardinal his privilege and particular protection for the author of those mythologies—now, without any fear, under so glorious and powerful a patronage, he securely presumed to write on.

And indeed it is observable, that in the book to which that epistle is prefixed, he has more freely than in the rest exposed the monks, priests, pope, decretals, Council of Trent, then sitting, etc.

That epistle is dated the 28th of January, 1552, and some write that he died in 1553. By the following epigram, printed before his last book,

Rabelais seems to have been dead before it was published,—

> Rabelais est-il mort ?   Voici encore un livre !
> Non, sa meilleure part a repris ses esprits,
> Pour nous faire present de l'un de ses ecrits
> Qui le rend entre nous immortel et fait vivre.
> *Nature quite.*

The signature seems to be an anagram of Jean Turquet, father of the historian Louis Mayerin Turquet.

This satirical work employed our Rabelais only at his spare hours; for he tells us that he spent no time in composing it, but that which he usually allowed himself for eating ; yet it has deserved the commendations of the best of serious writers; and particularly of the great Thuanus, whose approbation alone is a panegyric. And if we have not many other serious tracts by its author, the private affairs of Cardinal du Bellay, in which he was employed, and his profession as a physician and a curate, may be supposed to be the cause of it. Yet he published a Latin version of the Aphorisms of Hippocrates, and with them some of Galen's works, which, for its faithfulness and purity of style, has been much esteemed by the best judges of both: nor is Vorstius, who attempted the same, said to have succeeded so well. Rabelais also wrote several French and Latin epistles, in an excellent style, to several great and learned men, and particularly to Cardinal de Chatillon, the Bishop of Maillezais, and Andrew Tiraqueau, the famous civilian. Those epistles do not only show that he was a man fit for negotiations, but that he had gained at Rome the friendship of several eminent prelates. He likewise wrote a book, called Sciomachia, and of the feasts made at Rome, in the palace of Cardinal du Bellay, for the birth of the Duke of Orleans, printed at Lyons, in 8vo, by Sebast. Gryphius, 1549. And there is an Almanack for the year 1553, calculated by him for the meridian of Lyons, and printed there, which shows that he was not only a grammarian, poet, philosopher, physician, civilian, and theologian, but also an astronomer. Besides, he was a very great linguist, being well skilled in the French, German, Italian, Spanish, Latin, Greek, and Hebrew tongues ; and we see in his letters, that he also understood Arabic, which he had learned at Rome, of a Bishop of Caramith.

Some write, that Rabelais died at Meudon; but Dom Pierre de St Romuald says, that Dr Guy Patin, royal professor at Paris, who was a great admirer of Rabelais, assured him, that he caused himself to be brought from his cure to Paris, where he lies buried in St Paul's churchyard, at the foot of a great tree, still to be seen there (1660). He died in a house in the street called La Rue des Jardins, in St Paul's parish at Paris, about the year 1553, aged 70 years. But his fame will never die.

Stephen Pasquier, advocate-general, one of the most learned and judicious writers of his age; Joachim du Bellay, Archdeacon of Paris, named to the archbishopric of Bourdeaux ; Peter Boulanger, Peter Ronsard, once prince of the French poets, Jean Antoine de Baif, and many more of the best pens of his age, honoured his memory with epitaphs, and a great number of learned men have made mention of him in their writings ; as Wm. Budé, master of the requests, alias Budæus, in Epistolis Græcis Jac. Aug. de Thou, president in the court of parliament at Paris, alias Thuanus, Hist. lib. 38 et Commentar. de Vitâ suâ, lib. 6. Theod. Beza. Clement Marot, who inscribed to him an imitation, in French, of the 21st epigram of Martial's fifth book, 'Si tecum mihi, Chare Martialis, etc.' Hugh Salel, that translated Homer's Iliad into French. Stephen Dolet, a French and Latin poet, burned for being a Protestant, at Paris, 1545. Peter Ronsard. Stephen Pasquier, in his Recherches de la France, and in the first and second books of his Lettres. Jean Cecile Frey. Francis Bacon, Lord Verulam, in his book of the Advancement of Learning. Andrew Du Chesne, in his book Des Antiquitez de France. Thevet, Hist. de Jean Clopinel : Gab. Mic. de la Roche Maillet, Vies des Illust. Personnages. Fran. Grudé, Seigneur de la Croix du Maine, in his Bibliothèque. Ant. du Verdier, Sieur de Vauprivas, Conseiller du Roy. Franc. Ranchin, doctor of physic at Montpellier. Scævola de Sainte Marthe, Conseiller du Roy, etc., alias Samarthanus, lib. primo Elog. Clarorum Virorum. Sir William Temple, in the second part of his Miscellanea. C. Sorel, first Historiographer of France, in his Bibliothèque Française. Dr Ant. Van Dale, de Oraculis et Consecrationibus. Monsieur Costar, dans son Apologie. M. Menage. Romuald, in the third part of his Thrésor Chronologique ; and several others, named in a book called Floretum Philosophicum, that mentions many particulars of his life, and the names of those that have spoke of him. A curate of Meudon, in honour of his predecessor, also caused to be printed whatever is writ in his praise, which books I have not been able to find. There is also a large account of Rabelais in the Grand Historical French Dictionary.

Sir Wm. Temple says in his *Miscellanea*, Part II.:—The great wits among the moderns have been,

19

in my opinion, and in their several kinds, of the French Rabelais and Montaigne. Rabelais seems to have been father of the ridicule, a man of excellent and universal learning, as well as wit; and though he had too much game given him for satire in that age, by the customs of courts and of convents, of processes and of wars, of schools and of camps, of romances and legends, yet he must be confessed to have kept up his vein of ridicule, by saying many things so smutty and profane, that a pious man could not have afforded, though he had never so much of that coin about him. And it were to be wished that the wits who have imitated him had not put too much value upon a dress that better understandings would not wear (at least in public) and upon a compass they gave themselves, which some other men cannot take.

And Coleridge says: 'Beyond a doubt Rabelais was among the deepest, as well as boldest, thinkers of his age. His buffoonery was not merely Brutus's rough stick, which contained a rod of gold : it was necessary as an amulet against the monks and legates. Never was there a more plausible, and seldom, I am persuaded, a less appropriate line, than the thousand times quoted—

Rabelais laughing in his easy chair

of Mr Pope. The caricature of his filth and zanyism show how fully he both knew and felt the danger in which he stood. I could write a treatise in praise of the moral elevation of Rabelais's work, which would make the church stare, and the conventicle groan, and yet would be truth, and nothing but the truth. I class Rabelais with the great creative minds of the world, Shakspeare, Dante, Cervantes, etc.'

THE

PREFACE,

WHEREIN IS GIVEN AN ACCOUNT OF THE DESIGN AND
NATURE OF THIS WORK, AND A KEY TO SOME
OF ITS MOST DIFFICULT PASSAGES

THE History of Gargantua and Pantagruel has
always been esteemed a master-piece of wit and
learning, by the best judges of both. Even the
most grave and reserved among the learned in many
countries, but particularly in France, have thought
it worthy to hold a place in their closets, and have
passed many hours in private with that diverting
and instructive companion. And as for those whose
age and profession did not incline them to be reserved, all France can witness that there has been
but few of them who could not be said to have their
Rabelais almost by heart : since mirth could hardly
be complete among those that love it, unless their
good cheer were seasoned with some of Rabelais's
wit.

Many large editions of that book have not sufficed
the world, and, though the language in which it is
written be not easily understood now, by those who
only converse with modern French books, yet it has
been reprinted several times lately, in France and
Holland, even in its antiquated style.

21

Preface

Indeed, some are of opinion that the odd and quaint terms used in that book add not a little to the satisfaction which is found in its perusal; but yet this can only be said of such of them as are understood; and when a reader meets with many words that are unintelligible (I mean to him that makes it not his business to know the meaning of dark and obsolete expressions), the pleasure which what he understands yields him is in a greater measure allayed by his disappointment; of which we have instances when we read Chaucer, and other books, which we do not thoroughly understand.

Sir Thomas Urquhart has avoided that obscurity in this following translation of Rabelais, so that most English readers may now understand that author in our tongue, better than many of the French can do in theirs. To do Rabelais justice, it was necessary that a person, not only master of the French, but also of much leisure and fancy, should undertake the task. The translator was not only happy in these things, but also in being a learned physician, and having, besides, some Frenchmen near him, who understood Rabelais very well, and could explain to him the most difficult words; and I think that, before the first and second books of Rabelais, which are all that was formerly printed of that author in English, there were some verses by men of that nation in praise of his translation.

It was too kindly received, not to have encouraged him to English the remaining three books, or at least the third—the fourth and fifth being in a manner distinct, as being Pantagruel's Voyage. Accordingly he translated the third book, and probably would have finished the whole had not death prevented him. So, the said third book, being found long after in manuscript among his papers,

somewhat incorrect, a gentleman who is not only
a very great linguist, but also deservedly famous for
his ingenious and learned compositions, was lately
pleased to revise it, as well as the two first, which
had been published about thirty years ago, and are
extremely scarce. He thought it necessary to make
considerable alterations, that the translation might
have the smartness, genuine sense, and the very
style and air of the original; but yet, to preserve
the latter, he has not thought fit to alter the style of
the translation, which suits as exactly with that of
the author as possible, neither affecting the polite-
ness of the most nice and refined of our modern
English writers, nor yet the roughness of our antiquated authors, but such a medium as might neither
shock the ears of the first, nor displease those who
would have an exact imitation of the style of
Rabelais.

Since the first edition of those two books of
Rabelais was so favourably entertained, without the
third, without any account of the author, or any
observations to discover that mysterious history, it
is hoped that they will not meet with a worse usage,
now they appear again so much improved, with the
addition of a third, never printed before in English,
and a large account of the author's life ; but prin-
cipally since we have here an explication of the
enigmatic sense of part of that admirable mytho-
logist's works, both of which have been so long
wanted, though never till now published in any
language.

The ingenious of our age, as well as those who
lived when Rabelais composed his Gargantua and
Pantagruel, have been extremely desirous of discovering the truths which are hid under the dark
veil of allegories in that incomparable work. The

great Thuanus found it worthy of being mentioned in his excellent history, as a most ingenious satire on persons who were the most distinguished in the kingdom of France by their quality and employments ; and without doubt he, who was the best of all our modern historians, and lived soon after it was writ, had traced the private design of Rabelais, and found out the true names of the persons whom he has introduced on this scene, with names, not only imaginary, but generally ridiculous, and whose actions he represents as ridiculous as those names. But as it would have been dangerous, having unmasked those persons, to have them exposed to public view, in a kingdom where they were so powerful ; and as most of the adventures, which are mystically represented by Rabelais, relate to the affairs of religion, so those few who have understood the true sense of that satire have not dared to reveal it.

In the late editions, some learned men have given us a vocabulary, wherein they explain the names and terms in it which are originally Greek, Latin, Hebrew, or of other tongues, that the text might thus be made more intelligible, and their work may be useful to those who do not understand those tongues. But they have not had the same success in their pretended explications of the names which Rabelais has given to the real actors in this farce; and thus they have, indeed, framed a key, but, if I may use the allegory, it was without having known the wards and springs of the lock. What I advance will doubtless be owned to be true by those who may have observed that by that key none can discover in those Pythagorical symbols (as they are called in the author's prologue to the first book) any event that has a relation to the history of those to whom the names, mentioned by Rabelais, have been applied by those that made that pretended key. They tell us in it, that King Grangousier is the same as King Louis XII. of France, that Gargantua is Francis I. and that Henry II. is the true name of Pantagruel; but we discover none of Louis XII.'s features in King Grangousier, who does none of the actions which history ascribes to that prince, so that the King of Siam, or the Cham of Tartary, might as reasonably be imagined to be Grangousier, as Louis XII. As much may be said of Gargantua and of Pantagruel, who do none of the things that have been remarked by historians as done by the Kings Francis I. and Henry II. of France.

This reason, which of itself is very strong, will much more appear to be such, if we reflect on the author's words in the prologue to the first book: 'In the perusal of this treatise,' says he, 'you shall find another kind of taste, and a doctrine of a more profound and abstruse consideration, which will disclose to you the most glorious doctrine, and dreadful mysteries, as well in what concerneth your religion, as matters of the public state and life economical;' mysteries which, as he tells us, are the juice and substantial marrow of his work. To this reason I add another as strong and evident. It is, that we find in Grangousier, Gargantua, and Pantagruel, characters that visibly distinguish them from the three Kings of France which I have named, and from all the other kings their predecessors.

In the first place, Grangousier's kingdom is not France, but a state particularly distinct from it, which Gargantua and Pantagruel call Utopia.

Secondly, Gargantua is not born in the kingdom of France, but in that of Utopia.

Thirdly, he leaves Paris, called back by his father,

that he might come to the relief of his country, which was attacked by Picrochole's army.

And, finally, Francis I. is distinguished from Gargantua, in the 39th chapter of the first book, when Friar John des Entonneures says, in the presence of Gargantua, and eating at his table, 'Had I been in the time of Jesus Christ, I would have kept him from being taken by the Jews in the garden of Olivet, and the devil fail me, if I should have failed to cut off the hams of those gentlemen apostles, who ran away so basely after they had well supped, and left their good master in the lurch; I hate that man worse than poison that offers to run away when he should fight and lay stoutly about him. Oh, if I were but King of France for fourscore or a hundred years, by God, I should whip, like cut-tail dogs, these runaways of Pavia : a plague take them,' etc.

But if Francis I. is not Gargantua, likewise Pantagruel is not Henry II., and if it were needful, I could easily show, that the authors of that pretended key have not only been mistaken in those names, but in all the others, which they undertook to decipher, and that they only spoke at random, without the least grounds or authorities from history.

All things are right so far ; but the difficulty lieth not there : we ought to show who are the princes that are hid under the names of Grangousier, Gargantua, and Pantagruel, if yet we may suppose them to be princes. But such a discovery cannot be very easily made, because most of their actions are only described in allegories, and in so confused and enigmatic a manner, that we do not know where to fix. This must be granted; yet it is not an impossible thing ; and if we can but once unmask Panurge, who is the ridiculous hero of the piece, we

may soon guess by the servant, and the air and figure
of his master, who Pantagruel is.

We find these four characters in Panurge:

1. He is well skilled in the Greek, Hebrew,
and Latin tongues; he speaks High and Low
Dutch, Polish, Spanish, Portuguese, English, Latin,
etc.

2. He is learned, understanding, politic, sharp,
cunning, and deceitful in the highest degree.

3. He publicly professes the Popish religion,
though he in reality laughs at it, and is nothing less
than a Papist.[1]

4. His chief concern, next to that of eating, is a
marriage, which he has a desire, yet is afraid to
contract, lest he should meet with his match : that
is, a wife even as bad as himself.

I do not know if those who, by the pretended
key, have been induced to believe that Panurge was
the Cardinal of Amboise in a disguise, have been
pleased to observe these four qualities; but I am
sure that nothing of all this can be applied to that
prelate, unless it be, that in general he was an able
minister of state. But all four were found in John
de Montluc, Bishop of Valence and Die, who was
the eldest brother of the Marshal de Montluc, the
most violent enemy which the Huguenots had in
those days.

1. Historians assure us,[2] that he understood the
Eastern tongues, as also the Greek and the Latin,
the best of any man in his time ; and in sixteen
embassies to many princes of Europe, to whom he
was sent, in Germany, England, Scotland, Poland,

---

[1] The writer means that Panurge is not conspicuous for any
religious views ; but that he is less papistically inclined than
towards any other form of religion.

[2] Brantôme. Beza Hist. Eccles.

27

Constantinople, he doubtless learned the living tongues, which he did not know before.

2. He gained a great reputation in all those embassies,[3] and his wit, his skill, his penetration, and his prudence, in observing a conduct that contented all persons, were universally admired. But he even outdid himself in the most difficult of all those embassies, which was that of Poland, to the throne of which kingdom he caused Henry de Valois, Duke of Anjou, to be raised, in spite of the difficulties, which the massacre of Paris, that was wholly laid to his charge in Poland (he having been one of the chief promoters of it), created concerning his election. His toils and his happy success, in those important negotiations, caused him to take this Latin verse for his motto—

Quæ regio in terris nostri non plena laboris?

3. The whole kingdom of France, and particularly the court, knew that he was a Calvinist, and he himself did not make a mystery of it, as appears by his preaching their doctrine once before the queen in a hat and cloak, after the manner of the Calvinists, which caused the Constable de Montmorency to say aloud, 'Why do not they pull that minister out of the pulpit?' Nay, he was even condemned by Pius IV. as a heretic, but that Pope having not assigned him judges *in partibus*, according to the laws of the kingdom, he kept his bishopric; and the Dean of Valence, who had accused him of being a Calvinist, not being well able to make good his charge, Montluc, who had mighty friends, caused him to be punished for it; also, after his death, his contract of marriage with

---

[3] Brantôme. Dupleix. Sponde. Maimbourg. Beza.

28

a gentlewoman called Anne Martin was found, yet
he still kept in the Roman Church, and still enjoyed
the revenues of his bishopric, as if he had been the
most bigoted Papist in that kingdom. The considerations that kept him from abjuring solemnly
the errors of the Church of Rome, were, that Calvin
let him know, that according to his reformation
there could be no bishops; he owned that this
obstacle would not, perhaps, have hindered him
from leaving that communion, could his kitchen
have followed him in the other: excepting that
particular, he was altogether for a reformation, and
in all things favoured its professors, and it is what
Rabelais has observed, when he makes him conclude
all his discourses in many languages with saying,
that 'Venter famelicus auriculis carere dicitur :⁴ at
this time, I am in a very urgent necessity to feed,
my teeth are sharp, my belly empty, my throat dry,
and my stomach fierce and burning ; all is ready.
If you will but set me to work, it will be as good
as a balsamum for sore eyes, to see me gulch and
ravin it. For God's sake give order for it.'
    4. His chief concern, next to that of living
plentifully, was that of his marriage, and as we have
observed, he married, and had a son whom he
owned, and who was afterwards legitimated by the
parliament ; it is the same who is famous in history
by the name of Balagny, and who was afterwards
Prince of Cambray ; his father caused him to be sent
into Poland, about the Duke of Anjou's election,
of which we have spoke, and he was very serviceable
to that duke in it. Now, it is that marriage of the
Bishop of Valence, that so much perplexes him by
the name of Panurge, in Rabelais's third book, and

⁴ Book ii. chap. 9.

29

which is the occasion of Pantagruel's Voyage to the Holy Bottle in the fourth and fifth.

It is much to be admired how a bishop, that openly sided with the Calvinists, who was also a monk, yet married, and living with his wife, whom he had regularly wedded, could enjoy one of the best bishoprics in France, and some of the chief employments at court. He must doubtless have been extremely cunning, and have had a very particular talent to keep those envied posts in the church and state, in spite of all those disadvantages, in the midst of so many storms raised against him and the Reformation, by enemies that had all the forces of the kingdom in their power, and could do whatever they pleased.

This prudence and craftiness is described to the life by our author, when he makes Panurge relate how he had been broached upon a spit by the Turks, all larded like a rabbit, and in that manner was roasting alive; when calling on God that he might deliver him out of the pains wherein they detained him for his sincerity in the maintenance of his law, the turn-spit fell asleep by the divine will; and Panurge, having taken in his teeth a fire-brand by the end that was not burned, cast it in the lap of his roaster ; with another set the house on fire, broached on the spit the Turkish lord who designed to devour him, and at last got away, though pursued by a great number of dogs, who smelled his lecherous half-roasted flesh ; and he threw the bacon, with which he had been larded, among them.

It is observable, that there he exclaims against the Turks about their abstaining from wine, which, perhaps, may refer to the Church of Rome's denying the cup in the eucharist to the laity, at which particularly Montluc was offended. To lard a man is

a metaphor often used by the French, to signify, to
accuse and reproach, and so he was even before he
had his bishopric ; throwing a fire-brand with his
mouth on the turnspit's lap, may be the hot words
which he used to clear himself, and with which he
charged his adversaries; and his spitting and burning the Turkish lord may, perhaps, mean the advantage which he had over them.[5]   The spectacles
which afterwards he wore on his cap, may signify
the caution which he was always obliged to take to
avoid a surprise; and his having a flea in his ear, in
French, signifies the same.[6]   His forbearing to wear
any longer his magnificent cod-piece, and clothing
himself in four French ells of a coarse brown russet
cloth, show that, as he was a monk, he could not
wear a cod-piece, as was the fashion in those days for
the laity; or, perhaps, it denotes his affecting to
imitate the simplicity of garb which was observable
in Calvinist preachers.

This subaltern hero of the farce, now found to be
the Bishop of Valence, by the circumstances and
qualifications already discovered, that cannot properly
belong to any other, may help us to know, not only
Pantagruel, to whom he had devoted himself, but
also Gargantua and Grangousier, the father and
grandfather of Pantagruel.

History assures us, that Montluc, Bishop of Valence, owed his advancement to Margaret de Valois,
Queen of Navarre, and sister to King Francis I.
She took him out of a monastery, where he was no
more than a Jacobin friar, and sent him to Rome,
whereby he was raised to the rank of an ambassador,
which was the first step to his advancement.

Thus Pantagruel should be Anthony de Bourbon,

---

[5] Book iii. chap 7.   [6] La puce a l'oreille.

31

Preface

Duke of Vendosme, King Henry IV.'s father, and Louis XIV.'s great grandfather. He was married to Jeanne d'Albret, the only daughter of the said Queen Margaret, and of Henry d'Albret, King of Navarre. Thus he became their son, and King of Navarre, after the death of the said Henry d'Albret, whom I take to be Gargantua : consequently his father, John d'Albret, King of Navarre, excommunicated by Pope Julius III. and deprived of the best part of his kingdom by Ferdinand, King of Arragon, should be Grangousier.

The verses before the third book (printed in 1546) discover that Pantagruel is Anthony de Bourbon, afterwards King of Navarre. The author dedicates it to the soul of the deceased Queen of Navarre, Margaret de Valois, who died in Brittany, in the year 1549 (and was therefore living at the time the verses were published). She had openly professed the Protestant religion ; and in 1534, her ministers, of whom the most famous were Girard Ruffy (since Bishop of Oleron in Navarre), Couraud and Berthaud, preached publicly at Paris by her direction, upon which a fierce persecution ensued. Her learning and the agreeableness of her temper were so extraordinary, as well as her virtue, that she was styled the tenth Muse, and the fourth Grace. She has written several books ; particularly one of poetry called the Marguerite des Marguerites, and another in prose called the Hexameron or Les Nouvelles Nouvelles : of which novels some might in this age seem too free to be penned by a lady, but yet the reputation of her virtue has always been very great, which shows, that though in that age both sexes were less reserved in their writings than we are generally in this, they were not more remiss in their actions. Let us consider the above-cited verses.

32

This *corps concords*, this conjugate body, that grows
so conformable to that queen's rules, and leads the
life of a traveller, who only desires to arrive at his
journey's end, being as it were in apathy—what
should it be but Henry d'Albret, who had survived
that queen, his consort, and could love nothing after
her in this world, endeavouring at the same time to
wean himself from its vanities, to aspire to a better,
according to that wise princess's pious admonitions?
Nor can the good Pantagruel be any other than
Anthony de Bourbon, whom we have already
named.

To this proof I add another, which admits of no
reply; it is, that the language which Pantagruel
owns to be that of Utopia and his country is the
same that is spoken in the provinces of Bearn and
Gascony, the first of which was yet enjoyed by the
King of Navarre. Panurge having spoken to him
in that language, 'Methinks I understand him,' said
Pantagruel; 'for either it is the language of my
country of Utopia, or it sounds very much like it.'[7]
Now those who are acquainted with the different
dialects of the French tongue, need but read to find
that Panurge had spoken in that of Gascony.
' *Agonou dont oussys vous desdaignez algarou,*' etc.

Besides, Gargantua, who is King of Utopia, is said
to be born in a state near the Bibarois, by which the
author, perhaps, does not only allude to *bibere* (drinking), but to Bigorre, a province, which was still
possessed by the King of Navarre, or at least to the
Vivarez, which may be reckoned among the provinces that are not far distant from that of Foix,
which also belonged to that king, his mother being
Catherine de Foix. That in which Gargantua was

[7] Book ii. chap. 9.

born is Beusse, which, though it also alludes to
drinking, yet, by the transmutation of B into V
(generally made by those nations as well as by many
others), seems to be the ancient name of Albret, viz.,
Vasates. I might add, that Grangousier is described
as one that was well furnished with hams of Bayonne,
sausages of Bigorre and Rouargue, etc.,[8] but none of
Bolognia; for he feared the Lombard *boconne* (or
'poisoned bit,' the Pope being indeed his enemy).
We are told that he could not endure the Spaniards;[9]
and mention is made also by Grangousier of the wine
that grows, 'not,' says he, 'in Brittany, but in this
good country of Verron,' which seems to be Bearn.[10]
I might instance more of this; but as I know how
little we ought to rely upon likeness of names to
find out places and colonies, I will only insist upon
the word Utopia, which is the name of Grangousier's
kingdom, and by which the author means Navarre,
of which Gargantua was properly only titular king,
the best part of that kingdom, with Pampelune, its
capital city, being in the King of Spain's hands: so
that state was as it were no more on earth, as to
any benefit he enjoyed by it; and it is what the
word Utopia, from οὐ and τόπος, signifies, viz., what
is not found, or a place not to be found. We have,
therefore, here four actors in the Pantagruelian farce,
three Kings of Navarre and the Bishop of Valence
bred up and raised in that house: we might add two
personæ mutæ, Catherine de Foix, Queen of Navarre,
married to John d'Albret; and she, therefore, should
be Gargamelle, as Margaret de Valois, married to his
son, Henry King of Navarre, should be Badebec.
  Picrochole is doubtless the King of Spain, who
deprived John d'Albret of that part of Navarre which

[8] Book i. chap. 3.   [9] Book i. chap. 8.   [10] Book i. chap. 13.

34

is on the side of the Pyrenean mountains that is next
to Spain. This appears by the name of Picrochole,
and by the universal monarchy of which he thought
himself secure.

The word Picrochole is made up of two, πιχρός
bitter, and χολή choler, bile, or gall, to denote the
temper of that king, who was nothing but bitterness
and gall. This doubly fits Charles V.; first with
relation to Francis I., against whom he conceived
an immortal hatred; and to Henry d'Albret, whose
kingdom he possessed, and whom he lulled with the
hopes of a restitution which he never designed;
which was one of the chief causes of the war that
was kindled between that king and the Emperor
Charles V., which lasted during both their reigns.
Besides, Charles V. was troubled from time to time
with an overflowing of bile; so that finding himself
decaying, and not likely to live much longer, after he
had raised the siege of Mets, as he had done that of
Marseilles before, being commonly as unfortunate as
his generals were successful, he shut himself up in a
monastery, where that distemper was the chief cause
of his death. The hope of universal monarchy, with
which that emperor flattered himself, was a chimera
that possessed his mind till he resigned his crown, and
which he seemed to have assigned with it to Philip
II. his son and successor.

This frenzy, which in his thirst of empire possessed him wholly, is very pleasantly ridiculed by
Rabelais.[11]   The Duke of Small-trash, the Earl of
Swash-buckler, and Captain Durtail, make Picrochole (in Rodomontado) conquer all the nations in
the universe.   I suppose that our satirist means by
these three, some grandees of Spain; for their king,

[11] Book i. chap. 33.

35

Preface

Picrochole, bids them be covered. After many
imaginary victories, they speak of erecting two
pillars to perpetuate his memory, at the Straits of
Gibraltar; by which he ridicules Charles V.'s
devise, which was two pillars, with *Plus Ultra* for
the motto. Then they make him go to Tunis and
Algiers (which Charles V. did), march to Rome, and
cause the Pope to die with fear; whereat Picrochole
is pleased, because he will not then kiss his pantoufle,
and longs to be at Loretto. Accordingly we know
that, in 1527, his army had taken Rome by storm,
plundered it and its churches, ravished the nuns, if
any would be ravished, and having almost starved the
Pope, at last took him prisoner; which actions of a
Catholic king's army, Sandoval, a Spanish author, only
terms *Opera non santa*. Then Picrochole, fancying
himself master already of so many nations, most
royally gratifies those who so easily made him
conquer them; to this he gives Caramania, Suria to
that, and Palestine to the third ; till at last a wise
old officer speaks to him much as Cyneas did to
Pyrrhus, and with as little success as that philosopher.

As it was not our author's design to give us a
regular history of all that happened in this time, he
did not tie himself up to chronology, and sometimes
joined events which have but little relation to each
other. Many times also the characters are double,
as perhaps is that of Picrochole. In the Menagiana,
lately published, which is a collection of sayings,
repartees, and observations by the learned Menage,
every one of them attested by men of learning and
credit, we are told that Messieurs de Sainte Marthe
assured him that the Picrochole of Rabelais was their
grandfather, who was a physician at Frontevraut.
These MM. de St Marthe are the worthy sons of the

famous Samarthanus, who gave so high a character of
Rabelais among the most celebrated men of France,
and who themselves have honoured his letters with
large notes, and showed all the marks of the greatest
respect for his memory.

Rabelais, who had more reason to write mystically
than any, may then be allowed equal freedom in his
allegories; and without fixing only the character of
Picrochole on Charles V., we may believe that it
refers as well to his predecessor, Ferdinand, King of
Arragon and of Castile, by Queen Isabella, his wife,
that deprived John d'Albret of his kingdom of
Navarre; for that Spaniard was as bitter an enemy,
as cunning, and at least as fatal to the house of
Navarre as his successor.

John d'Albret was an open-hearted, magnificent,
generous prince, but easy, and relying wholly on his
ministers; being given to his pleasures, which often
consisted in going privately to eat and drink with his
subjects, and inviting himself to their houses; however, he loved books, and was a great lover of
heraldry, nicely observing the pedigrees, coats, and
badges of honour of families, which perhaps makes
Rabelais open his scene with referring us to the
great Pantagruelian Chronicle (by which he begins
his second book) for the knowledge of that genealogy
and antiquity of race by which Gargantua is descended to us, how the giants were born in this
world, and how from them, by a direct line, issued
Gargantua: then he bids us not to take it ill, if he
for the present passes it by, though the subject be
such, that the oftener it were remembered, the more
it will please your worships; by which he exposes
that prince's and some gentlemen's continual ap-
plication to a vain search into the dark and fabulous
times for pedigrees, as Rabelais says, from the giants;

for many would be derived from something greater
than man. Then he makes his kings giants, because
they are so in power; and sometimes what serves the
whole court and attendants is by him applied wholly
to the king, as eating, clothing, strength: and then
by that he ridicules the romances of those days,
where giants are always brought in, as well as
magicians, witches, single men routing whole armies,
and a thousand other such fabulous stories. He has
also ridiculed the variety of doubtful though ancient
originals, in the odd discovery of the manuscript;
and, in the 9th chapter, the distinction of colours
and liveries, which took up that prince's time, due
to higher employments, as worthily as the rest of
heraldry. There he tells us that Gargantua's colours
or liveries were white and blue; by which his
father would give to understand, that his son was to
him a heavenly joy. Thence, with as much fancy
as judgment, he takes an opportunity to laugh at the
lame and punning devices or impresses of those days,
in which, however, Paulus Jovius had already given
rules to make better; yet, after all, I believe that by
Gargantua's colours, Rabelais also alludes to King
Henry d'Albret, and Marguerite his queen, who
were sincerely for a reformation; so the white may
signify innocence, candour, and sincerity; and the
blue, piety or heavenly love. Perhaps also as
Godefroy d'Estissac,[12] Bishop of Maillezais, in his
coat, gave, paley, of six pieces argent and azure, he
had a mind to celebrate the colours of his patron.

The account of Gargantua's youthful age, chap.
11, agrees very well with that which historians give
us of the way of bringing up Henry IV. of France,
by his grandfather, Henry d'Albret, who is the same

[12] Epist. de Rabelais.

with Gargantua.[13] That great monarch was in his
tender age inured by that old prince to all sorts of
hardships, for he caused him to be kept in the
country, where he ordered they should let him run
among the poor country boys, which the young
prince did, sometimes without shoes or hat, being
fed with the coarsest fare; so that, having by those
means contracted a good habit of body, he was afterwards so hardened to fatigues, so vigilant and active,
and so easily pleased with the most homely diet, that
it did not a little contribute to the advantage which
he had over the League, whose chief, the Duke de
Mayenne, was of a disposition altogether different.

The education of Gargantua by the sophisters is
a satire on those men,[14] and the tedious methods of
the schools, showing the little improvement that was
made in Henry d'Albret's studies as long as he was
under Popish governors, and the ill life that the
young gentlemen of the Roman church led ; as, on
the contrary, the benefit of having good tutors, and
the difference between the Romans and the Protestants,[15] carefully and piously educated at the
dawn of the Reformation; for there is no doubt that,
though Henry d'Albret did not dare to profess it, the
people in Navarre being all papists, and there being
obstacles enough to the recovery of that kingdom,
lost by his father, without raising more, yet he
heartily hated the popish principles, and the King of
Arragon and Castile, who, merely on the pretence of
John d'Albret's alliance with Louis XII., at the
time of his excommunication, had seized his country,
and held it by the Pope's gift; so we find that the
Reformers no sooner preached against bulls and in-

---

[13] Mezeray. Hardouin de Prefix. Hist. Henry IV.
[14] Book i. chap. 21.   [15] Book i. chap. 23.

dulgences, the taking away the cup in the eucharist, and transubstantiation, but that Marguerite, the wife of King Henry d'Albret, and sister to Francis I., owned herself to be one of the new opinion, and as powerfully defended its professors as she could. Any one may see, by the two chapters of Gargantua's education by Ponocrates, that the author treats of a Protestant prince, and of Gargantua's being brought to a reformed state of life: for he says, that when Ponocrates knew Gargantua's vicious manner of living, he resolved to bring him up in a much different way, and requested a learned physician of that time, called Master Theodorus, seriously to prepend how to bring him to a better course: he says, that the said physician purged him canonically, with anticyrian hellebore, by which medicine he cleared all that foulness and perverse habit of his brain, and by this means Ponocrates made him forget all that he had learned under his ancient preceptors. Theodorus is a very proper name for a divine, signifying 'gift of God,' from Θεου and δῶρον, and that great master of thought, Father Malebranche, gives it to the divine who is one of the interlocutors in the admirable metaphysical dialogues, which he calls Conversations Chrestiennes; so that, as Rabelais tells us, Theodorus was a physician for the mind, that is, one of the new preachers, and perhaps Berthaud, that of Queen Marguerite.

By the anticyrian [16] hellebore, with which he purged Gargantua's brain, may be meant powerful arguments, drawn from reason and the scripture, opposed to the authority of the Popish Church. After this purge we find Gargantua awaked at four in the morning, and, while they were rubbing him,

[16] Ἀντικυρία, potestas, apud Suidam.

some chapter of the holy scripture aloud, and clearly, with a pronunciation fit for the matter, read to him, and, according to the purpose and argument of that lesson, oftentimes giving himself to worship, adore, pray, and send up his supplications to that good God whose word did show His majesty and marvellous judgment. That chapter and the next are admirable, as well as many more; nor can we ever have a more perfect idea of the education of a prince, than is that of his Gargantua, whom he represents all along as a man of great honour, sense, courage, and piety; whereas under his other masters, in the chapters before, we find him idle, and playing at all sorts of games. Nothing can better demonstrate the great genius and prudence of our author, who could submit to get together so many odd names of trifling things, to keep himself out of danger, and grace the counterpart which is so judicious and so grave. He had told us first, that Gargantua, under his former pedagogues, after a good breakfast, went to church, a huge greasy breviary being carried before him in a great basket; that there he heard twenty-six or thirty masses; that this while came his matin-mumbler (chaplain) muffled about the chin (that is, with his cowl), round as a hoop, and his breath pretty well antidoted with the vine-tree syrup; that with him he mumbled all his kyriels, and, as he went from the church, sauntering along through the cloisters, ridded more of St Claude's pater-nosters than sixteen hermits could have done. So that there we find him a Papist, and in the following chapter, as I have said, a Protestant.

Without doubt, the sophisters, under whom Gargantua [17] did not improve, were some noted men

[17] Book i. chap. 14.

in his age. I have not yet discovered who they were.

As for Don Philip of Marais, Viceroy of Papeligosse,[18] who advises Grangousier to put his son under another discipline, he may perhaps be Philip, son to the Mareschal of Navarre; the title of Don being taken by the Navarrois, and Marais seems Mareschal.

Gargantua is sent with Ponocrates to Paris by his father, 'that they might know,' says he, 'what was the study of the young men in France.'[19] This shows that Grangousier was not king of it, and that Gargantua was a stranger there.

Many who take him to be Francis I. think that his huge great mare is Madame d'Estampes, that king's mistress, and explain that mare's skirmishing with her tail, whereby she overthrew all the wood in the county of Beauce, by a gift which, they say, he made her of some of its forests. They say also that the king was desirous to buy her a necklace of pearls, and that, partly on that account, he would have got some money of the citizens of Paris; but they being unwilling to comply with his demand, the king and his mistress threatened to sell the bells of Our Lady's Church (the cathedral) to buy his lady a necklace; and that this has given occasion to say, that Gargantua designed to hang those bells at his mare's neck.[20]

I will offer here a conjecture on that story of the bells: we find, in the seventeenth, eighteenth and nineteenth chapters of the first book, that Master Janotus de Bragmardo, a sophister, is sent to Gargantua to recover the bells, and makes a wretched speech to him about it: I am sensible that it was

---

[18] Book i. chap. 15.   [19] Chaps. 15 and 16.   [20] Book i. chap. 17.

partly his design to ridicule the universities, which at that time deserved no better, in France. But in particular, I believe he aimed at Cenalis, a doctor of Sorbonne, and afterwards Bishop of Avranches; for I find that this prelate had wrote a treatise, wonderfully pleasant,[21] concerning the signs whereby the true church may be distinguished from the false; in it he waives the preaching of the gospel, and administration of the sacraments, and pretends to prove that bells are the signs which essentially distinguish the church of Rome from the reformed, who at that time had none, but used to assemble privately at the letting off of a musket in the High Street, which was a sign by which they knew that it was time to meet to perform divine service. Cenalis on this triumphs, as if he had gained his point, and runs on in a long antithesis, to prove that bells are the signs of the true church, and guns the mark of the bad. 'All bells,' says he, 'sound; but all guns thunder: all bells have a melodious sound; all guns make a dreadful noise: bells open heaven; guns open hell: bells drive away clouds and thunder; guns raise clouds, and mock the thunder.' He has a great deal more such stuff, to prove that the church of Rome is the true church, because, forsooth, it has bells, which the other had not.

The taking away the bells of a place implies its conquest, and even towns that have articled are obliged to redeem their bells: perhaps the taking away the great bells at Paris was the taking away the privileges of its university, or some other; for Paris may only be named for a blind. Thus the master beggar of the friars of St Anthony, coming

---

[21] Hist. de Jean Crespin.

Preface

for some hog's purtenance (St Anthony's hog is
always pictured with a bell at his neck) who, to
be heard afar off, and to make the bacon shake in
the very chimneys, had a mind to filch and carry
those bells away privily, but was hindered by their
weight—that master beggar, I say, must be the head
of some monks, perhaps of that order in the Faux-
bourg St Antoine, who would have been substituted
to those that had been deprived; and the petition
of Master Janotus is the pardon which the university begs, perhaps for some affront resented by the
prince; for those that escaped the flood, cried, 'We
are washed *Par ris;*' that is, for having laughed.
Rabelais, *en passant*, there severely inveighs against
the grumblers and factious spirits of Paris; which
makes me think that, whether the scene lies there
or elsewhere, as in Gascony, some people of which
country were Henry d'Albret's subjects, still this
was a remarkable event. In the prologue to the
fourth book, Jupiter, busied about the affairs of
mankind, cries, ' Here are the Gascons cursing,
damning and renouncing, demanding the re-establishment of their bells.' I suppose that more is
meant than bells, or he would not have used the
word re-establishment.

But it is time to speak of the great strife and
debate raised betwixt the cake-bakers of Lerné, and
those of Gargantua's country; whereupon were
waged great wars.[22] We may easily apply many
things concerning these wars to those of Navarre,
between the house of d'Albret and King Ferdinand
and Charles V. Thus Les Truans, or, as this translation renders it, the inhabitants of Lerné, who, by
the command of Picrochole their king, invaded and

[22] Book i. chap. 25.

plundered Utopia, Gargantua's country, are the
Spanish soldiers, and Lerné is Spain. The word
truand, in old French, signifies an idle lazy fellow,
which hits pretty well the Spaniards' character; the
author having made choice of that name of a place
near Chinon, because it alludes to the Lake Lerna,
where Hercules destroyed the Lernæan hydra, which
did so much hurt in the country of Argos. Thus
Spain was a Lerna of ills to all Europe, while, like
France, it aspired to universal monarchy; but it
was so more particularly to Navarre, in July 1512,
when King John d'Albret and Queen Catherine de
Foix, the lawful sovereigns, were dispossessed by
Ferdinand, King of Arragon, almost without any
resistance. The said King John, desirous of peace,
sent Don Alphonso Carillo, Constable of Navarre,
in the quality of his ambassador, to Ferdinand, to
prevent the approaching mischief; 'But he was
so ill received,' says the History of Navarre,[23] dedicated to King Henry IV. and printed with his
privilege, 'that he was glad to return to his king
with speed, and related to him that there was no
hope left to persuade the King of Arragon to a
peace, and that Louis de Beaumont, Earl of Lerins,
who had forsaken Navarre, daily encouraged Ferdin-
and to attack that kingdom.' So that this embassy
resembles much that of Ulric Gallet to Picrochole,
who swears by St James, the saint of the Spaniards.
In November 1512, Francis Duke of Angoulême,
afterwards king, was sent with King John d'Albret,
by Lewis XII. to recover Navarre, having with him
several of the great lords in France, and a great
army, which possessed itself of many places, but
the rigour of the season obliged them to raise the

---

[23] Hist. de Navarre par C. Secretaire et Interpret. du Roy.

siege of Pampeluna. And in 1521, another army, under the command of Andrew de Foix, Lord of Asperault, entered Navarre, and wholly regained it,[24] but it was lost again soon after by the imprudence of that general, and the avarice of Saint Colombe, one of his chief officers.

Those that will narrowly examine history will find that many particulars of the wars, in the first of Rabelais, may be reconciled to those of Navarre; but I believe that he means something more than a description of the fights among the soldiers, by the debate raised betwixt the cake-sellers or fouassiers of Lerné, and the shepherds of Gargantua. Those shepherds, or pastors, should be the Lutheran and Calvinist ministers, whom John and Henry d'Albret favoured, being the more disposed to adhere to the reviving gospel which they preached, by the provoking remembrance of the Pope's and King of Spain's injurious usage; and for that reason Queen Marguerite did not only profess the Protestant religion, but, after the death of Henry d'Albret, Queen Jane, their daughter, married to Anthony de Bourbon, was a zealous defender of it till she died; and her son Henry, afterwards raised to the throne of France, publicly owned himself a Protestant, till his impatient desire of being peaceably seated on it made him leave the better party to pacify the worse.

The cake-sellers of Lerné are the priests, and other ecclesiastics of Spain; as also all the missificators, of the church of Rome. Rabelais calls them cake-mongers, or fouassiers, by reason of the host, or sacramental wafer, which is made of dough, between a pair of irons, like the cakes or fouasses in Poitou, where Rabelais lived, and is said to be tran-

---

[24] Memoires de Martin du Bellay.

substantiated into Christ's body, when consecrated by the priest.

The subject of the debate, as Rabelais terms it, between those cake-sellers and the shepherds, is the first's refusal to supply the latter with cakes, to eat with the grapes which they watched. 'For,' as Rabelais observes, 'it is a celestial food to eat for breakfast fresh cakes with grapes;' by which he alludes to the way of receiving the communion among the Protestants, who generally take that celestial food fasting, and always with the juice of the grape, that is, with wine, according to the evangelical institution. Now the cake-mongers, or popish priests, would not consent to give cakes, that is to say, bread, but would only give the accidents of the cakes, or, to speak in their own phrase, the accidents of the bread; and it is well known that this was the chief occasion of our separation from the church of Rome.

Upon the reasonable request of the shepherds, the cake-sellers, instead of granting it, presently fell to railing and reviling, adding, after a whole litany of comical, though defamatory epithets, that coarse, unraunged bread, or some of the great brown household loaf, was good enough for such shepherds, meaning that the gross notions of transubstantiation ought to satisfy the vulgar. The shepherds reply modestly enough, and say that the others used formerly to let them have cakes, by which must be understood the times that preceded the doctrine of transubstantiation. Then Marquet, one of the cake-merchants, treacherously invites Forgier to come to him for cakes, but, instead of them, only gives him a swingeing lash with his whip over thwart the legs, whereupon he is rewarded by the other with a broken pate, and falls down upon his mare, more

47

Preface

like a dead than a living man, wholly unfit to strike
another blow.

These two combatants are the controvertists of
both parties. The Papist immediately begins to rail
and abuse his adversary; the Lutheran confounds
him in his replies, and, for a blow with a whip,
treacherously given, very fairly disables his enemy.

This is the judgment that Rabelais, a man of wit
and learning, impartially passes on both parties. If
any would seek a greater mystery in that grand
debate, as Rabelais calls it, which term, I believe,
he would hardly have used for a real fight, let them
imagine that he there describes the conference at
Reinburgh, where Melancthon, Bucer, and Pistorius
debated of religion against Eccius, Julius Pflug, and
John Gropper, and handled them much as Forgier
did Marquet.

But this exploit of Forgier being inconsiderable,
if compared to those of Friar John des Entonneures,
or *of the funnels*, as some corruptly call him, we
should endeavour to discover who is that brave
monk that makes such rare work with those that
took away the grapes of the vineyard. By the pretended key, which I think fit to give you after this,
since it will hardly make up a page, we are told that
our Friar John is the Cardinal of Lorraine, brother
to the Duke of Guise: but that conjecture is certainly groundless; for though the princes of his
house were generally very brave, yet that cardinal
never affected to show his courage in martial achieve-
ments, and was never seen to girt himself for war,
or to fight for the cause which he most espoused;
besides, had he been to have fought, it would have
been for Picrochole. It would be more reasonable
to believe that Friar John is Odet de Coligny Cardinal de Chatillon, Archbishop of Tholouse, Bishop

and Earl of Beauvais, Abbot of St Benign, of Dijon, of Fleury, of Ferrières, and of Vaux de Cernay: for that prelate was a man of courage, no ways inferior to his younger brothers, the Admiral and the Lord d'Andelot.[25] Besides, he was an enemy to Spain, and a friend to Navarre; then he was a Protestant, and helped his brothers, doing great service to those of his party, and was married to Elizabeth de Hauteville, Dame de Thoré, a lady of great quality. Pope Pius IV., in a private consistory, deprived him for adhering to his brothers, but he neither valued the Pope nor his censures; he died in England in 1571, and lies interred in Canterbury Cathedral, having been made a Cardinal by Clement VII. at his and Francis I.'s interview at Marseilles in 1533. I own that what he did for the Protestant cause was chiefly after the death of Rabelais, and that some have represented him as a man wholly given to his ease; but Rabelais, whose best friend he was, knew his inclinations even when he composed this work, which made him dedicate the fourth part of it to him; and it is chiefly to that brave cardinal that we are obliged for that book and the last of this mysterious history;[26] since, without the King's protection, which he obtained for Rabelais, he had resolved to write no more, as I have already observed. And for his being addicted to his pleasures, that exactly answers the name of his abbey of Theleme, of which those that are members do what they please, according to their only rule, *Do what thou wilt*, and to the name of the abbey, θέλημα, *Voluntas*. Perhaps Rabelais had also a regard to θάλαμος, which often signifies a nuptial chamber, to show that our valiant monk was

[25] Vide Thuan. Samarthan. Ciacon. Du Bouchet. d'Aubigné, lib. 4. Sponde in Annal. Hist. Eccles. Beza. Petrameller.
[26] Lib. 4, Epist. Dedicat.

married: thus the description of the abbey shows us a model of a society free from all the ties of others, yet more honest by the innate virtues of its members; therefore its inscription excludes all monks and friars, inviting in all those that expound the holy gospel faithfully, though others murmur against them. Indeed, I must confess that he makes his friar swear very much; but this was to expose that vice, which, as well as many others, reigned among ecclesiastics in his age. Besides, the cardinal had been a soldier; and the men of that profession were doubtless not more reserved then than they are now.

I presume to say more, though, as all that I have said already, I humbly offer it as bare and uncertain conjecture: why may we not suppose that our author has a mind to give us, after his manner, a sketch of the great Luther? He was also a monk, and a jolly one too; 'being' as Rabelais says, 'a clerk even to the teeth in matter of breviary.' The vineyard, and consequently the wine which is saved, is the cup in the communion, which through his means, when taken away by the popish priests, was, in spite of Charles the Emperor, also King of Spain, and his soldiers, restored to the Protestants in Germany. The prior, who calls Friar John 'drunken fellow' for troubling the divine service, may be the Pope and the superior clergy.

Then Friar John throwing off his great monk's habit, and laying hold on the staff of the cross, is Luther's leaving his monastery, to rely on Christian weapons, the merit of his Redeemer. The victory obtained against those that disorderly ravaged the vineyard and took away the grapes, is his baffling the arguments of his opposers; and their being out of order, means the ignorance of the papists. The

little monkitos that proffer their help to Friar John,
and who, leaving their outer habits and coats upon
the rails, make an end of those whom he had already
crushed, are those monks and other of the clergy,
much inferior to Luther, who followed his reformation, and wrote against those whom he had in a
manner wholly confuted.

It is known, that at the Council of Trent the
Germans thirsted very much after the wine in the
eucharist, and that they were as eager for the abolish-
ing of the canons that enjoined celibacy to the
clergy, as for the restitution of the cup to the laity.
They used to have the words of our Saviour, ' Bibite
ex hoc omnes,' marked in golden characters in all
their Bibles, made songs and lampoons on the robbers
of the cup, as they called them. They had also a
design to have cups in all their standards and ensigns
of war, and the picture of the cup in all the churches
of their communion, as the Hussites of Bohemia had
done, which occasioned this distich by a poet of the
Roman church :

> Tot pingit calices Bohemorum terra per urbes,
> Ut credas Bacchi numina sola coli.

Indeed, what is said of Friar John, chap. 41, 42,
and 43, may induce us to believe, that the man who
has the greatest share in the character of the monk
did not absolutely cast off his frock, but far from it,
we see that the friar kept it on, to preserve himself
from his enemies, and desired no other armour for
back and breast, and after Gargantua's followers had
armed him cap-à-pié against his will, his armour was
the cause of an unlucky accident, which made him
call for help, and swear that he was betrayed, while
he remained hanged by the ears on a tree. So he
afterwards threw away his armour, and took to him

the staff of the cross: holding himself invulnerable with his monkish habit. Accordingly when Captain Drawforth is sent by Picrochole with 1600 horsemen thoroughly besprinkled with holy water, and who, to be distinguished from their enemies, wore a stole instead of a scarf (for so it should have been in the 43rd chapter, and not star, as it is there printed); we find that Friar John having frighted them all away, Drawforth only excepted, that bold enemy, with his utmost strength, could not make his lance pierce our monk's frock, and was soon knocked down by him with the staff of the cross: and found out to be a priest by his stole.

This confirms what has been said, that all this war is chiefly a dispute of religion; and this part of it seems to relate to Cardinal Chatillon, because he was secure within his ecclesiastical habit; the author sometimes, as I have said, joining several characters together. Thus the monk's discourse at table is not only applicable to that cardinal, but also to Montluc Bishop of Valence, who makes his first appearance on our doctor's stage, in the second act, by the name of Panurge; for Friar John being desired to pull off his frock; 'Let me alone with it,' replies he, 'I'll drink the better while it is on. It makes all my body jocund; did I lay it aside, I should lose my appetite:' so, many in those days, as well as in these, loved the benefice more than they hated the religion. Some will say that the request made then to Friar John was only that he should ease himself of his monastic frock while he was at table, but Rabelais would not have made his monk refuse such a request; he knew that some of the princes of the clergy had in his time, at the French court, and in the King's presence, taken a greater liberty; for there had been a ball in Lewis XII.'s reign, where

two cardinals danced before him among the rest;
and in another, given him by Joanne Jacomo
Trivulse, several princes and great lords had danced
in friars' habits. The monk talks with a great deal
of freedom at Gargantua's table, and swears that he
kept open house at Paris for six months; then he
talks of a friar that is become a hard student, then
says, that for his part he studies not at all, justifying
himself for this conduct in false Latin; after this he
abruptly starts a new matter, and lets his fancy run
after hares, hawks, and hounds, and thus he goes on
by sallies, and admirably humours the way of talking
of the young court abbots in France. Now probably
the cardinal, who did not set up for a man of learning, being of great quality, allowed himself liberty
accordingly, making hunting one of his recreations;
and indeed what Gargantua says concerning Friar
John, in the next chapter,[27] hits Cardinal Chatillon's
character exactly: there having taxed most monks
with mumbling out great store of legends and psalms,
which they understand not at all, and interlarding
many pater-nosters, with ten times as many ave-
maries, without thinking upon, or apprehending the
meaning of what they say, which he calls mocking
of God, and not prayers; he says, 'that all true
Christians, in all places, and at all times, send up
their prayers to God, and the spirit prayeth and
intercedes for them, and God is gracious to them:
now such a one,' adds he, 'is our Friar John, he is no
bigot,' etc.

What Grangousier says to the French pilgrims
shows that he was no bigot, and was not King of
France; when speaking of some superstitious
preachers, one of whom had called him heretic, he

[27] Book i. chap. 40.

53

Preface

adds, ' I wonder that your king should suffer them in their sermons to publish such scandalous doctrine in his dominions.' Then Friar John says to the pilgrims, that while they are thus upon their pilgrimage, the monks will have a fling at their wives. After that, Grangousier bids them not be so ready to undertake those idle and unprofitable journeys, but go home and live as St Paul directs them, and then God will guard them from evils which they think to avoid by pilgrimages.

What has been observed puts it beyond all doubt, that our jesting author was indeed in earnest when he said, that he mystically treated of the most high sacraments, and dreadful secrets, in what concerns our religion. I know that immediately after this, he passes off with a banter, what he had assured very seriously; but this was an admirable piece of prudence; and whoever will narrowly examine his writings, will find, that this virtue is inseparably joined with his wit, so that his enemies never could have any advantage over him.

But not to comment upon several other places in his first book, that the ingenious may have the pleasure of unriddling the rest of it themselves, I will only add, that his manner of ending it is a master-piece surpassing the artful evasion which, as I have now observed, is in its introduction.

It is an enigma, as indeed is the whole work: I could only have wished that it had been proper to have put it into a more modish dress (for then doubtless it would more generally have pleased). But I suppose that the gentleman who revised this translation thought it not fit to give the graces of our modern enigmas to the translation of a prophetical riddle in the style of Merlin. Gargantua piously fetches a very deep sigh, when he has heard it read,

Preface

and says, that he perceives by it, that it is not now
only that people called to the faith of the gospel are
persecuted; but happy is the man that shall not be
scandalized, but shall always continue to the end, in
aiming at the mark, which God by His dear Son has
set before us, etc. Upon this the monk asks him,
what he thought was signified by the riddle?
What? says Gargantua, the decrease and propagation
of the divine truth. That is not my exposition, says
the monk, it is the style of the prophet Merlin;
make as many grave allegories and tropes as you
will; I can perceive no other meaning in it; but
a description of a set at tennis in dark and obscure
terms. By this riddle, which he expounds, he
cunningly seems to insinuate that all the rest of his
book, which he has not explained, wholly consists of
trifles; and what is most remarkable, is, that he
illustrates the truths which he had concealed, by the
very passages, wherewith he pretends to make them
pass for fables, and thus blinds, with too much light,
those enemies of truth, who would not have failed to
have burned him alive in that persecuting age, had
he had less wit and prudence than they showed
ignorance and malice.

I need not enlarge much on the other books, by
reason of the discoveries made in the first that relate
to them. The first chapter of the second gives us
Pantagruel's pedigree from the giants: it has been
observed by a learned man some years ago, that the
word giant, which the interpreters of the scripture
have set in their versions, stands there for another,
that means no more than prince in the Hebrew; so
perhaps our author was the more ready to make his
princes giants, though, as I have said, his chief design
was tacitly to censure, in this, John d'Albret and
such others as (like one in Brittany, that took for his

motto, Antequam Abraham esset, sum) were too proud of an uncertain empty name. His description of the original of giants, and the story of Hurtali's bestriding the ark, is to mock those in the Talmud and other legends of the Rabbins; for he tells us, that when this happened, the calends were found in the Greek almanacks, and all know that ad Græcas calendas, is as much as to say never; for the Greeks never reckoned by calends. Yet what he tells of the earth's fertility in medlars, after it had been imbrued with the blood of the just, may be allegorical; and those who, by feeding on that fair large delicious fruit, became monstrous, may be the converts of that age, who, by the popish world, were looked upon as monsters. The blood of martyrs, which was profusely spilt in that age, has always been thought prolific even to a proverb; and the word mesles in French, and medlars in English, equally imports meddling. Thus in French, 'Il se mesle de nos affaires,' he meddles with our business; so the medlars may be those who busied themselves about the Reformation.

The great drought at the birth of Pantagruel, is that almost universal cry of the laity for the restitution of the cup in the sacrament, at the time that Anthony de Bourbon Duke of Vendosme was married to the heiress of Navarre, which was in October 1548, the Council of Trent then sitting. For thence we must date his birth, since by that match he afterwards gained the title of King, besides Bearn, Bigorre, Albret, and several other territories; and we are told, Book iii. chap. 48, that Pantagruel, at the very first minute of his birth, was no less tall than the herb Pantagruelian (which unquestionably is hemp); and a little before that, it is said, that its height is commonly of five or six feet. The death

56

of Queen Marguerite, his mother-in-law, that soon followed, made our author say, that when Pantagruel was born, Gargantua was much perplexed, seeing his wife dead, at which he made many lamentations. Perhaps this also alludes to the birth of King Edward VI., which caused the death of his mother, Queen Jane Seymour. King Henry VIII. is said to have comforted himself with saying, that he could get another wife, but was not sure to get another son. Thus, here we find Gargantua much grieved and joyful by fits, like Talboy in the play, but at last comforting himself with the thoughts of his wife's happiness and his own, in having a son, and saying, that he must now cast about how to get another wife, and will stay at home and rock his son.

In the 6th chapter, we find Pantagruel discoursing with a Limousin, who affected to speak in learned phrase. Rabelais had, in the foregoing chapter, satirized many persons, and given a hint of some abuses in the universities of France; in this he mocks some of the writers of that age, who, to appear learned, wholly filled their works with Latin words, to which they gave a French inflection. But this pedantic jargon was more particularly affected by one Helisaine of Limoges, who, as Boileau says of Ronsard, en Français parlant Grec et Latin (speaking Greek and Latin in French), thought to have refined his mother tongue. So Rabelais, to prevent the spreading of that contagion, has not only brought that Limousin author on his Pantagruelian stage, but wrote a letter in verse, all in that style, in the name of the Limousin scholar, printed at the end of the Pantagruelian prognostication. Pasquier, who lived at that time, has made the like observation on that chapter, when in his second book of letters, p. 53, he says, ' Pour l'ornement de nostre langue, et nous

57

aider mesmes du Grec et du Latin, non pour les
escorcher ineptement comme fit sur nostre jeune
age Helisaine, dont nostre gentil Rabelais s'est
mocqué fort à propos en la personne de l'escolier
Limosin qu'il introduit parlant à Pantagruel en un
langage escorché Latin.

The 7th chapter, wherein he gives a catalogue of
the books in St Victor's library, is admirable, and
would require a large comment, it being a satire
against many writers and great affairs in that age, as
well as against those who either make collections of
bad books, or seek no others in libraries; but I have
not leisure to read over a great number of books that
ought to be consulted for such a task.

The cause which was pleaded before Pantagruel
by the Lords Suck-fizle and Kiss-breech,[28] seems to
be a mock of the famous trial concerning two
duchies, four counties, two viscounties, and many
baronies and lordships, to which Loyse de Savoye,
the mother of Francis I., laid claim. Charles de
Bourbon, Constable of France, was possessed of
them; but because he had refused to marry her, she
made use of some titles which she had to them to
perplex him; and though she could not, even with
the King her son's favour, cast the Constable, yet they
were sequestered into the King's hands, and the final
determination put off.

The 18th, 19th, and 20th chapters treat of a great
scholar in England, who came to argue by signs with
Pantagruel, and was overcome by Panurge. I do not
well know on whom to fix the character of Thaumast
that scholar, whose name may not only signify an
admirer, but an admirable person, or one of those
schoolmen who follow the doctrine of Thomas

[28] Book ii. chaps. 10, 11, 12, 13.

58

Aquinas, in opposition to that of Scotus: and I find as little reason to think, that any would have come to confer with Anthony de Bourbon of geomancy, philosophy, and the cabalistic art. Indeed, Sir Thomas More went ambassador to Francis I.; and Erasmus, who lived some time in England, also came to Paris; but I cannot think that either may pass for the Thaumast of Rabelais. Perhaps he hath made him an Englishman, merely on purpose to disguise the story; and I would have had some thoughts of Henricus Cornelius Agrippa who came to France and died there; but I will prove, when I examine the third book, that he has brought him on the stage by the name of Her Trippa. So it is not impossible but that he may have meant Hieronymus Cardan of Milan, who flourished in that age, and was another dark cabalistic author. The first has said, Occult. Philos. l. i, c. 6, that he knew how to communicate his thoughts by the species of sight in a magical way, as Pythagoras was said to do, by writing anything in the body of the moon, so as it should be legible to another at a vast distance; and he pretends to tell us the method of it in his book, De Vanitate Scientiarum. Cardan also has writ concerning private ways of imparting our thoughts, Subtilit. 1, 17, and De Variet. Rerum, lib. 12; but these ways of signifying our thoughts by gestures, called by the learned Bishop Wilkins, Semæology, are almost of infinite variety; according as the several fancies of men shall impose significations upon such signs as are capable of sufficient difference. And the venerable Bede has made a book only of that, commonly styled Arthologia or Dactylologia, which he calls Lib. de Loquelâ par Gestum Digitorum, sive de Indigitatione. So that perhaps our author made his Thaumast an Englishman, not to reflect on Bede, but because that learned

59

father is the most ancient and famous author that has written a book on that subject.

I have read of a public debate, much like that of Thaumast and Panurge, and as probable, said to have been held at Geneva. The aggressor lifted up his arm and closed three of his fingers and his thumb, and pointed with the remaining finger at his opponent; who immediately pointed at him again with two. Then the other showed him two fingers and one thumb; whereupon his antagonist shook his closed fist at him. Upon this the aggressor showed him an apple; and the other looking into his pocket found a bit of bread, and in a scornful way let him see it; which made him that begun the dispute yield himself vanquished. Now when the conqueror was desired to relate what their signs signified: he with whom I disputed, said he, threatened first to put out one of my eyes, and I gave him to understand that I would put out both his; then he threatened to tear both mine, and take off my ˙nose; upon which I showed him my fist, to let him know that I would knock him down; and as he perceived that I was angry, he offered me an apple to pacify me as they do children; but I showed him that I scorned his present, and that I had bread, which was fitter for a man.

The Dipsodes,[29] that had besieged the city of the Amaurots, are the Flemings, and other subjects of the Emperor Charles V. that máde inroads into Picardy, and the adjacent territories, of which Anthony of Bourbon was not only governor, but had considerable lordships in those parts. The Flemings have always been brisk topers; and for this reason are called Dipsodes, from διψάω, *sitio*, διψώδης,

---

[29] Book ii. chap. 23.

thirsty; and he calls Picardy and Artois, the land
of the Amaurots, from the word ἀμαυρὸς, *obscurus*
or *evanidus;* perhaps because they are in the north
of France; or that parts of them were in the hands
of the enemy.

The next exploit is that in the 29th chapter,
where we find how Pantagruel discomfited the three
hundred giants armed with freestone, and Loupgarou,
their captain. The death of Loupgarou, in the
presence of his giants, may relate to the taking of
Liliers, a town between Bapaume and Aire: it
molested very much the country that belonged to
the French, and was seated near a marsh; yet
notwithstanding the advantage of the season and its
resolute garrison, the Duke of Vendosme, having
caused a large breach to be made, and being ready
to storm the place, the besieged desired to capitulate,
and after many parleys, surrendered the town on
dishonourable terms.

By accident the ammunition of the besiegers had
taken fire, and even some of the carriages of the
artillery were burned; which may perhaps have
made our author say, in the foregoing chapter, that
Carpalim having set on fire the enemy's ammunition,
the flame having reached the place where was their
artillery, he was in great danger of being burned;
or, perhaps, this alludes to the Duke of Vendosme's
setting Liliers on fire, and destroying it quite, after
he had taken it. For our author writes not like an
historian, but like a poet, who ought not to be
blamed for anachronisms. However, it is certain,
that the relief of Terouenne, and then the surrender
of Liliers, were Anthony de Bourbon's two first
exploits; the one soon after the other. Then the
300 giants armed with freestone, which Pantagruel
struck down like a mason, by breaking their stony

armour, mowing them down with the dead body of
Loupgarou, are a great number of castles about
Liliers, Terouenne, Saint Omer, Aire, and Bethune,
which Anthony of Bourbon demolished, immediately
after he had taken Liliers, and then passed through
Terouenne, which is the city of the Amaurots,
which he went to relieve; by whose inhabitants
Pantagruel is so nobly received in the 31st. We
may also suppose, that by King Anarchus, Rabelais
means the plundering, lawless boors that sheltered
themselves in those castles, who were afterwards
reduced to sell herbs. This is, Anarchus's being
reduced to cry green sauce in a canvas jacket.

The Duke of Vendosme marched next, without
any resistance, through the Upper Artois, took
Bapaume in his way, which is doubtless the
Almyrods, called so from ἁλμυρώδης, Salsuginosus,[30]
or salted people, who resolved to hold out against
Pantagruel; yet only to have honourable conditions.
It seems to me, that this is meant of the castle of
that town, which held out against the duke only for
terms; all the inhabitants of the town having retired
into that small place, where there was but one well,
whose water had been altogether exhausted in two
days (to which, perhaps, relates the salt which
Pantagruel put into the mouths of his enemies), and
they were ready to submit to mercy, with halters at
their necks;[31] but the King, who had already sent
many expresses to the duke, ordering him to march
to join him with all speed, and neither to stop at
Bapaume or any where else, sent him angrily fresh
orders, wherein he charged him of his allegiance to
join him that day at Chasteau in Cambrezis, on
pain of incurring his displeasure. So the duke, to

---

[30] Book ii. chap. 32.   [31] Memoires de Guil. du Bellay, Liv. 10.

the great joy of the besieged, and his greater sorrow, raised his camp, and came to the King. Neither does our author speak of the surrender of the Almyrods; but makes Pantagruel's forces be overtaken with a great shower of rain, and then tells us how Pantagruel covered a whole army with his tongue. For they began, says he, to shiver and tremble, to crowd, press, and thrust close to one another; which when he saw, he bid his captains tell them that it was nothing; however, that they should put themselves into order, and he would cover them; and he drew out his tongue only half way, and covered them all. I find that the duke, before he took Liliers, and besieged the castle of Bapaume, sent to the King to desire him to send him a month's pay to his forces, and then he could take some frontier towns, and even Bapaume; but the King sent him no money, and, on the contrary, ordered him to march on to meet him; but before he had that answer, he had taken Liliers. So his soldiers, who wanted their pay and clothes, being also vexed for having, · by the King's fault, missed taking the booty in the castle of Bapaume, were displeased, and in bad circumstances; but upon this the duke spoke to the King, and got them their arrears and clothes. And this is what Rabelais calls covering an army with his tongue. As for what follows, it seems an imitation of Lucian's whale in his true history; as the news which Epistemon brings from hell, in the 30th chapter, is also a copy of that author; and what ours says he saw in Pantagruel's mouth is only to blind the rest, which seems to me so plain, like most of the discoveries I here publish, that I wonder that none ever gave an account of any of them in the space of above one hundred and forty years.

Preface

The sickness of Pantagruel, chap. 33, is his disgust upon this disappointment at Bapaume; or some real sickness that seized him.

There the author concludes his second book, that was published some time after the first, which we may perceive by what he tells us of the monks, and their bigoted cullies, who had already tried to find something in it that might render him obnoxious to the law; which caused him to be somewhat more reserved in matters of religion in that and the following, than he was afterwards in the fourth and fifth.

Panurge is the chief actor in the third act of our Pantagruelian play. We find him there much perplexed with uncertainties; his mind fluctuating between the desire of entering into a matrimonial engagement, and the fear of having occasion to repent it. To be eased of his doubt, he consults several persons, all famous for some particular skill in removing anxieties of mind; and there our learned and ingenious satirist displays his knowledge and his fancy to admiration. ·

But before that, we find Pantagruel, in the first chapter, transporting a colony of Utopians into Dipsodie; for which Rabelais gives a very good reason, and proves himself a master at politics as well as at other things. To explain that passage, we must know that the Duke of Vendosme garrisoned out of Picardy some of the places that had been taken in Artois, fixing also there some of his vassals and tenants, who were very numerous thereabouts; and as he was born among them, viz. at La Fere, in 1518, he had a particular love for them.

In the second chapter Panurge is made Laird of Salmygondin in Dipsodie, and wasteth his revenue before it comes in. I can apply this to nothing but the gift of some benefice to Montluc by the Duke of Vendosme or the Queen of Navarre, afterwards his mother-in-law; which benefice not being sufficient to supply him in his extravagancies, something more considerable was bestowed on him; which, having set him at ease, gave him occasion to reflect on his former ill conduct, and grow more thrifty; so that afterwards he entertained some thoughts of marriage, and probably was married when Rabelais wrote.

Among those whom Panurge consults, the Sybil of Panzoust is the first whose right name is difficult to be discovered. The pretended key in the French makes her a court lady; but its author seems never to have read Rabelais, or at least not to have understood him, if we may judge of it by the names which he, in spite of reason, has set against some of those in our author. Among four or five short explanations of as many passages in Rabelais, also printed in the French, one of them tells us, that by the Sybil of Panzoust, our author means a gentlewoman of that place, near Chinon, who died very old, and always lived single, though importuned by her friends to marry when she was young. But Rabelais having in this book very artfully made his Panurge consult men of different professions famous in his time, to be eased of his doubt, I do not believe that he would have begun by a woman altogether unknown to the learned world; yet not but that he may have made choice of the name of Panzoust to double the character, if he knew that such an antiquated she-thing lived there. I have endeavoured to discover who might be that Sybil, but dare not positively fix that character on any. St Theresa, a Spanish nun, who lived in that age, might come in for a share; she has writ several books, and was already famous

Preface

when Rabelais lived; she had very odd notions; and discovered perhaps as much madness as sanctity. I find another noted crack-brained bigot, who was old at that time, and lived at Venice; it is one whom several great men have mentioned by the name of *Virgo Veneta.* Guillaume Postel, amongst the rest, a very learned Jesuit, and very famous in that age for philosophy, calls her Mother Joan, and had such a veneration for her, that he thought the reparation of the female sex not yet perfected, and that such a glorious work was reserved for her. But Florimond de Raymond excuses him in this, and says, that he only designed to praise her for the great services which she had done him in his travels.

In the one and twentieth chapter Panurge consulteth with Raminagrobis, an old French poet, who was almost upon the very last moment of his life. This poet was William Cretin, treasurer of the king's chapel, who had lived under Charles VIII., Louis XII., and Francis I., as may be seen by his works. Never was man more celebrated by the writers of his age. John le Maire dedicated to him his three first books of the illustrations of France, and speaks of him as of the man to whom he owed all things. Geoffroy Toré, in his Champ Fleury, says, that Cretin in his chronicles of France had outdone Homer and Virgil. And even Marot inscribed to him his epigrams.

The Rondeau, which Raminagrobis gives to Panurge upon his resolution as to his marriage, Prenez-la, ne la prenez pas, etc., that is, Take, or not take her, off or on, etc., is taken out of Cretin, who had addressed it to Guillaume de Refuge, who had asked his advice, being in the same perplexity. However, Rabelais makes him die like a good Protestant, and afterwards turns off cunningly what

66

the other had said against the popish clergy, who
would not let him die in peace.

I ought not to omit a remark printed in the last
Dutch edition of this book, concerning what Panurge
says of Cretin: 'He is, by the virtue of an ox, an arrant
heretic; a thorough-paced, rivetted heretic. I say,
a rooted combustible heretic; one as fit to burn, as
the little wooden clock at Rochelle; his soul goeth
to thirty thousand carts-full of devils.' Rabelais there
reflects on the sentence of death passed on one of
the first that owned himself a Protestant at Rochelle.
He was a watchmaker, and had made a clock all of
wood, which was esteemed an admirable piece;
but because it was the work of one condemned for
heresy, the judges ordered, by the said sentence, that
the clock should be burned by the common hang-
man, and it was burned accordingly. We must also
observe that the adjective clavelé, that is full of nails
or rivetted, is brought in because that watchmaker,
who was very famous for his zeal, was named
Clavelé.

In the 24th chapter Panurge consults Epistemon,
who perhaps may be Guillaume Ruffy, Bishop of
Oleron, one of Queen Marguerite's ministers, who
had been some time in prison for preaching the Reformation, and was afterwards made bishop in the
King of Navarre's territories, having without doubt
dissembled like many others. Thus his descent into
hell, in the second book, may be his prison: I own
that he is with Pantagruel in the wars, but so is
Panurge, and this is done to disguise the characters;
I am the more apt to believe him a clergyman, because he understands Hebrew very well, which few
among the laity do, and none else in our author,
besides Panurge, who calls him his dear gossip.
Then his name denotes him to be a thinking, con-

sidering man, and as he was Pantagruel's pedagogue, so probably Ruffy initiated or instructed the duke in the doctrine of the new preachers.

Enguerrant, whom Rabelais taxes with making a tedious and impertinent digression about a Spaniard, is Enguerrant de Monstrelet, who wrote La Chronique et Annales de France.

In the same chapter, he speaks of the four Ogygian islands near the haven of Sammalo; by this he seems to mean Jersey, Guernsey, Sark, and Alderney. As Queen Marguerite lived a while and died in Brittany, our actors may be thought sometimes to stroll thither. Calypso was said to live at the island Ogygia; Lucian, amongst the rest, places her there, and Plutarch mentions it in the book of the face that appears in the circle of the moon.

Her Trippa, is undoubtedly Henricus Cornelius Agrippa burlesqued. Her is Henricus or Herricus, or perhaps alludes to Heer, because he was a German, and Agrippa is turned into Trippa, to play upon the word tripe. But for a farther proof, we need but look into Agrippa's book, de Occult. Philosoph. lib. 1. cap. 7. De Quatuor Elementorum Divinationibus, and we shall find the very words used by Rabelais of Pyromancy, Acromancy, Hydromancy, etc.; besides, Agrippa came to Francis I., whom our author calls the great King, to distinguish him from that of Navarre.

Friar John des Entonneures, or, of the Funnels, as he is called in this translation, advises Panurge to marry; and whether by that brave monk we understand Cardinal Chatillon, or Martin Luther, the character is kept, since both were married; neither was the latter wholly free from Friar John's swearing faculty, if it be true that being once reproved about it, he replied, 'Condonate mihi hoc qui fui

Monachus.' He is called also des Entomeures from
ἐντομή, ἐντέμνειν, to cut and make incisions, which
was our monk's delight, who is described as a mighty
trencher-man.

Hippothadeus, the theologian, may perhaps be
Philip Shwartzerd, alias Melancthon; for he
speaks too much like a Protestant to be the King's
confessor; neither could Montluc be supposed to
desire his advice.

Rondibilis, the physician, is doubtless Gulielmus
Rondeletius. Thuanus remarks, in the thirty-eighth
book of his history, that Gul. Rondelet of Montpellier died 1566, and that, though he was a learned
physician, Rabelais had satirized him.

I am not so certain of the man whom Trouillogan
personates; he calls him an Ephectic and Pyr-
rhonean philosopher. Molière has imitated the
scene between Trouillogan and Panurge, in one of
his plays, and M. de la Fontaine, the story of Hans
Carvel, and that of the devil of Pope-Figland, in his
inimitable Contes et Nouvelles.

There was a jack-pudding in France in that age,
called Triboulet, but I believe that the fool whom
our author describes in the 38th chapter is one more
considerable, though less famous. I cannot guess
why he has heaped up so many adjectives on that
fool, unless it be to show the excess of his folly, and
to mock some of the authors of that age, who often
bestowed a large train of such unnecessary attendants
on a single noun substantive.

Marotte is a word very much used by the French,
signifying a fool's bauble or club, and the word Fou,
given by Rabelais to Triboulet, implies a mad,
crack-brained, or inconsiderate man, and also a
jester; the word idiot being more used in French,
for what we properly call a fool: now Clement

69

Marot, the best poet in the reign of Francis I., whose valet de chambre he was styled, was a notable jester, and is said to have played many merry tricks that bordered somewhat on extravagance; besides, many among the vulgar mistaking the enthusiasm of poets for madness, have but a small opinion of the wisdom of most of them. But these considerations do not seem to me strong enough to make me believe that Rabelais would have passed so severe a censure on that poet, who was then but lately dead, an exile for his religion, and had made honourable mention of him in his works, they being undoubtedly intimate friends.

Judge Bridlegoose, who decided causes by the chance of dice, and was arraigned for prevarication at the bar of the parliament of Mirelingois, resembles much a judge of Montmartre, who they say could neither write nor read, yet had been a judge many years; and being once called into question in a superior court, owned his ignorance as to the point of writing and reading, but affirmed that he knew the law; and desiring that the cause of which an appeal had been made from his jurisdiction might be examined, he was found to have done justice, and his sentence and authority were confirmed.

I have said before, that the herb Pantagruelion is *Hemp ;* Rabelais makes Pantagruel load a great quantity of it on board his ships, and indeed it is one of the most useful things in the world, not only at sea, but also at land. The curious and pleasing description of that plant makes up the rest of this third book.

I hope that I have said enough to show that what appears trivial and foolish in this work is generally grave and of moment when seriously examined, and humbly submit all I have said to the judgment of the learned.

Our Rabelais's work is a satire of the kind of those

which, from Menippus, were called -Menippæan
by his imitator Varro, the most learned among the
Romans; having given that name to that which he
made, because, like that cynic philosopher, in it he
had treated of grave matters in a merry joking style.
That satire, or, as Tully calls it, that *poema varium et
elegans*, was at once a mixture of prose and several
sorts of verse; of Greek and of Latin; of philology
and of philosophy. Yet, since Strabo says that by
them he got the name of σπουδογελοῖος, or Joco-
serius, we may believe that there was morality in
them; but that, as in our Rabelais, not being
obvious, some thought them trifling; like many in
our age, who find it much easier to judge and find
fault than to understand.

I could wish that among the other sorts of writing
which, in some things, have been imitated by our
author, I might not reckon Petronius Arbiter; yet I
only say this as to his immodesty; for otherwise, as
that consul, under some amorous fictions, has concealed a close and ingenious satire on the vices that
reigned in Nero's court, and was as nice and good a
judge of polite learning as of dissolute pleasures,
without doubt he is to be followed and admired:
and, indeed, his fable was esteemed to be like the
Greek satiric poems, which Plato says consisted of
fictions whose hidden sense differed very much from
the superficial signification of the words; since
Macrobius, while he distinguishes fables made barely
to please from those that at once divert and instruct,
has placed that of Petronius among the latter.

Our author's works are also an imitation of Democritus and of Socrates, if we may compare writings
with actions; for those two philosophers used to be
still merry, and freely ridiculed whatever was a fit
subject of raillery.

Preface

Now Rabelais chiefly pursues his subject by jesting and exposing, ridiculing and despising what he thinks deserves such an usage; and it is but seldom that he makes use of railing, or sullen biting reproofs.

In short, it is a mixture, or, if I may use the expression, an olio, of all the merry, serious, satirical, and diverting ways of writing, that have hitherto been used. But still mirth is predominant in the composition, and, like a pleasing tartness, gives the whole such a relish, that we ever feed on it with an eager appetite, and can never be cloyed with it.

To imitate it, is not only *periculosæ plenum opus aleæ*, but almost an impossible task; nor is it easily to be defined. We see that it is historical, romantic, allegorical, comical, satirical; but as sometimes all these kinds of writing are united in one passage, at others they appear severally.

As for the mixture of odd, burlesque, barbarous, Latin, Greek, and obsolete words, which is seen in his book, it is justifiable, as it serves to add to the diversion of the reader. About twenty years before it was composed, Theophilus Folengi, a monk born at Mantua, of a noble family who is hardly known now otherwise than by the name of Merlinus Coccaius, had put out his Liber Macaronicorum, which is a poetical rhapsody, made up of words of different languages, and treating of pleasant matters in a comical style. The word macarone in Italian signifies a jolly clown, and maccaroni a sort of cakes made with coarse meal, eggs, and cheese, as Thomasin observes.

This mixture of languages, and of odd and fantastic terms, has been censured by Vavassor, chiefly, because he pretends that the ancients never used it, though none will deny that they mixed words and verses of different kinds. As for the puns, clenches,

72

conundrums, quibbles, and all such other dregs or
bastard sorts of wit, that here and there have crept in
among the infinite number of our author's ingenious
and just conceptions, I will not apologise in their
behalf, otherwise than by showing that Aristophanes
and Plautus have strewed them more lavishly through
their works, which are partly of the nature of
this.

Mirth being so desirable a thing, so beneficial to
the body and to the mind, and laughing one of the
distinguishing characters of mankind, our author may
be said not to have advantaged the world a little, in
composing this merry treatise. He justifies himself
in his dedication to Cardinal Chatillon, for his
comical expressions, by representing the case which
many disconsolate and sick persons had received by
them; and he says before his first book, *Le rire est le
propre de l'homme ;* or, as it has been Englished, 'To
laugh is proper to the man.' Even Cæsar had writ a
whole book of merry and witty sayings; and Balzac,
a great enemy to burlesque, has said, 'That mankind
was not a little obliged to the man who sometimes
could make Augustus merry.'

Nor has our author only aimed at mirth, though he
has partly made it subservient to his chief design.
He knew that the learned and the ignorant, by
different motives, delight in fables, and that the love
of mirth being universal, the only way to cause his
sentiments to be most known and followed, was to
give them a merry dress.

He saw that vice was not to be conquered in a
declamatory war, and that the angry railing lectures
of some well-meaning men were seldom as effectual
to make it give ground, as the gay yet pointed
railleries of those who seem unconcerned; the latter
convincing us effectually, while the others, with

Preface

their passionate invectives, persuade us of nothing, but that they are too angry to direct others.

This gay way of moralizing has also nothing of the dry mortifying methods of those philosophers who, striving to demonstrate their principles by causes and a long series of arguments, only rack the mind; but its art and delicacy is not perceived by every reader: consequently many people will not easily find out the inward beauties of the works of Rabelais; but he did not intend that every one should perceive them, though every one may be extremely diverted by the outward and obvious wit and humour. Painting has its grotesque and bold touches, which seem irregular to the vulgar, only pleased with their oddness; while masters, through the antic features and rough strokes, discover an exact proportion, a softness and a boldness together, which charm them to an unspeakable degree. So in artful jests and ironies, in that *lusus animi* and judicious extravagance, what seems mean and absurd is most in sight, and strikes the vulgar; but better judgments under that coarse outside discover exquisite wit, just and sublime thoughts, vast learning, and the most profound reasonings of philosophy.

It is true, that those whose temper inclines them to a stoical severity will not have the same taste; and, indeed, rallying seldom or never becomes them; but those who would benefit themselves by the perusal of Rabelais need not imitate his buffoonery; and it is enough if it inwardly move us, and spread there such seeds of joy as will produce on all sorts of subjects an infinite number of pleasant reflections. In those places that are most dangerous, a judicious reader will curb his thoughts and desires, considering that the way is slippery, and thus will easily be safe; with wise reflections moderating his affections.

It is even better to drink some too strong wines, tempering them with water, which makes them but the more pleasant, than to confine ourselves to flat and insipid liquors, which neither affect the palate nor cheer us within. The Roman ladies used to view the wrestlers naked in the cirque, and one of them discreetly said, that a virtuous woman was not more scandalized at their sight than at that of a statue, of which great numbers were naked in all places.

Thus the sight of those females at Sparta, who danced naked, being only covered with the public honesty, made no ill impression on the beholders. We may pass over, with as much ease, the impurities of our historian, as we forgive to excellent painters nudities, which they too faithfully represent; and we may only admire and fix our eyes on the other parts of the piece. *Omnia sana sanis.*

The age in which our author wrote was not so reserved in words as this, and perhaps he has not so much followed his own genius in making use of gross or loose expressions, as he has endeavoured to accommodate his way of writing to the humour of the people, not excepting a part of the clergy of those times. Now we ought not to blame those authors who wrote in former ages for differing from us in several things; since they followed customs and manners which were then generally received, though now they seem to us improper or unjust. To discover all the beauties in their works, we must awhile lay aside the thoughts of our practice, if it contradicts theirs; otherwise all books will be very short-lived, and the best writers, being disheartened with the thoughts of the speedy oblivion or contempt of their works, will no longer strive to deserve an immortal fame, which fantastic posterity would deny them.

75

Preface

After all, as I could wish that some expressions, which I will not only call too bold and too free, but even immodest and profane, had not been in this book, I would not have those persons to read it whose lives are so well regulated, that they would not employ a moment of which they might not give an account without blushing; nor those whose minds, not being ripened by years and study, are most susceptible of dangerous impressions. Doubtless they may do much better than to read this book.

Some, therefore, will think, that either it was not to be translated, or ought to have been translated otherwise; and that, as in the most handsome faces there are always some lines which we could wish were not there; so, if those things, which here may shock some persons, had been omitted or softened, it would more justly and more generally have pleased: I suppose that the translator would have done so, had he not been afraid to have taken out some material thing, hid under the veil of some unhappy expression, instead of taking away a bare trifle.

But as what may be blameable in this book bears no proportion with the almost infinite number of admirable and useful things which are to be found in it, the ingenious ought not to be deprived of it. Lucian's works, notwithstanding a thousand passages in them against modesty and religion, have been handed down to us by the primitive Christians, which they would not have done, had they not been sensible that they could do much more good than harm.

The art of writing has caused much mischief, which made the ancients say, that its inventor had sown serpents' teeth. Yet who would be without the use of letters? We may as well cut out our tongue, that world of wickedness, as it is called in

76

scripture. Weak minds may turn good things to the worst use, and even sacred writings have produced ill effects: readers are often more blameable than authors, and should like bees gather honey out of poetical flowers, instead of sucking the poison like spiders. The cause of the ill actions of most men is not in books, but in the wicked disposition of their hearts; and the soft melancholy with which the most chaste romances often cloud the mind, thus making way for violent passions, is much more to be feared than a work of this nature.

As long as those and some of our plays are in the hands of the weaker sex; that Catullus, Ovid, Juvenal, and Martial are learned by heart in schools by men children; and a thousand other books, more dangerous, prostituted to the ignorant vulgar; Rabelais's works, in ·which there is more morality, as well as more wit and learning, than in most that are read, may be allowed a place among the best.

PETER MOTTEUX.

N.B. At the end of the late French editions of Rabelais, without the least reason, the Dipsodes were said to be Lorrains. Friar John was said to be Cardinal de Lorraine. Gargantua was said to be Francis I. Grangousier was said to be Lewis XII. Great mare of Gargantua, Madame d'Estampes. Her Trippa, a great magician. Hippothadeus, the king's confessor. Lerné, Bresse. Loupgarou, ·Amiens. Pantagruel, Henry II. Sybil of Panzoust, a court lady. Panurge, Cardinal d'Amboise. Picrochole, Piedmont. Salmygondin, Benefices. Theleme, Protocol of the Council of Trent. Xenomanes, the chancellor.

These are all the names said to belong to these three books, and unjustly called a key to them.

THE LIST

SOME OF THE NAMES

MENTIONED IN THE FIRST, SECOND, AND THIRD BOOKS
OF RABELAIS, EXPLAINED IN THE PREFACE.

THE antidoted franfreluches	{ A satire on the Pope, Emperor, etc.
Grangousier . . .	John d'Albret, King of Navarre
Gargamelle	{ Catherine de Foix, Queen of Navarre
Gargantua . . .	{ Henry d'Albret, King of Navarre
Badèbec	Margaret de Valois, his Queen
Pantagruel	Anthony de Bourbon
Panurge	Montluc, Bishop of Valence.
Friar John of the funnels	{ Cardinal Chatillon, also Martin Luther
Utopia	Navarre
Beusse	Albret
Verron	Bearn
Bibarois	Vivarez
Picrochole	King of Spain
Lerné	Spain
Cake-bakers of Lerné .	The Popish priests
The cakes	Bread in communion
Truands of Lerné . .	The Spanish army
Philip Marais, Viceroy of } Papeligosse . . . }	Philip, son to the Mareschal of Navarre

78

List of Names

Theodorus, the physician for the brain . . . . — Berthaud, a Protestant divine

White and blue, Gargantua's colours . . . . — Innocence, piety, Bishop of Maillezais's colours

Epistemon . . . . — Ruffy, Bishop of Oleron

Anticyrian hellebore . . — The Holy Scripture

Vine of Sevillé . . . — Cup in the Eucharist

Janotus de Bragmardo . . — Cenalis, Bishop of Avranches, also a head of a college

Gargantua's Mare . . . — A lady

Master beggar of St Anthony . — The provincial father of that order

Ulrick Gallet . . . — Constable of Navarre, also Ulrick Zuinglius

Giants . . . . . — Princes

Gargantua's shepherds . . — Lutheran preachers

The medlars . . . . — The Reformers

The thirstiness of Gargantua and the great drought at Pantagruel's birth . . — The cry for the restitution of the wine in the Eucharist

The Limosin scholar . . — Helisaine, a pedantic author

The catalogue of the books in St Victor's library at Paris . . . . — A satire on some books in that library, now one of the best in France

The cause between Kiss-breech and Suck-fizzle . . . — A trial between the mother of Francis I. and Const. Bourbon

Kiss-breech . . . . — Poyet, chancellor

Suck-fizzle . . . . — Monthelon, lord-keeper

Thaumast, the English scholar — Sir Thomas More, and Hieronymus Cardan

The Dypsodes . . . — Netherlanders

The city of the Amaurotes . — Terouenne

The Amaurotes . . . — Picardy

Loupgarou . . . . — The town of Liliers

The giants armed with freestone . . . . — Castles near Liliers, Saint Omer, etc.

King Anarchus made to cry green sauce in a canvas jacket . . . . — Boors that sheltered themselves there

The Almyrods . . . — Bapaume

Pantagruel covering an army with his tongue . . . — Anthony Bourbon, obtaining clothes for his army

The sickness of Pantagruel . — His disgust

The colony of Utopians sent into Dypsodie . . . — His vassals in Picardy, settled in the Low Countries

List of Names

Good friends, my readers, who peruse this book,
Be not offended, whilst on it you look;
Denude yourselves of all deprav'd affection,
For it contains no badness nor infection;
'Tis true that it brings forth to you no birth
Of any value, but in point of mirth;
Thinking therefore how sorrow might your mind
Consume, I could no apter subject find;
    One inch of joy surmounts of grief a span;
    Because to laugh is proper to the man.

BOOK I

THE INESTIMABLE LIFE OF THE
GREAT GARGANTUA, FATHER OF PANTAGRUEL,
HERETOFORE COMPOSED BY M. ALCOFRIBAS,[1]
ABSTRACTOR OF THE QUINTESSENCE, A
BOOK FULL OF PANTAGRUELISM

THE AUTHOR'S PROLOGUE

Most noble and illustrious drinkers, and you thrice precious pockified blades (for to you, and none else do I dedicate my writings), Alcibiades, in that dialogue of Plato's, which is entitled, 'The Banquet,' whilst he was setting forth the praises of his school-master, Socrates (without all question the prince of philosophers), amongst other discourses to that purpose said, that he resembled the Sileni.[2] Sileni of old were little boxes, like those we now may see in the shops of apothecaries, painted on the outside with wanton toyish figures, as harpies, satyrs, bridled geese, horned hares, saddled ducks, flying goats, thiller harts, and other such counterfeited pictures, at pleasure, to excite people unto laughter, as Silenus

---

[1] *Alcofribas Nasier*, anagram of François Rabelais.
[2] *Sileni.*—From Σιλλαίνω, to jeer, banter, scoff at.

83

himself, who was the foster-father of good Bacchus,
was wont to do; but within those capricious caskets
called Sileni, were carefully preserved and kept
many rich and fine drugs, such as balm, ambergreese,
amomon, musk, civet, with several kinds of precious
stones, and other things of great price. Just such
another thing was Socrates; for to have eyed his
outside, and esteemed of him by his exterior
appearance, you would not have given the peel
of an onion for him, so deformed he was in body,
and ridiculous in his gesture. He had a sharp-
pointed nose,[3] with the look of a bull and countenance of a fool; he was in his carriage simple, boorish
in his apparel, in fortune poor, unhappy in his wives,
unfit for all offices in the commonwealth, always
laughing, tippling and merry, carousing to every one,
with continual gibes and jeers, the better by those
means to conceal his divine knowledge. Now,
opening this box you would have found within it
a heavenly and inestimable drug, a more than
human understanding, an admirable virtue, matchless
learning, invincible courage, inimitable sobriety,
certain contentment of mind, perfect assurance, and
an incredible disregard of all that for which men
commonly do so much, watch, run, sail, fight, travel,
toil, and turmoil themselves.

Whereunto (in your opinion) doth this little
flourish of a preamble tend? For so much as you,
my good disciples, and some other jolly fools of ease
and leisure, reading the pleasant titles of some books
of our invention, as Gargantua, Pantagruel, Whippot,
the Dignity of Codpieces, of Pease and Bacon, with
a commentary, etc., are too ready to judge that there

---

[3] *Sharp-pointed nose.*—Yet, in all the antique gems, he is
represented with a blunt, round, bottle-nose.

is nothing in them but jests, mockeries, lascivious
discourse, and recreative lies; because the outside
(which is the title) is usually, without any farther
inquiry, entertained with scoffing and derision. But
truly it is very unbeseeming to make so slight
account of the works of men, seeing yourselves
avouch that it is not the habit that makes the monk,
many being monasterially accoutred, who inwardly
are nothing less than monachal; and that there are
of those that wear Spanish caps, who have but little
of the valour of Spaniards in them. Therefore is it,
that you must open the book, and seriously consider
of the matter treated in it. Then shall you find
that it containeth things of far higher value than the
box did promise; that is to say, that the subject
thereof is not so foolish, as by the title at the first
sight it would appear to be.

And put the case, that in the literal sense you
meet with purposes merry and solacious enough, and
consequently very correspondent to their inscrip-
tions, yet must not you stop there as at the melody
of the charming Syrens, but endeavour to interpret
that in a sublimer sense, which possibly you intended
to have spoken in the jollity of your heart. Did
you ever pick the lock of a cupboard to steal a
bottle of wine out of it? Tell me truly, and, if
you did, call to mind the countenance which then
you had. Or, did you ever see a dog with a marrow-
bone in his mouth—the beast of all others, says
Plato, lib. 2, de Republica, the most philosophical?
If you have seen him, you might have remarked
with what devotion and circumspectness he wards
and watcheth it; with what care he keeps it; how
fervently he holds it; how prudently he gobbets it;
with what affection he breaks it; and with what
diligence he sucks it. To what end all this?

What moveth him to take all these pains? What are the hopes of his labour? What doth he expect to reap thereby? Nothing but a little marrow. True it is that this little is more savoury and delicious than the great quantities of other sorts of meat, because the marrow (as Galen testifieth, 3, Facult. Nat. and 11, de Usu Partium) is a nourishment most perfectly elaboured by nature.

In imitation of this dog, it becomes you to be wise to smell, feel, and have in estimation these fair, goodly books stuffed with high conceptions, which though seemingly easy in the pursuit, are in the cope and encounter somewhat difficult. And then like him, you must, by a sedulous lecture and frequent meditation, break the bone and suck out the marrow; that is, my allegorical sense, or the things I to myself propose to be signified by these Pythagorical symbols; with assured hope, that in so doing, you will at least attain to be both well-advised and valiant by the reading of them; for, in the perusal of this treatise, you shall find another kind of taste, and a doctrine of a more profound and abstruse consideration, which will disclose unto you the most glorious doctrines and dreadful mysteries, as well in what concerneth our religion, as matters of the public state and life economical.

Do you believe, upon your conscience, that Homer, whilst he was couching his Iliads and Odysses, had any thought upon those allegories, which Plutarch, Heraclides Ponticus, Eustathius, Cornutus, squeezed out of him, and which Politian[4]

4 *Which Politian filched.*—M. le Duchat plainly proves that Rabelais wrongs Politian very much by this expression (*derobé*), and that he did it to pleasure his friend Budæus, who, it is well known, was jealous, as well as his friend Lascaris, of Politian's great reputation.

filched again from them? If you trust it, with
neither hand nor foot do you come near to my
opinion, which judgeth them to have been as little
dreamed of by Homer, as the gospel sacraments
were by Ovid, in his Metamorphoses; though a
certain gulligut friar,5 and true bacon-picker, would
have undertaken to prove it, if, perhaps, he had met
with as very fools as himself, and as the proverb
says, 'a lid worthy of such a kettle.'

If you give any credit thereto, why do not you the
same to these jovial new Chronicles of mine?
Albeit, when I did dictate them, I thought thereof
no more than you, who possibly were drinking the
whilst, as I was. For in the composing of this
lordly book, I never lost nor bestowed any more, nor
any other time, than what was appointed to serve me
for taking of my bodily refection, that is, whilst I
was eating and drinking. And, indeed, that is the
fittest and most proper hour, wherein to write these
high matters and deep sentences: as Homer knew

5 *Gulligut friar*, *etc.*—In the French, *Frère Lubin*. Satirical
writers have been a long time in possession of, and consequently
claim by prescription, a right to call the whole posse of monks,
in general, Frères Lubins, though, more properly, it seems to
appertain to the Franciscans, not so much on account of the
colour of their habit (grey, like a wolf, *loup*), as because their
patriarch (St Francis) did so indulgently call brother, the wolf
which had done so much damage to the inhabitants of Gubio.
As for St Lubin, Bishop of Chartres, who died about the middle
of the 6th century, his Latin name in the Martyrologies, is
Leobinus. To bring this nearer home, the *Frère Lubin* whom
Rabelais here alludes to is not a Franciscan friar, but an English
Jacobin (white Friar), who explained Ovid's Metamorphoses
allegorically. His book, in 4to, was printed at Paris, in 1509,
by Josse Badius, and was intituled, ' Metamorphosis Ovidiana
moraliter, à Magistro Thoma Walleys Anglico, de professione
Prædicatorum sub sanctissimo Patre Dominico, explanata.' It
had appeared at Bruges, in folio, even in the year 1484, in
French, printed by Colard Mansion.

very well, the paragon of all philologues, and Ennius, the father of the Latin poets, as Horace calls him, although a certain sneaking jobbernol alleged that his verses smelled more of the wine than oil. So saith a Turlupin[6] or a new start-up grub of my books; but a turd for him. The fragrant odour of the wine, oh! how much more dainty, pleasant, laughing, celestial, and delicious it is, than that smell of oil! and I will glory as much when it is said of me, that I have spent more on wine than oil, as did Demosthenes, when it was told him, that his expense on oil was greater than on wine. I truly hold it for an honour and praise to be called and reputed a frolic Gaulter[7] and a Robin Goodfellow; for under this name am I welcome in all choice companies of Pantagruelists. It was upbraided to Demosthenes, by an envious, surly knave, that his Orations did smell like the sarpler, or wrapper of a foul and filthy oil vessel. For this cause interpret you all my deeds and sayings, in the perfectest sense; reverence the cheese-like brain[8] that feeds you with these faire

---

[6] *Turlupin.*—In the French Tirelupin. M. le Duchat says, Tirelupin (for so Rabelais always spells it) was a nick-name given, in 1372, to a certain sort of cynic-like people, who lived upon lupins, which they gathered (*tirèrent*) up and down the fields.

[7] *Merry-Walter.*—In French, Bon Gaultier. Certain proper names have particular ideas affixed to them for ridiculous reasons. For instance, nothing being more common than cuckoldom, and the name of John, cuckolds are therefore called Johns or Jans. Gaultier (*Walter*) means a pleasant companion, in allusion to *gaudir*, to play the good-fellow (from *gaudere*, in Latin). Nicodemus is a foolish fellow, or *ninny-hammer*, from *nigaut* and *nice*, which last word has not the meaning of our word nice, but means dull. *Agnes* means harmless, inoffensive, lamb-like, from agneau, in Latin, *agnus.*

[8] *Cheese-like brain.*—*Cerveau caseiforme*, a word of Rabelais' coining, to express the resemblance of the brain to soft cheese.

billevezees, and trifling jollities, and do what lies in
you to keep me always merry. Be frolic now, my
lads, cheer up your hearts, and joyfully read the rest,
with all the ease of your body and profit of your
reins. But hearken, joltheads, you viedazes,[9] or
dickens take ye, remember to drink a health to me
for the favour again, and I will pledge you instantly,
Tout ares-metys.

CHAPTER I

OF THE GENEALOGY AND ANTIQUITY OF GARGANTUA

I MUST refer you to the great Chronicle of Pantagruel
for the knowledge of that genealogy and antiquity of
race by which Gargantua is come unto us. In it
you may understand more at large how the giants
were born in this world, and how from them by a
direct line issued Gargantua, the father of Pantagruel:
and do not take it ill, if for this time I pass by it,
although the subject be such, that the oftener it were
remembered, the more it would please your worshipful
Seniorias; according to which you have the authority
of Plato in Philebo and Gorgias; and of Flaccus,[10]
who says that there are some kinds of purposes (such
as these are without doubt), which, the frequentlier
they be repeated, still prove the more delectable.

Would to God every one had as certain knowledge of his genealogy since the time of the ark of
Noah until this age. I think many are at this day

---

[9] *Vietzdazes.*—Ass-visaged (Provençal).
[10] Hæc placuit semel, hæc decies repetita placebit. Horat.
Art. Poet.

emperors, kings, dukes, princes, and popes on the
earth, whose extraction is from some porters and
pardon-pedlars; as on the contrary, many are now
poor wandering beggars, wretched and miserable,
who are descended of the blood and lineage of great
kings and emperors, occasioned, as I conceive it, by
the transport and revolution of kingdoms and empires,
from the Assyrians to the Medes, from the Medes to
the Persians, from the Persians to the Macedonians,
from the Macedonians to the Romans, from the
Romans to the Greeks, from the Greeks to the
French.

And to give you some hint concerning myself,
who speak unto you, I cannot think but I am come
of the race of some rich king or prince in former
times; for never yet saw you any man that had a
greater desire to be a king, and to be rich, than I
have, and that only that I may make good cheer, do
nothing, nor care for anything, and plentifully enrich
my friends, and all honest and learned men. But
herein do I comfort myself, that in the other world
I shall be so, yea, and greater too than at this present
I dare wish. As for you, with the same or a better
conceit consolate yourselves in your distresses, and
drink fresh if you can come by it.

To return to our wethers,[11] I say, that by the
sovereign gift of heaven, the antiquity and genealogy
of Gargantua hath been reserved for our use more

---

[11] *To return to our wethers.*—In the French, *revenons à nos
moutons*—a proverb taken from the old French play of Patelin,
where a woollen draper is brought in, who, pleading against his
shepherd concerning some sheep the shepherd had stole from him
would ever and anon digress from the point, to speak of a piece
of cloth which his antagonist's attorney had likewise robbed him
of, which made the judge call out to the draper, and bid him
'return to his muttons.'

full and perfect than any other except that of the
Messias, whereof I mean not to speak; for it belongs
not unto my purpose, and the devils, that is to say,
the false accusers and dissembled gospellers, will
therein oppose me. This genealogy was found by
John Andrew in a meadow, which he had near the
pole-arch, under the olive-tree, as you go to Narsay:
where, as he was making a cast-up of some ditches,
the diggers with their mattocks struck against a great
brazen tomb,[12] and unmeasurably long, for they could
never find the end thereof, by reason that it entered
too far within the sluices of Vienne. Opening this
tomb in a certain place thereof, sealed on the top
with the mark of a goblet, about which was written
in Hetrurian letters 'HIC BIBITUR,' they found nine
flagons, set in such order [13] as they used to rank their
skittles in Gascony, of which that which was placed
in the middle had under it a big, fat, great, grey,
pretty, small, mouldy, little pamphlet, smelling
stronger, but no better, than roses. In that book,
the said genealogy was found written all at length,
in a chancery hand, not in paper, not in parchment,
nor in wax, but in the bark of an elm tree; yet so
worn with the long tract of time, that hardly could
three letters together be there perfectly discerned.

I, though unworthy, was sent for thither, and with

---

[12] *A great brazen tomb.*—In a place called Civaux, within two
leagues of Chauvigni, in Lower Poitou, there is still to be seen,
almost even with the surface of the earth, a great number of
stone tombs, for near two leagues together, in a circle, particularly
near the River Vienne, wherein likewise, it is thought, are many
more of those tombs. This is what Rabelais here alludes to, and
the tradition of the country is, that they enclosed the bodies of a
prodigious number of Visigoth Arians, defeated by Clovis.

[13] *In such order.*—Not all upon a line, as in some places, and at
a certain game, but upon three parallel lines, three pins on each
line, as here with us.

much help of those spectacles, whereby the art of
reading dim writings, and letters that do not clearly
appear to the sight, is practised, as Aristotle teacheth
it; did translate the book, as you may see in your
Pantagruelising, that is to say, in drinking stiffly to
your own heart's desire, and reading the dreadful and
horrific acts of Pantagruel.   At the end of the book
there was a little treatise, entituled the 'Antidoted
Fanfreluches; or, a Galimatias of extravagant conceits.'   The rats and moths, or (that I may not lie)
other wicked beasts, had nibbled off the beginning:
the rest I have hereto subjoined, for the reverence I
bear to antiquity.

CHAPTER II

THE ANTIDOTED FANFRELUCHES:[14] OR, GALIMATIAS OF
EXTRAVAGANT CONCEITS FOUND IN AN ANCIENT
MONUMENT

No sooner did the Cymbrians' overcommer
Pass through the air to shun the dew of summer,
But at his coming straight great tubs were fill'd,
With pure fresh butter down in showers distill'd:

[14] *Antidoted Fanfreluches.*—This piece is a snare laid by Rabelais
for such of his readers as shall ridiculously set up for cunning
people.   He would have been very much puzzled, were he to
have been obliged to unriddle his antidoted conundrums.   It
matters nothing to say, he qualified them in this manner, and
made them so obscure by way of antidote against any offence
they might have given had they been more intelligible.   My
answer is, he very well foresaw that even this obscurity would set
the curious more agog to dive into the mystery thereof.   Have
not Nostradamus' Prophecies met with commentators ?   Have

Wherewith when water'd was his grandam heigh,
Aloud he cried, Fish it, sir, I pray;
Because his beard is almost all beray'd;
Or, that he would hold to'm a scale he pray'd.

To lick his slipper, some told was much better,
Than to gain pardons, and the merit greater.
In th'interim a crafty chuff approaches,
From the depth issued, where they fish for roaches;
Who said, Good sirs, some of them let us save,
The eel is here, and in this hollow cave
You'll find, if that our looks on it demur,
A great waste in the bottom of his fur.

To read this chapter when he did begin,
Nothing but a calf's horns were found therein;
I feel, quoth he, the mitre which doth hold
My head so chill, it makes my brain take cold.
Being with the perfume of a turnip warm'd,
To stay by chimney hearths himself he arm'd,
Provided that a new thill-horse they made
Of every person of a hair-brain'd head.

They talked of the bunghole of Saint Knowles,
Of Gilbathar and thousand other holes,
If they might be reduc'd t' a scarry stuff,
Such as might not be subject to the cough:

we not seen divers and sundry explications of the famed Enigma
of Bologna, Ælia Lælia Crispis? Joseph Scaliger used to say
Calvin was wise in not writing upon the Apocalypse. For my
part, without· profanely comparing Rabelais' conundrums with
the works of St John, I shall always hold those to be prudent
men who do not offer to explain the Book of Revelation.
Grammatical notes indeed may be allowed of, but shame and
eternal derision on those who shall make historical ones on it,
and, having made them, shall publish them to the world.

Since ev'ry man unseemly did it find,
To see them gaping thus at ev'ry wind:
For, if perhaps they handsomely were clos'd,
For pledges they to men might be expos'd.

In this arrest by Hercules the raven
Was flayed at her [his] return from Lybia haven.
Why am not I, said Minos, there invited?
Unless it be myself, not one's omitted :
And then it is their mind, I do no more
Of frogs and oysters send them any store:
In case they spare my life and prove but civil,
I give their sale of distaffs to the devil.

To quell him comes Q. B. who limping frets
At the safe pass of trixy crackarets:
The boulter, the grand Cyclops' cousin, those
Did massacre, whilst each one wip'd his nose:
Few ingles [15] in this fallow ground are bred,
But on a tanner's mill are winnowed.
Run thither all of you, th' alarms sound clear,
You shall have more [16] than you had the last year.

[15] *Ingles.*—It means a bardachio, a catamite; the French word
is *boulgrin.* M. le Duchat says, Some people will have this
fallow field to be the field of the Roman Church, which, in
Rabelais' opinion, was not at that time cultivated as it ought;
and the Boulgrins means the French Lutherans, whom he calls
boulgrins, as being descended from the Vaudois, who were called
boûgres, from Bulgaria, over which they were spread. Rabelais,
by the *Tanner's Mill,* intimates, that till his time few persons had
undertaken to reform the Western Church, or to separate from it,
without leaving their skin behind them, as the saying is.
[16] *You shall have more, etc.*—If the Protestants' interpretation of
this place be right, Rabelais here foretells the heretics of his time
that they will be still more roughly treated than their ancestors
were.

Short while thereafter was the bird of Jove
Resolv'd to speak, though dismal it should prove;
Yet was afraid, when he saw them in ire,
They should o'erthrow quite flat, down dead,
   th' empire.
He rather chus'd the fire from heaven to steal,
To boats where were red-herrings put to sale;
Than to be calm 'gainst those who strive to brave us,
And to the Massorets' fond words enslave us.

All this at last concluded gallantly,
In spite of Até and her hern-like thigh,[17]
Who, sitting, saw Penthesilea ta'en,
In her old age, for a cress-selling quean.
Each one cried out, Thou filthy collier toad!
Doth it become thee to be found abroad?
Thou hast the Roman standard filch'd away,
Which they in rags of parchment did display.

Juno was born, who under the rainbow,
Was a bird-catching with her duck below:
When her with such a grievous trick they plyed,
That she had almost been bethwacked by it.
The bargain was, that, of that throat-full, she
Should of Proserpina have two eggs free;
And if that she thereafter should be found,
She to a hawthorn hill should be fast bound.

Seven months thereafter lacking twenty-two,
He, that of old did Carthage town undo,

---

[17] *Hern-like thigh.*—The Até of the Greeks was a goddess who excited tumults and quarrelings, and Rabelais gives a hern, or heron's thigh, that is, long and light, as a heron's is, because Homer (Iliad 9), in order to insinuate that dissensions are very swift in arriving, and often for the slightest cause, paints that goddess very swift and light of foot.

Did bravely midst them all himself advance,
Requiring of them his inheritance;
Although they justly made up the division,
According to the shoe-welt-laws decision,
By distributing store of brews and beef
To these poor fellows that did pen the brief.

But th' year will come, sign of a Turkish bow,
Five spindles yarn'd and three pot-bottoms too,
Wherein of a discourteous king the dock
Shall pepper'd be under an hermit's frock.
Ah ! that for one she hypocrite you must
Permit so many acres to be lost!
Cease, cease, this vizard may become another,
Withdraw yourselves unto the serpent's brother.[18]

'Tis in times past that he who is shall reign
With his good friends in peace now and again.
No rash nor heady prince shall then rule crave,
Each good will its arbitrement shall have;
And the joy, promised of old as doom
To the heaven's guests, shall in its beacon come.
Then shall the breeding mares, that benumb'd were,
Like royal palfreys ride triumphant there.

And this continue shall from time to time,
Till Mars be fettered for an unknown crime;
Then shall one come, who others will surpass,
Delightful, pleasing, matchless, full of grace.

---

[18] *Serpent's brother.*—I take it to be a burlesque curse for ' Go to
hell.' The devil, every one knows, is called a serpent, because of
that serpent which beguiled our first parents. See Apocalypse,
c. 12 and 20. Serpent's brother for serpent, as fraterculus'gigantis
for gigas in Juvenal. Sat. iv. v. 98.

Cheer up your hearts, approach to this repast,
All trusty friends of mine; for he's deceas'd
Who would not for a world return again.
So highly shall time past be cry'd up then.

He who was made of wax shall lodge each member
Close by the hinges of a block of timber.
We then no more shall Master ! Master ! whoot.
The swaggerer, who th' alarum bell holds out,
Could one seize on the dagger which he bears,
Heads would be free from tingling in the ears,
To baffle the whole storehouse of abuses;
And thus farewell Apollo and the Muses.

CHAPTER III

HOW GARGANTUA WAS CARRIED ELEVEN MONTHS IN HIS MOTHER'S BELLY

GRANGOUSIER was a good fellow in his time, and
notable jester; he loved to drink neat, as much as
any man that then was in the world, and would
willingly eat salt meat. To this intent he was
ordinarily well furnished with gammons of bacon,
both of Westphalia, Mayence and Bayonne,[1] with

---

[1] *Gammons of bacon, both of Westphalia, Mayence and Bayonne.*—
M. le Duchat observes,—the hams (for so jambon, with an
addition of place, means; otherwise a gammon) of Mayence, and
those of Bayonne, continue still in great request. The former
have their name from Mayence (Mentz), not because they are
cured there, but because these hams, which come from Westphalia,
used formerly to be sold there, at a fair which has since been
transferred to Francfort on the Maine. As for Bayonne hams,
the finest come to Paris, where they make pies of them for the
best tables. See the Queen of Navarre's Heptameron, Nouv. 28.

store of dried neat's tongues, plenty of links, chitter-
lings and puddings, in their season; together with
salt beef and mustard, a good deal of hard roes of
powdered mullet called botargos,[2] great provision of
sausages, not of Bolonia (for he feared the Lombard
Boccone[3]), but of Bigorre, Longaulnay, Brene, and
Rouargue.   In the vigour of his, age he married
Gargamelle,[4] daughter to the King of the Parpaillons,

[2] *Botargos.*—Duchat says,—In Provence they call Botargues the
hard roe of the mullet, pickled in oil and vinegar.   The mullet
(muge) is a fish which is catch'd about the middle of December;
the hard roes of it are salted against Lent, and this is what is
called *Boutargues*, a sort of *boudins* (puddings), which have nothing
to recommend them but their exciting thirst.

[3] *For he feared the Lombard Boccone.*—' Car il craignoit li
Bouconi de Lombard.'   Bocconi in Italian signifies a mouthful of
anything (from the Latin bucca, the hollow part of the cheek),
but in French it signifies poison, or a poisoned bit absolutely.
See Cotgrave, Miege, Boyer, Richelet, etc. etc.   The reason of
this may be gathered from Duchat's note, viz.:—The sausages
that come from Bolognia la Grasse (the fat or fertile), in Italy,
are in high renown for their goodness (and very justly, teste
meipso); and what Rabelais here insinuates is, that for all it was
so delicious a morsel, so excellent a thing to eat, Grangousier
would never touch it, because he feared ' the Lombard bit.'   Now
the reader is to know, that the Italians, who are accused of
being not over-scrupulous at poisoning their enemies, bore an
extreme hatred to Louis XII. after he had made war upon them,
in order to recover the Duchy of Milan, which belonged to him
by lineal descent from Valentina of Milan, his grandmother, and
which is composed of the ancient Lombardy.   'God keep us
from three things ; the scrivener's *et cætera* ; the apothecary's *qui
pro quo* ; and *the Lombard bit*,' was a common proverb in Oliver
Maillard's time (Serm. 35 of the Advent).   Of these proverbial
expressions, which are quoted by H. Stephens in c. 6 of his
Apology for Herodotus, the last may have taken its rise from the
aforesaid Valentina (Duchess of Milan) being violently suspected
of foul play towards the King Charles VI. and attempting to
poison him, to make way for that king's brother, her husband, to
mount the throne.

[4] *Gargamelle, daughter to the King of the Parpaillons.*—
Parpaillon in some parts of France is the papillon (butterfly).

a jolly pug, and well-mouthed wench. These two
did oftentimes do the two-backed beast together,
joyfully rubbing and frotting their bacon against one
another, in so far, that at last she became great with
child of a fair son, and went with him unto the
eleventh month; for so long, yea longer, may a
woman carry her great belly, especially when it is
some master-piece of nature, and a person pre-
destinated to the performance, in his due time, of
great exploits.   As Homer says that the child
which Neptune begot upon the Nymph was borne
a whole year after the conception, that is in the
twelfth month.   For, as Aulus Gellius saith, lib. 3,
this long time was suitable to the majesty of
Neptune, that in it the child might receive his
perfect form.   For the like reason Jupiter made the
night wherein he lay with Alcmena last forty-eight
hours, a shorter time not being sufficient for the
forging of Hercules, who cleansed the world of the
monsters and tyrants wherewith it was opprest.   My
masters, the ancient Pantagruelists, have confirmed
that which I say, and withal declared it to be not
only possible, but also maintained the lawful birth
and legitimation of the infant born of a woman in
the eleventh month after the decease of her husband.
Hypocrates, lib. de alimento.   Plinius, lib. 7, cap. 5.
Plautus, in his Cistellaria.   Marcus Varro in his
Satyre inscribed, The Testament, alleging to this
purpose the authority of Aristotle.   Censorinus, lib.

Gargamelle is a burlesque word for the gullet, the weasand.
Gargante in Spanish signifies the same thing.   The Greeks have
their γαργαρεὼν, and all these words, as well as the *gurges* of
the Latins, the *gorgo* of the Italians, the *gargoüille* of the French,
the *gargle* of the English, *gorgelen* of the Hollanders, *gegurgel* of
the Germans, etc., have been formed from that noise the throat
makes in gargling one's mouth.

99

de die natali. Arist., lib. 7, cap. 3 and 4, de natura animalium. Gellius, lib. 3, cap. 16. Servius, in his exposition upon this verse of Virgil's Eclogues, Matri longa decem, etc., and a thousand other fools, whose number hath been increased by the lawyers ff. de suis, et legit l. intestato. paragrapho. fin. and in Auth. de restitut. et ea quæ parit in xi. mense. Moreover upon these grounds they have foisted in their Robidilardick, or Lapiturolive law. Gallus ff. de lib. et posth. l. sept. ff. de stat. hom. and some other laws, which at this time I dare not name.[5] By means whereof the honest widows may without danger play at the close buttock game with might and main, and as hard as they can for the space of the first two. months after the decease of their husbands. I pray you, my good lusty springal lads, if you find any of these females that are worth the pains of untying the cod-piece-point, get up, ride upon them, and bring them to me; for, if they happen within the third month to conceive, the child shall be heir to the deceased, if, before he died, he had no other children, and the mother shall pass for an honest woman.

When she is known to have conceived, thrust forward boldly, spare her not, whatever betide you, seeing the paunch is full. As Julia, the daughter of the Emperor Octavian, never prostituted herself to her belly-bumpers but when she found herself with child, after the manner of ships that receive not their steersman till they have their ballast and lading. And if any blame them for this their rataconniculation and reiterated lechery upon their pregnancy and big-

---

[5] *Which at present I dare not name. By which laws the widows,* *etc.*—Thus the text of Rabelais stands, and this profusion of quotations is probably designed to ridicule that affectation in the writers of his time.

bellicdness, seeing beasts, in the like exigent of their
fulness, will never suffer the male-masculant to
encroach them, their answer will be, that those are
beasts, but they are women, very well skilled in the
pretty vails, and small fees of the pleasant trade and
mysteries of superfetation: as Populia heretofore
answered, according to the relation of Macrobius, lib.
2, Saturnal. If the devil would not have them to
bag, he must wring hard the spigot,[6] and stop the
bung-hole.

CHAPTER IV

HOW GARGAMELLE, BEING GREAT WITH GARGANTUA, DID EAT A HUGE DEAL OF TRIPES

THE occasion and manner how Gargamelle was
brought to bed and delivered of her child, was thus:
and, if you do not believe it, I wish your bum-gut
may fall out and make an escapade. Her bum-gut,
indeed, or fundament escaped her in an afternoon,
on the third day of February, with having eaten at
dinner too many godebillios. Godebillios are the
fat tripes of coiros. Coiros are beeves fattened at
the cratch in ox stalls, or in the fresh guimo
meadows. Guimo meadows are those that for their
fruitfulness may be mowed twice a year. Of those
fat beeves they had killed three hundred sixty-seven
thousand and fourteen, to be salted at Shrovetide,
that in the entering of the spring they might have

----

[6] *He must wring hard the spigot.*—Rabelais means, that after a
woman has been three months a widow, she should be cautious for
fear of accidents which may hurt her reputation.

plenty of powdered beef wherewith to season their mouths at the beginning of their meals, and to taste their wine the better. They had abundance of tripes, as you have heard, and they were so delicious, that everyone licked his fingers. But as the devil would have it,[1] for all men could do, there was no possibility to keep them long in that relish ; for in a very short while they would have stunk, which had been an indecent thing. It was therefore concluded that they should be all of them gulched up, without losing anything. To this effect they invited all the burghers of Sainais, of Suillé, of the Roche-Clermaud, of Vaugaudry, without omitting the Coudray Monpensier, the Gué de Véde,[2] and other their neighbours, all stiff drinkers, brave fellows, and good players at nine-pins. The good man Grangousier took great pleasure in their company, and commanded there should be no want nor pinching for anything. Nevertheless he bid his wife eat sparingly, because she was near her time, and that these tripes were no very commend-able meat. They would fain,[3] said he, be at the

[1] *But as the devil would have it.*—In the original it is, 'Le grande diablerie à quatre personnaiges.' M. le Duchat tells us it is an expression used by the people of Poitou, to signify, 'le malheur voulut,' as if we should say, by devilish ill luck such or such a thing happened. The rise of it was this: in the amphi-theatre of Doué and at St Maxent in Poitou, they heretofore used to act religious plays, with more or fewer actors, among whom were commonly some devils, who were hereafter to torment hardened sinners, world without end. These pious theatrical representations were called petite, or grande diablerie. Petite (little devilry) when there were less than four devils; grande, when there were four; whence the proverb comes, faire le diable à quatre, to make a more than ordinary hellish hurly-burly.

[2] *Gué de Vede, etc.*—All these places are either appertaining to Poitou, or adjoining to Chinon, Rabelais' town.

[3] *They would fain, etc.*—In Alsace, where they are great eaters

chewing of ordure, that would eat the case wherein
it was. Notwithstanding these admonitions, she did
eat sixteen quarters, two bushels, three pecks, and a
pipkin full. Oh, the fair fecality wherewith she
swelled, by the ingrediency of such shitten stuff!

After dinner they all went out in a hurle, to the
grove of the willows, where, on the green grass, to
the sound of the merry flutes and pleasant bagpipes,
they danced so gallantly, that it was a sweet and
heavenly sport to see them so frolic.

CHAPTER V

HOW THEY CHIRPED OVER THEIR CUPS

THEN did they fall upon the chat of victuals, and
some belly furniture to be snatched at in the very
same place. Which purpose was no sooner mentioned, but forthwith began flagons to go, gammons
to trot, goblets to fly, great bowls to ting, glasses to
ring. Draw, reach, fill, mix, give it me without
water. So my friend, so, whip me off this glass [1]
neatly, bring me hither some claret, a full weeping
glass till it run over. A cessation and truce with
thirst. Ha, thou false fever, wilt thou not be gone?
By my figgins, godmother, I cannot as yet enter in
the humour of being merry, nor drink so currently

of tripe, and where Rabelais lived some time, they have a proverb,
which may run thus in English :—

> Scrape tripe as clean as e'er you can,
> A tythe of filth will still remain.

[1] *Whip*, *etc.*—*Fouette moi ce verre*, whip me that glass, turn up
the bottom or breech of it, as when you whip a child.

103

as I would. You have catch'd a cold, gammer?
Yea, forsooth, sir. By the belly of Sanct Buff, let
us talk of our drink: I never drink but at my
hours, like the Pope's mule. And I never drink
but in my breviary,[2] like a fair father guardian.
Which was first, thirst or drinking? Thirst, for
who in the time of innocence would have drunk
without being athirst? Nay, sir, it was drinking;
for privatio præsupponit habitum. I am learned,
you see; Fœcundi calices quem non fecere disertum?
We poor innocents[3] drink but too much without
thirst. Not I truly, who am a sinner, for I never
drink without thirst, either present or future. To
prevent it, as you know, I drink for the thirst to
come. I drink eternally. This is to me an eternity
of drinking, and drinking of eternity. Let us sing,
let us drink, and tune up our roundlays. Where is
my funnel? What, it seems I do not drink but by
an attorney? Do you wet yourselves to dry, or do
you dry to wet you? Pish, I understand not the
rhetoric (theoric I should say), but I help myself
somewhat by the practice. Beast, enough! I sup,
I wet, I humect, I moisten my gullet, I drink, and
all for fear of dying. Drink always and you shall
never die. If I drink not, I am a ground dry,
gravelled and spent. I am stark dead without drink,
and my soul ready to fly into some marsh amongst
frogs; the soul[4] never dwells in a dry place, drought

[2] *In my breviary.*—That is, at the time when he was canonically
required to read his breviary.
[3] *Innocents.*—These are monks, who call the hood of their
habit the biggin or cap of innocence. But their words will
bear an allusion to what is said of some innocent people who are
tortured with water forced down their throats to make them confess.
[4] *The soul, etc.*—Upon those words of St Augustin, 'Anima
certè, quia spiritus est, in sicco habitare non potest,' reported in
2d part of the decree, Caus. 32, etc.

kills it. Oh, you butlers, creators of new forms,
make me of no drinker a drinker, perenity and
everlastingness of sprinkling, and bedewing me
through these my parched and sinewy bowels. He
drinks in vain, that feels not the pleasure of it.
This entereth into my veins, the pissing tool and
urinal vessels shall have nothing of it. I would
willingly wash the tripes of the calf which I
apparelled this morning. I have pretty well now
ballasted my stomach and stuffed my paunch. If
the papers of my bonds and bills could drink as well
as I do, my creditors would not want for wine when
they come to see me, or, when they are to make any
formal exhibition of their rights to what of me they
can demand. This hand of yours spoils your nose.
Oh, how many other such will enter here before
this go out ! What, drink so shallow ? It is enough
to break both girds and pettrel. This is called a cup
of dissimulation, or flaggonal hypocrisy.

What difference is there between a bottle and a
flagon ? Great difference ; for the bottle is stopped
and shut up with a stopper, but the flagon with a
vice. Bravely and well played upon the words !
Our fathers drank lustily, and emptied their cans.
Well cacked, well sung ! Come, let us drink ; will
you send nothing to the river ? Here is one going
to wash the tripes. I drink no more than a sponge.
I drink like a Templar Knight. And I, tanquam
sponsus. And I, sicut terra sine aqua. Give me a
synonymon for a gammon of bacon. It is the
compulsory of drinkers: it is a pully. By a pully-
rope 5 wine is let down into the cellar, and by a
gammon into the stomach. Hey ! now, boys, hither,

5 *A pully-rope, etc.*—Thus we say, a red herring is a shoeing-
horn to a pot of ale.

some drink, some drink. There is no trouble in it.
Respice personam, pone pro duo, bus non est in usu.
If I could get up as well as I can swallow down, I
had been long ere now very high in the air.
Thus became Tom Toss-pot rich ; thus went in
the tailor's stitch. Thus did Bacchus conquer
Inde ;[6] thus Philosophy, Melinde.[7] A little rain
allays a great deal of wind ; long tippling breaks the
thunder. But, if there came such liquor from my
ballock, would you not willingly thereafter suck
the udder whence it issued. Here page, fill ! I
prythee, forget me not, when it comes to my turn,
and I will enter the election I have made of thee
into the very register of my heart. Sup, Guillot,
and spare not, there is somewhat in the pot. I
appeal from thirst, and disclaim its jurisdiction.
Page, sue out my appeal in form. This remnant in
the bottom of the glass must follow its leader. I
was wont heretofore to drink out all, but now I
leave nothing. Let us not make too much haste ;
it is requisite we carry all along with us. Hey day,
here are tripes fit for our sport, and, in earnest,
excellent godebillios of the dun ox (you know) with
the black streak. Oh, for God's sake, let us lash
them soundly, yet thriftily. Drink, or I will—.

[6] *Thus did Bacchus conquer Inde.*—That is, all the conquests
Bacchus made in the Indies are no more than the chimerical
projects of drinkers when the wine gets into their noddles.
[7] *Thus Philosophy, Melinde.*—The sages of Portugal, having
undertaken to convert the people of Melinde, wrought upon them
as much by drinking as reasoning, which afterwards made the
conquests of the whole country easy to the Portuguese. The
translator has here made too free with his author. The two
first lines of Rabelais, are—

Ainsi se fit Jacques Cueur riche;
Ainsi prounctent boys en friche, etc.

No, no, drink, I beseech you. Sparrows will not eat unless you bob them on the tail, nor can I drink if I be not fairly spoke to. The concavities of my body are like another hell for their capacity. Lagonædatera.[8] There is not a corner nor cony-burrow in all my body where this wine doth not ferret out my thirst. Ho, this will bang it soundly. But this shall banish it utterly. Let us wind our horns by the sound of flagons and bottles, and cry aloud that whoever hath lost his thirst come not hither to seek it. Long clysters of drinking are to be voided without doors. The great God made the planets, and we make the platters neat.[9] I have the word of the gospel in my mouth, Sitio. The stone called Asbestos is not more unquenchable than the thirst of my paternity. Appetite comes with eating, says Angeston,[10] but the thirst goes away with drinking. I have a remedy against thirst, quite contrary to that which is good against the biting of a mad dog. Keep running after a dog, and he will never bite you; drink always before the thirst, and it will never come upon you. There I catch you, I awake you. Argus had a hundred eyes for his sight, a butler should have (like Briareus) a hundred hands wherewith to fill us wine indefatigably. Hey now, lads, let us moisten [11] ourselves, it will be time to

[8] *Lagonædatera.*—It should be, as it is in Rabelais, *lagona edatera.* These two words are no other than Biscayan, and mean, ' partner, some drink.'

[9] *Platters neat.*—' Plates neat,' would come nearer the French pun, viz., *planetts,* and *plats netz.*

[10] *Angeston.*—This, in all probability, alludes to Jerom le Hangest, a doctor of Paris, a great school divine, and a barbarous writer of those times, and serves to show that it was not, as has been thought, Amyot, Bishop of Auxerre, who first brought up this saying.

[11] *Let us moisten, etc.*—He before had said, in this chapter, Do

dry hereafter. White wine here, wine, boys!
Pour out all in the name of Lucifer, fill here, you,
fill and fill (peascods on you) till it be full. My
tongue peels. Lans tringue ; to thee, countryman, I
drink to thee, good fellow, comrade [12] to thee, lusty,
lively ! Ha, la, la, that was drunk to some purpose,
and bravely gulped over. Oh, lachryma Christi,[13] it
is of the best grape ? I' faith, pure Greek,[14] Greek !
Oh, the fine, white wine ! upon my conscience, it is
a kind of taffatas wine ; [15] hin, hin, it is of one ear,[16]

you wet yourselves to dry, or do you dry to wet you ? This is
not unlike the song of an old testy toper—

> Remplis ton verre vuide,
> Vuide ton verre plein.
> Je ne puis souffrir dans ta main,
> Un verre ni vuide ni plein.

> Fill, fill your glass, which empty stands,
>   Empty it and let it pass ;
> For I hate to see in people's hands
>   A full or empty glass.

[12] *Comrade.—Compaygn*, an old French word, to which has
succeeded *compagnon*, though *compain* is still used in Languedoc and
Picardy. Caninius says it comes from the Latin *compaganus*, not
from *com* and *panis*.

[13] *Oh, lachryma Christi.*—Within eight miles of Viterbo, and
two days' journey from Rome, on the descent of a hill inclosed
within the territory of the little town of Montefiascone, grows the
excellent Moscatello wine, otherwise called *Lachryma Christi*,
from a neighbouring abbey which boasts of being possessed of a
tear just like that at Vendôme.

[14] *Pure Greek.—Deviniere* in the original, not Greek. *Deviniere*
was the vineyard belonging to the author's father, and the place
where he was born. Sir T. U. might take *deviniere* to be meant
of the wine, as if it was *divine*, Greek wine.

[15] *Taffatas wine.*—As smooth and pleasing to the taste as
taffeta is to the feeling.

[16] *Wine of one ear.*—It is a proverbial expression for exceeding
good wine. I have introduced the same with good success
(Præfiscinè dico ; verbo absit invidia) in some parts of Leicester-

well wrought, and of good wool. Courage, comrade ;
up thy heart, Billy ! We will not be beasted at this
bout, for I have got one trick. Ex hoc in hoc.
There is no enchantment, nor charm there, every one
of you hath seen it. My apprenticeship is out, I am
a free man of this trade.[17] I am prester Macé, Prish,
Brum ! I should say, master passé. Oh, the
drinkers, those that are a-dry, oh, poor, thirsty souls !
Good page, my friend, fill me here some, and crown
the wine,[18] I pray thee. A la Cardinale ![19] Natura
abhorret vacuum. Would you say that a fly could
drink in this ? This is after the fashion of Switzer-
land. Clear off, neat, supernaculum ! Come, therefore, blades to this divine liquor, and celestial juice,
swill it over heartily, and spare not ! It is a decoction of nectar and ambrosia.

shire, and elsewhere, speaking of *good ale*, ale of *one ear :* bad ale,
ale of two ears. Because when it is good, we give a nod with *one
ear ;* if bad, we shake our head, that is, give a sign with both *ears*
that we do not like it.

[17] *I am a free man of this trade.*—*Je suis presbtre Macé,* he
would say, *maître passé,* but his tongue tripped, being fuddled. As
if any of us, in our cups, should say, The Chicop of Bichester
loves beggs and acon, instead of The Bishop of Chichester loves
eggs and bacon. A play of words on the benedictine René Macé,
chronicler of Francis I.

[18] *Crown the wine.*—Pour on till the wine seems to crown my
glass. Homer and Virgil use this expression more than once.
Writing the words *pour on*, puts me in mind of an honest, faithful
drunkard, who, being called upon, when he lay snoring upon the
floor, to get up, and not leave his wine behind him, answered,
Pour it upon me.

[19] *A la Cardinale.*—A brimmer. Rouge-bord, a red brim (for
red wine) is another word for a brimmer, synonymous to cardinale :
for rouge-bord means a red brim, as I said, and cardinale means a
cardinal's hat, which is red.

109

CHAPTER VI

WHILST they were on this discourse and pleasant tattle of drinking, Gargamelle began to be a little unwell in her lower parts; whereupon Grangousier arose from off the grass, and fell to comfort her very honestly and kindly, suspecting that she was in travail, and told her that it was best for her to sit down upon the grass under the willows, because she was likely very shortly to see young feet, and that therefore it was convenient she should pluck up her spirits, and take a good heart of new at the fresh arrival of her baby; saying to her withal, that although the pain was somewhat grievous to her, it would be but of short continuance, and that the succeeding joy would quickly remove that sorrow, in such sort that she should not so much as remember it. On with a sheep's courage,[1] quoth he. Dispatch this boy, and we will speedily fall to work for the making of another. Ha! said she, so well as you speak at your own ease, you that are men! Well then, in the name of God, I'll do my best, seeing that you will have it so; but would to God

---

[1] *On with a sheep's courage.*—Have at least as much courage as an ewe sheep that is going to yean. Instead of these words, *on with a sheep's courage,* to those inclusively, *seeing you will have it so,* we find in the edition of Dolet, agreeably to those of Francis Justus, 1534 and 1535, the following words :—' I will prove it,' said he. ' Our Saviour says in the Gospel, Joannis xvi., A woman, when she is in travail, hath sorrow, because her hour is come ; but as soon as she is delivered of the child, she remembereth no more the anguish. Ha, said she, you say well, and I had much rather hear such sentences of the Gospel, and find myself the better for it, than to hear the Life of St Margaret, or such like canting hypocritical trumpery.'

that it were cut off from you ! What, said Grangousier ? Ha, said she, you are a good man indeed,
you understand it well enough. What, my member ?
said he. By the goat's blood, if it please you, that
shall be done instantly; cause bring hither a knife.
Alas, said she, the Lord forbid, and pray Jesus to
forgive me ! I did not say it from my heart, therefore
let it alone, and do not do it neither more nor less
any kind of harm for my speaking so to you. But
I am like to have work enough to do to-day, and all
for your member, yet God bless you and it.

Courage, courage, said he, take you no care of the
matter, let the four foremost oxen do the work.[2] I
will yet go drink one whiff more, and if, in the
meantime, anything befal you that may require my
presence, I will be so near to you, that, at the first
whistling in your fist, I shall be with you forthwith.
A little while after she began to groan, lament
and cry. Then suddenly came the midwives from
all quarters, who groping her below, found some
peloderies,[3] which was a certain filthy stuff, and of a

[2] *Let the four foremost oxen do the work.*—Let your reliance be
on the vigour and stretching-leatherness of the suffering part ; for
we see but very few women, however weakly they be, but what
happily get over the condition you are in. *Let the four foremost
oxen do the work*, is a proverbial expression in the province of
Poitou, where, not having horses enough to draw their waggons
and carts, they usually draw with three couple of oxen, if they go
far, and the way is bad. The four foremost, which are always
the ablest, follow each other very close, but they are at a considerable distance from the two hillers, that when the cart or wain
is set fast in a slough, these four, which are made to do it, may
draw out of the mire the two others, together with the waggon
or cart.

[3] *Peloderies.*—*Pellauderies,* Rabelais spells it. Cotgrave con-
strues it, filthy matter, beastly or ugly stuff. M. le Duchat says,
it is the shreds, parings, clippings and scrapings of beasts' hides
and skins, from *peau* (*pellis* in Latin.) In Normandy they call
pellautier, a worker in hides, a pelter we may say in English.

III

taste truly bad enough. This they thought had been
the child, but it was her fundament that was slipt
out with the mollification of her straight entrail
which you call the bum-gut, and that merely by
eating of too many tripes, as we have showed you
before. Whereupon an old ugly trot in the company, who had the repute of an expert she-physician,
and was come from Brisepaille,4 near to Saint
Genou, three score years before, made her so
horrible a restrictive and binding medicine, and
whereby all her larris, arse-pipes and conduits were
so oppilated, stopped, obstructed and contracted,
that you could hardly have opened and enlarged
them with your teeth, which is a terrible thing
to think upon; seeing the devil at the mass5 at

4 *Come from Brisepaille, near to St Genou.*—In Languedoc and
in Dauphiny, to say of a woman that she is come from Brisepaille,
near St Genou, so many years ago, is to call her an old whore,
and literally, though punningly, signifies that the straw (*paille*)
of her bed has been long since bruised (*brisée*) with the knees
(*genoux*) of her belly-bumpers. These three make *Brise Paille
Genou.*

5 *Seeing the devil at mass, etc.*—This is not very clear, as the
translator has managed it. Perhaps the reader will understand
it better when he has perused the following note of M. le Duchat,
which is this : Peter Grosnet, in his Collection of Cato's Golden
Sayings and other Moral Sentences, relates this story in the
following terms :—

> Two gossips prating in a church,
> The dev'l, who stood upon the lurch,
> In short-hand, on a parchment roll,
> Writ down their words ; and when the scroll
> Could hold no more (it was so full),
> His devilship began to pull
> And stretch it with his teeth, which failing,
> He knocked his head against the railing.
> St Martin laughed, though then at mass,
> To see the devil such an ass,
> To think the parchment roll, or e'en a skin,
> Could hold two women's chat, when they begin.

The birth of Gargantua.

Saint Martin's was puzzled with the like task, when with his teeth he had lengthened out the parchment whereon he wrote the tittle-tattle of two young mangy whores. By this inconvenience the coty- ledons of her matrix were presently loosened, through which the child sprang up and leaped, and so, entering into the hollow vein, did climb by the diaphragm even above her shoulders, where the vein divides itself into two, and from thence taking his way towards the left side, issued forth at her left ear. As soon as he was born, he cried not as other babes use to do, Miez, miez, miez, miez, but with a high, sturdy, and big voice shouted about, Some drink, some drink, some drink, as inviting all the world to drink with him. The noise hereof was so extremely great, that it was heard in both the countries at once, of Beauce [6] and Bibarois. I doubt me that you do not thoroughly believe the truth of this strange nativity. Though you believe it not, I care not much: but an honest man, and of good judgment, believeth still what is told him, and that which he finds written.

Is this beyond our law, or our faith; against reason or the Holy Scripture? For my part, I find nothing in the sacred Bible that is against it. But tell me, if it had been the will of God, would you say that he could not do it? Ha, for favour sake, I beseech you, emberlucock or impulregafize your spirits with these vain thoughts and idle conceits;

---

[6] *Beauce and Bibarois.*—Beusse (for so Rabelais spells it) is a large town, which gives name to a little river, formed by divers springs near Loudun. The Bibarois is nothing else but the Vivarets, as the Gascons pronounce that word. Rabelais here reflects upon the country of Beusse and Vivarets, as if the in- habitants were great *drinkers, Buveurs (bibitores,* if I may use that Latin word, to answer the French *bibaroys*) and *būverie (bibbing),* by way of pun upon Beusse.

for I tell you, it is not impossible with God; and, if
he pleased, all women henceforth should bring forth
their children at the ear. Was not Bacchus engendered out of the very thigh of Jupiter? Did
not Roquetaillade come out of his mother's heel, and
Crocmoush from the slipper of his nurse? Was not
Minerva born of the brain, even through the ear of
Jove? Adonis, of the bark of a myrrh tree; and
Castor and Pollux of the doupe of that egg[7] which
was laid and hatched by Leda? But you would
wonder more, and with far greater amazement, if I
should now present you with that chapter of Plinius,
wherein he treateth of strange births, and contrary
to nature, and yet am I not so impudent a liar as he
was. Read the seventh book of his Natural History,
chap. 3, and trouble not my head any more about
this.

CHAPTER VII

AFTER WHAT MANNER GARGANTUA HAD HIS NAME
GIVEN HIM, AND HOW HE TIPPLED, BIBBED,
AND CURRIED THE CAN

THE good man Grangousier, drinking and making
merry with the rest, heard the horrible noise which
his son had made as he entered into the light of this
world, when he cried out, Some drink, some drink,

---

[7] *Doupe of that egg.*—I know not what *doupe* means, unless it
is Scotch for *double*. Leda was indeed double-egged ; for Jupiter
turned himself into a swan, and lay with her just after her
husband ; by them two she had two eggs ; of one came Pollux
and Helena; of the other, Castor and Clytemnestra. Rabelais'
words are only *de la cocque d'un oeuf.* [*Doup* is a north-country
word for the buttocks.]

114

some drink; whereupon he said in French, Que
grand tu as et souple le gousier ! that is to say, How
great and nimble a throat thou hast ! Which the
company hearing said, that verily the child ought to
be called Gargantua; [1] because it was the first word
that after his birth his father had spoke, in imitation
and at the example of the ancient Hebrews; whereunto he condescended, and his mother was very well
pleased therewith. In the meanwhile, to quiet the
child, they gave him to drink a tirelarigot, that is,
till his throat was like to crack with it; then was he
carried to the font, and there baptized according to
the manner of good Christians.

Immediately thereafter were appointed for him
seventeen thousand nine hundred and thirteen cows
of the towns of Pautille and Brehemond, [2] to furnish
him with milk in ordinary, for it was impossible to
find a nurse sufficient for him in all the country,
considering the great quantity of milk that was
requisite for his nourishment; although there were
not wanting some doctors of the opinion of Scotus,
who affirmed that his own mother gave him suck,
and that she could draw out of her breasts one
thousand four hundred and two pipes, and nine pails
milk at every time.

Which indeed is not probable, and this point hath

[1] *Gargantua.*—This word is partly made up of these three words
before, *Grand tu as*, as the French pronounce it.
[2] *Pautille and Brehemond.*—The map of the Chinonois, Rabelais'
native country, places Potille on the River Vienne, within a
league of Chinon ; and Brehemont on the Loire, three leagues
from Chinon, on which it is dependent. Here are made those
cheeses which, by the French translator of Platina de Obsoniis, were
so highly valued, that in his translation printed in 1505, though
Platina does not take any notice of those cheeses, yet he has made
particular and very honourable mention of them ; wherein he has
been followed by Bruyerin, or La Bruyere Champier, l. 14, *de re
cibaria*, c. 8.

been found duggishly scandalous [3] and offensive to
tender ears, for that it savoured a little of heresy.
Thus was he handled for one year and ten months;
after which time, by the advice of physicians, they
began to carry him, and then was made for him a
fine little cart drawn with oxen, of the invention of
Jan Denio, [4] wherein they led him hither and thither
with great joy; and he was worth the seeing, for he
was a fine boy, had a burly physiognomy, and almost
ten chins. He cried very little, but beshit himself
every hour; for, to speak truly of him, he was
wonderly phlegmatic in his posteriors, both by
reason of his natural complexion, and the accidental
disposition which had befallen him by his too much
quaffing of the Septembral juice. Yet without a
cause did not he sup one drop ; for if he happened
to be vexed, angry, displeased or sorry, if he did fret,
if he did weep, if he did cry, and what grievous
quarter soever he kept, in bringing him some drink,
he would be instantly pacified, reseated in his own
temper in a good humour again, and as still and
quiet as ever. One of his governesses told me
(swearing by her fig), how he was so accustomed to
this kind of way, that, at the sound of pints and
. flagons, he would on a sudden fall into an ecstasy, as
if he had then tasted of the joys of paradise; so that
they, upon consideration of this his divine com-

---

[3] *Duggishly scandalous.—Mammallement scandaleuse.* Rabelais
here seems particularly to have in view the anathema pronounced
by the Universities of Lovain and Cologne, and afterwards by
Pope Leo X. in 1520, against the propositions of Luther, which,
as his very adversaries confessed, were not all equally heretical
and capital. See Sleidan, l. 2, and Fra. Paolo's History of the
Council of Trent.

[4] *Jan Denio.*—Rabelais calls him Jehan, not Jan, for Jan means
a cuckold, Denyau, not Denio. An ancient and honourable
family, most of them lawyers, both in Poitou and Bretagne.

116

plexion, would every morning, to cheer him up, play with a knife upon the glasses, on the bottles with their stopples, and on the pottle-pots with their lids and covers, at the sound whereof he became gay, did leap for joy, would loll and rock himself in the cradle, then nod with his head, monocordising [5] with his fingers, and barytonising [6] with his tail.

CHAPTER VIII

HOW THEY APPARELLED GARGANTUA

BEING of this age, his father ordained to have clothes made to him in his own livery, which was white and blue. To work then went the tailors, and with great expedition were clothes made, cut and sewed, according to the fashion that was then in request. I find by the ancient records or pancarts, to be seen in the chamber of accounts, or Court of the Exchequer, at Montsoreau,[1] that he was accoutred in manner as

[5] *Monocordising with his fingers.*—It should be *monochordising* with his fingers. Moving his fingers, as if he was about to play on the instrument called by the ancients monochord, because it had but one string. The monochord of the moderns has kept the same name (though it has several strings) because they are unisons.

[6] *Barytonising with his tail.*—The art of rhetoric, quoted by Borel, has the word barytoniser, but barytoner is better. It means yielding a grave tone or accent, βαρυτονεῖν ; Gargantua formed the acute accent with his fingers (by snapping them) and the grave with his bum.

[1] *Chamber of accounts at Montsoreau.*—Rabelais, placing the scene of his romance in Touraine, and part of the adjoining provinces, was resolved to settle a chamber of accounts at Montsoreau, a little town and comté in Anjou, on the Loire, alluding belike to the title of comtes, which belonged to the lords of Montsoreau, a family so eminent about the twelfth century, that Walter de Montsoreau is styled Most Christian Prince in an instrument of those times, as M. Menage has observed, as did likewise M. Pavillon before him.

followeth. To make him every shirt of his were taken up nine hundred ells of Chatcleraud linen, and two hundred for the gussets, in manner of cushions, which they put under his arm-pits. His shirt was not gathered nor plaited, for the plaiting of shirts [2] was not found out till the seamstresses (when the point of their needle was broken) began to work and occupy with the tail. There were taken up for his doublet, eight hundred and thirteen ells of white satin, and for his points fifteen hundred and nine dogs' skins and a half. Then was it that men began to tie their breeches to their doublets, and not their doublets to their breeches: for it is against nature,[3] as hath most amply been showed by Ockam [4] upon the exponibles of Master Haute chaussade.

[2] *Plaiting of shirts.*—The fashion began in Rabelais' time. 'Nam rugæ hæ, quid aliud sunt hoc tempore, quam nidi, aut receptacula pediculorum et pulicum,' says one in Vives. (Dial. intituled Vestitus, et deambulatio matutina.) The person who spoke thus did not like that new mode, it seems, and so says, the gathers of such shirts are fit for nothing but to harbour lice and fleas.

[3] *Against nature.*—Indeed it is neither natural nor possible to fasten or hang one thing to another thing which was lower than it.

[4] *Ockam.*—The copy in Rabelais' own hand-writing has it Olzam, in old characters, according to which, in the manuscripts, and many printed pieces of those times, the *k* is made like an *z*; whence it is, that not one of the editions I have yet seen has it Okam, or Ockam, which is that English doctor's true name ; but all of them Olkam, Olcam, or Olzam. Here below, in chap. 33, the printers have committed the same fault in the word Lubeck; for in the edition of Niery, 1573, we see Lubelz for Lubeck. In c. 40, l. 3, A.D. 1553, that edition has Stolzom for Stockholm, and in Prol. of l. 4, Ollzegon for Ockeghem, still carried on by the same blunder; nay, even those that worked for H. Stephens, on the best edition of his 'Apology for Herodotus, A.D. 1566,' have stumbled at the words Kyrielle and Lansquenets; instead of which they have put Lzirielle and Lansquenelz. [William of Occam, or Ockam, is said to have been a favourite author of

For his breeches were taken up eleven hundred
and five ells and a third of white broad-cloth.   They
were cut in the form of pillars, chamfered, channelled,
and pinked behind, that they might not overheat his
reins; and were, within the panes, puffed out with
the lining of as much blue damask as was needful;
and remark, that he had very good leg-harness,
proportionable to the rest of his stature.

For his codpiece were used sixteen ells and a
quarter of the same cloth, and it was fashioned on
the top like unto a triumphant arch most gallantly
fastened with two enamelled clasps, in each of which
was set a great emerald, as big as an orange; for, as
says Orpheus, lib. de lapidibus, and Plinius, libro
ultimo, it hath an erective virtue and comfort and
comfortative of the natural member.   The exiture,
out-jecting or out-standing of his codpiece, was of
the length of a yard, jagged and pinked, and withal
bagging, and strutting out with the blue damask
lining, after the manner of his breeches.   But had
you seen the fair embroidery of the small needlework pearl, and the curiously interlaced knots, by
the goldsmith's art set out and trimmed with rich
diamonds, precious rubies, fine torquoises, costly
emeralds, and Persian pearls, you would have compared it to a fair Cornucopia, or horn of abundance,
such as you see in antiques, or as Rhea gave to the
two nymphs, Amalthea and Ida, the nurses of Jupiter.

And, like to that horn of abundance, it was still

Luther's.   He wrote *A Dialogue between a knight and a clerk concerning the power spiritual and temporal*, in 1305 (printed at
Cologne and Paris in the 15th century), in order to disabuse the
clergy of their unreasonable expectations concerning the power or
the Pope over the temporalities of princes, which they hoped
would be exercised in such a way as to exempt the Church from
contributing either to the relief of the poor or the security of the
nation.]

gallant, succulent, droppy, sappy, pithy, lively, always flourishing, always fructifying, full of juice, full of flower, full of fruit, and all manner of delight. I avow God, it would have done one good to have seen him, but I will tell you more of him in the book which I have made of the Dignity of Codpieces. One thing I will tell you, that, as it was both long and large, so was it well furnished and victualled within, nothing like unto the hypocritical codpieces of some fond wooers, and wench-courters, which are stuffed only with wind, to the great prejudice of the female sex.

For his shoes were taken up four hundred and six ells of blue crimson velvet, and were very neatly cut by parallel lines, joined in uniform cylinders. For the soling of them were made use of eleven hundred hides of brown cows, shapen like the tail of a keeling.[5]

For his coat were taken up eighteen hundred ells of blue velvet, dyed in grain, embroidered in its borders with fair gilliflowers, in the middle decked with silver pearl, intermixed with plates of gold, and stores of pearls, hereby showing, that in his time he would prove an especial good fellow, and singular whip-can.

His girdle was made of three hundred ells and a half of silken serge, half white and half blue, if I mistake it not. His sword was not of Valentia, nor his dagger of Saragossa, for his father could not

---

[5] *Keeling.*—An unusual word as the Camb. Dict. says, for what the Latins, or rather Greeks, call salpa, that is, a stockfish. Rather, as Cotgrave says, a kind of small cod, whereof stockfish is made. He calls it a kneeling, but that must be a typographical error. Merlus is the French word. [Keeling is the common cod-fish—a name made use of by North-sea fishermen at the present day.]

endure these hidalgos borrachos maranisados como
diablos: but he had a fair sword made of wood, and
the dagger of boiled leather, as well painted and
gilded as any man could wish.

His purse was made of the cod of an elephant,
which was given him by Her Pracontal,[6] proconsul
of Lybia.

For his gown were employed nine thousand six
hundred ells, wanting two thirds, of blue velvet as
before, all so diagonally pearled, that by true perspective issued thence an unnamed colour, like that
you see in the necks of turtle-doves or turkey-cocks,
which wonderfully rejoiced the eyes of the beholders.
For his bonnet or cap were taken up three hundred
two ells and a quarter of white velvet, and the form
thereof was wide and round, of the bigness of his
head; for his father said, that the caps of the
Marrabaise fashion,[7] made like the cover of a pasty,
would one time or other bring a mischief on those
that wore them.   For his plume, he wore a fair great
blue feather, plucked from an Onocrotal of the
country of Hircania the wild, very prettily hanging

[6] *Her Pracontal.*—The sire Pracontal, of an ancient family in
Dauphiny.
[7] *Caps of the Marrabaise fashion.—Bonnetz à la Marrabaise,* i.e.,
à la Juiva, Jew fashion, and as they are worn by the Spaniards,
many of whom are counted a sort of Jews and Mahometans
concealed.—Marrabais seems to be a word compounded of
Maurus and Arabs, because the Moors and Arabians ruled a long
time in part of Spain; and as there were many Jews intermixed
among them, thence Marrabais means a Mahometan and a Jew.
And because the Spaniards are abusively named Marranes and
Marrabais, as if they held with the Jews ; therefore, when in
c. 22, l. 3, we read of the poet Raminagrobis—He is by God,
a witty, quick, and subtile sophister, I'll lay an even wager he is
a Marrabais, Rabelais undoubtedly means he is acute as the
Spaniards, who, as is well known, being much attached to school
divinity, were consequently great logicians.

down over his right ear. For the jewel or brooch which in his cap he carried, he had in a cake of gold, weighing three score and eight marks, a fair piece enamelled, wherein was pourtrayed a man's body with two heads, looking towards one another, four arms, four feet, two arses, such as Plato, *in Symposia*, says was the mystical beginning of man's nature; and about it was written in Ionic letters, Ἀγαπη οὐ ζητει τα ἑαυτης.

To wear about his neck, he had a golden chain, weighing twenty-five thousand and sixty-three marks of gold, the links thereof being made after the manner of great berries, amongst which were set in work green jaspers, engraven and cut dragon-like, all environed with beams and sparks, as King Nicepsos of old was wont to wear them: and it reached down to the very bust of the rising of his belly, whereby he reaped great benefit all his life long, as the Greek physicians know well enough. For his gloves were put in work sixteen otters'[8] skins, and three of the loup-garous or men-wolves[9] for the bordering of

---

[8] *Otters' skins.—Peaux de lutins.* Lutin in French is not an otter, but an hob-goblin. Loutre indeed is an otter, and Sir T. U. mistook it for the other, deceived by the similitude of the name, not of the thing : for there is no such thing as an hob-goblin; and for that reason Rabelais here introduces it; for what can be more imaginary than an hob-goblin's skin ?

[It is, however, worthy of notice that the otter's skin was used for glove-making in Izaak Walton's day.

' *Viator.* Why, sir, what's the skin worth ?

' *Huntsman.* 'Tis worth ten shillings to make gloves; the gloves of an *otter* are the best fortification for your hands against wet weather that can be thought of.'—*Compleat Angler,* 1655, p. 66.]

[9] *Men-wolves.—Loup-garous.* This word means a man who is said to transform himself, or thinks himself transformed into a wolf. See Cotgrave's various and different accounts of this imaginary creature.

them: and of this stuff were they made, by the
appointment of the Cabalists of Sanlouand.[10]　As
for the rings which his father would have him to
wear, to renew the ancient mark of nobility, he had
on the forefinger of his left hand a carbuncle as big
as an ostrich's egg, enchased very daintily in gold of
the fineness of a Turkey seraph.　Upon the middle
finger[11] of the same hand, he had a ring made of
four metals together, of the strangest fashion that
ever was seen; so that the steel did not crash
against the gold, nor the silver crush the copper.
All this was made by Captain Chappuys, and
Alcofribas his good agent.　On the medical finger of
his right hand, he had a ring made spireways, wherein
was set a perfect baleu ruby, a pointed diamond, and
a Physon emerald, of an inestimable value.　For
Hans Carvel, the King of Melinda's jeweller,
esteemed them at the rate of three score nine
millions eight hundred ninety-four thousand and
eighteen French crowns of Berry,[12] and at so much
did the Foucres of Augsburg[13] prize them.

[10] *Sanlouand.*—A priory on the Vienne, about a league from
Chinon.

[11] *Middle finger.*—Medical finger in the original: which among
the Greeks, indeed was the middle finger, ' quòd eo veteres Medici
miscerent pharmaca,' Alex. ab Alex.　Among the Latins it was
otherwise ; they called the ring-finger medicus, as well as
annularis.　See Camb. Dict. under Digitus, for the names and
reasons of all the fingers, as well as thumb.

[12] *Crowns of Berry.*—In the French, *Moutons à la grande Laine* :
well-wooled sheep.　A gold coin, on one side whereof was represented Jesus Christ, under the figure of a lamb, with these words
round it, ' Agnus Dei, qui tollis peccata mundi, miserere nobis.'
Rabelais often uses this word.

[13] *Foucres of Augsburg.*—*Fourques de Augsbourg.*　Rabelais, in
his first letter, tells us, they were vastly rich and very eminent
merchants ; for his words are, Next to the Fourques of Augsbourg
in Germany, Philip Strozzi, of Florence in Italy, is counted the
richest merchant in Christendom.—Their true name is Fugger,

123

CHAPTER IX

THE COLOURS AND LIVERIES OF GARGANTUA

GARGANTUA'S colours were white and blue, as I have
showed you before, by which his father would give
us to understand, that his son to him was a heavenly
joy; for the white did signify gladness, pleasure,
delight, and rejoicing, and the blue, celestial things.
I know well enough, that, in reading this, you laugh

and they are at this day counts of the Empire, of which they were
made barons by the Emperor Maximilian I. The Supplement to
Morery giving an account of the name Fuggers, I thought fit to
translate it. 'They were the richest merchants in Augsburg
(their native city) in Charles the Fifth's time, and obtained of
that Emperor a privilege, exclusive of all others, to bring from
Venice into Germany all the spiceries, which were distributed in
France, and all the neighbouring countries. As these spiceries at
that time came from the Levant, only by the Red Sea, and from
thence into the Mediterranean, they were very scarce and dear.
Whereby the Fuggers made so great a fortune, that they were
counted the wealthiest family throughout the Empire, insomuch
that they have a proverb in Germany, "Such a one is as rich as
the Fuggers," speaking of a person that is immensely rich, or has
an overgrown estate. This family is yet in great credit, and
makes a considerable figure, some in the army, others in the
Emperor's court. It is related of these rich merchants, as a very
singular thing, and curious to be known, that the Emperor
Charles V. in his return from Tunis, passing into Italy and from
thence through the city of Augsburg, took up his quarters at their
house ; that, to show their gratitude and their joy for the honour
he did them with his presence, one day, among their other
magnificent regalements of the Emperor, they put into the
chimney-place a faggot or bundle of cinnamon, which was a
very valuable commodity at that time ; then showing him a
promissory note they had of his, for a very large sum of money,
they set it on fire, and with it kindled the faggot, which yielded
an odour and a brightness, the more pleasing to the Emperor as
he saw himself quit of a debt which his affairs did not, at that
time, permit him to pay without some difficulty.'

at the old drinker, and hold this exposition of colours
to be very extravagant, and utterly disagreeable to
reason, because white is said to signify faith, and
blue, constancy. But without moving, vexing, heat-
ing or putting you in a chafe (for the weather is
dangerous), answer me, if it please you; for no other
compulsory way of arguing will I use towards you,
or any else; only now and then I will mention a
word or two of my bottle. What is it that induceth
you; what stirs you up to believe, or who told you
that white signifieth faith, and blue constancy?
An old paltry book, say you, sold by the hawking
pedlars and ballad-mongers, entitled 'The Blazon of
Colours.' Who made it? Whoever it was, he was
wise in that he did not set his name to it. But,
besides, I know not what I should rather admire in
him, his presumption or his sottishness. His presumption and overweening, for that he should
without reason, without cause, or without any
appearance of truth, have dared to prescribe, by his
private authority, what things should be denotated
and signified by the colour: which is the custom of
tyrants, who will have their will to bear sway instead
of equity, and not of the wise and learned, who, with
the evidence of reason, satisfy their readers. His
sottishness and want of spirit, in that he thought,
that without any other demonstration, or sufficient
argument the world would be pleased to make his
blockish and ridiculous impositions the rule of their
devices. In effect, according to the proverb, 'To a
shitten tail fails never ordure,' he hath found, it
seems, some simple ninny in those rude times of old,
when the wearing of high round bonnets was in
fashion, who gave some trust to his writings, according to which they carved and engraved their
apophthegms and mottos, trapped and caparisoned

their mules and sumpter-horses, apparelled their
pages, quartered their breeches, bordered their
gloves, fringed the curtains and valances of their
beds, painted their ensigns, composed songs, and,
which is worse, played many deceitful jugglings, and
unworthy base tricks undiscoveredly, amongst the
very chastest matrons. In the like darkness and
mist of ignorance are wrapped up these vain-glorious
courtiers, and name-transposers, who, going about in
their impresas to signify esperance [espoir], (that in
hope) have pourtrayed a sphere; and bird's pennes,
for pains; l'Ancholie (which is the flower colombine)
for melancholy; a horned moon or crescent, to show
the increasing or rising of one's fortune; a bench
rotten and broken, to signify bankrupt; non and a
corslet for non dur habit (otherwise non durabit, it
shall not last); un lit sans ciel, that is, a bed without
a tester, for un licentié, a graduated person, as,
bachelor in divinity, or utter barrister-at-law; which
are equivocals so absurd and witless, so barbarous
and clownish, that a fox's tail [1] should be fastened to
the neck-piece of, and a vizard made of a cowsherd
given to, everyone that henceforth should offer, after
the restitution of learning, to make use of any such
fopperies in France.

By the same reasons (if reasons I should call
them, and not ravings rather, and idle triflings about
words) might I cause paint a pannier, to signify that
I am in pain—a mustard-pot, that my heart tarries
much for it—one pissing upwards for a bishop—the
bottom of a pair of breeches for a vessel full of

---

[1] *A fox's tail, etc.*—A way of speaking borrowed from the
ancients, who were wont to treat in this manner such as they had
a mind should be laughed at. 'Veteres,' says the Scaligerana,
'iis quos irridere volebant, cornua dormientibus capiti imponebant,
vel *caudam vulpis*, vel quid simile.'

fart-hings—a codpiece for the office of the clerks of
the sentences, decrees or judgments, or rather (as the
English bears it), for the tail of a cod-fish—and a
dog's turd, for the dainty turret, wherein lies the
heart of my sweetheart.

Far otherwise did heretofore the sages of Egypt,
when they wrote by letters, which they called
Hieroglyphics, which none understood who were not
skilled in the virtue, property, and nature of the
things represented by them. Of which Orus Apollo
hath in Greek composed two books, and Polyphilus,[2]
in his Dream of Love, set down more. In France you
have a taste of them in the device[3] or impresa of my
Lord Admiral which was carried before that time by
Octavian Augustus. But my little skiff along these
unpleasant gulfs and shoals will sail no farther,

[2] *Polyphilus, etc.*—' Hypnerotomachia Poliphili, ubi omnia non
nisi somnium esse docet, atque obiter plurima scitu sanè quam
digna commemorat.' This is the inscription of the book, which
is a folio, printed at Venice by Aldus Manutius, A. 1499. M.
le Duchat gives a long, but not very advantageous character of
this book and its author. Alchymists think the philosopher's
stone may be found in it, if they had but the right key to it.
The author was a Venetian monk, Francisco Colonna, who
composed his strange love dream (it is nothing more) at Treviso
in 1467.

[3] *Device, etc.*—Rabelais, in two or three places, says positively,
Augustus' motto was ' Festina lentè,' with the device of an
anchor, a very heavy thing, and round it a dolphin, the swiftest
of fishes, if not of all creatures. And yet it is certainly true
that this very motto and device was the Emporor Titus'; that
of Augustus having been, as H. Stephen observes, Terminus
fulmini conjunctus, with the same words indeed, Festina lentè.
Rabelais often wrote by memory. The Admiral of France he
alludes to, is thought to be M. de Brion Chabot, whose device
was the Anchor and Dolphin, the one referring to his marine
employment, the other to his particular attachment to the
Dauphin. (I think a noble English peer has likewise for his
motto, Festina lentè, which, as it means On slow, there is no
occasion to name him.)

therefore must I return to the port from whence I came. Yet do I hope one day to write more at large of these things, and to show both by philosophical arguments and authorities, received and approved of, by and from all antiquity, what, and how many colours there are in nature, and what may be signified by every one of them, if God save the mould of my cap, which is my best wine-pot, as my grandam said.

CHAPTER X

OF THAT WHICH IS SIGNIFIED BY THE COLOURS WHITE AND BLUE

THE white therefore signifieth joy, solace, and gladness, and that not at random, but upon just and very good grounds: which you may perceive to be true, if, laying aside all prejudicate affections, you will but give ear to what presently I shall expound unto you.

Aristotle saith, that, supposing two things contrary in their kind, as good and evil, virtue and vice, heat and cold, white and black, pleasure and pain, joy and grief,—and so of others,—if you couple them in such manner, that the contrary of one kind may agree in reason with the contrary of the other, it must follow by consequence, that the other contrary must answer to the remnant opposite to that wherewith it is conferred. As for example, virtue and vice are contrary in one kind, so are good and evil. If one of the contraries of the first kind be consonant to one of those of the second, as virtue and goodness, for it is clear that virtue is good, so shall the other two

contraries, which are evil and vice, have the same
connexion, for vice is evil.

This logical rule being understood, take these two
contraries, joy and sadness, then these other two,
white and black, for they are physically contrary.
If so be, then, that black do signify grief, by good
reason then should white import joy. Nor is this
signification instituted by human imposition, but by
the universal consent of the world received, which
philosophers call Jus Gentium, the Law of Nations,
or an uncontrollable right of force in all countries
whatsoever. For you know well enough, that all
people, and all languages and nations, except the
ancient Syracusans,[1] and certain Argives, who had
cross and thwarting souls, when they mean outwardly
to give evidence of their sorrow, go in black; and all
mourning is done with black. Which general consent is not without some argument, and reason in
natur, the which every man may by himself very
suddenly comprehend, without the instruction of
any; and this we call the law of nature. By virtue
of the same natural instinct, we know that by
white all the world hath understood joy, gladness,
mirth, pleasure, and delight. In former times,
the Thracians and Grecians[2] did mark their good,

---

[1] *Syracusans.*—Plutarch, describing the magnificence of the
funeral ceremonies performed by the Syracusans to Timoleon,
says, they appeared thereat in their neatest, cleanest clothes,—
Πάντων καθαρὰς ἐθῆτας φορούντων. From whence Alexander
ab Alexandro, cap. 7 of l. 3 of his Genial Days, has taken occasion to write, that the custom of the Syracusans was to attend
funerals in a white robe. Wherein he has committed two faults,
here faithfully copied by Rabelais. First in talking of a white
robe, when Plutarch mentions no colour, but only the neatness of
their clothes; the other, for taking the extraordinary funeral
honours, done by the Syracusans to Timoleon, for a custom
established among them in all funerals.

[2] *Grecians.*—Cretans, in Rabelais.

propitious, and fortunate days with white stones, and their sad, dismal, and unfortunate ones with black. Is not the night mournful, sad, and melancholy? It is black and dark by the privation of light. Doth not the light comfort all the world? And it is more white than anything else. Which to prove, I could direct you to the book of Laurentius Valla against Bartolos; but an Evangelical testimony I hope will content you. In Matth. xvii., it is said, that, at the transfiguration of our Lord, Vestimenta ejus facta sunt alba sicut lux, his apparel was made white like the light. By which lightsome whiteness he gave his three apostles to understand the idea and figure of the eternal joys; for by the light are all men comforted, according to the word of the old woman, who, although she had never a tooth in her head, was wont to say, Bona lux.[3] And Tobit, chap. v., after he had lost his sight, when Raphael saluted him, answered, What joy can I have that do not see the light of heaven? In that colour did the angels testify the joy of the whole world, at the resurrection of our Saviour, John xx., and at his Ascension, Acts i. With the like colour of vesture did St John the Evangelist, Apoc. iv. 7, see the faithful clothed in the heavenly and blessed Jerusalem.

Read the ancient, both Greek and Latin histories, and you shall find, that the town of Alba (the first pattern of Rome) was founded, and so named by reason of a white sow that was seen there. You shall likewise find in those stories, that when any man, after he had vanquished his enemies, was by

---

[3] *Bona Lux.*—Φῶs ἀγαθὸν. 'Id est, Lumen bonum, vitæ lumen est. Id autem dictum est ab anu quapiam moriente, quam etiamnum juvabat vivere,' says Erasmus himself, under the name of Listrius, on the Φῶs ἀγαθὸν of the Encomium Moriæ, p. 64 of the Basle edition, 1676.

a decree of the senate, to enter into Rome trium-
phantly, he usually rode in a chariot drawn by white
horses : which, in the Ovatian Triumph, was also the
custom ; for by no sign or colour would they so
significantly express the joy of their coming, as by
the white.   You shall there also find, how Pericles,
the general of the Athenians, would needs have that
part of his army, unto whose lot befel the white
beans, to spend the whole day in mirth, pleasure,
and ease, whilst the rest were a-fighting.   A thousand
other examples and places could I allege to this
purpose, but that it is not here where I should do it.
    By understanding hereof, you may resolve one
problem, which Alexander Aphrodiseus hath accounted unanswerable,[4] why the lion, who, with his
only cry and roaring, affrights all beasts and dreads,
feareth only a white cock ?   For, as Proclus [5] saith,
' Libro de sacrificio et magia,' it is because the
presence, or the virtue of the sun, which is the
organ and promptuary of all terrestrial and sidereal
light, doth more symbolise and agree with a white
cock, as well in regard of that colour, as of his
property and specifical quality, than with a lion.
He saith furthermore, that devils have been often
seen in the shape of lions, which, at the sight of a
white cock, have presently vanished.   This is the

[4] *Unanswerable.*—Rabelais' word is insoluble, which the reader
will agree with me is the proper word here, to correspond with
solve before.   But this, by the bye, and only to show Rabelais'
correctness.   M. le Duchat says, the place where Alexander
Aphrodiseus declares this problem insoluble, is in his preface to
his Problems, where, however, M. le Duchat takes notice, that
that author does not actually say it is a white cock the lion
dreads, but only a cock.
    [5] *Proclus.*—Rabelais cites him again, l. 2, c. 1, yet neither
Proclus, nor Alexander Aphrodiseus, determines the colour of the
cock.

cause why Galli (so are the Frenchmen called,
because they are naturally as white as milk, which
the Greeks call Gala) do willingly wear in their caps
white feathers, for by nature they are of a candid
disposition, merry, kind, gracious, and well-beloved,[6] and for their cognizance and arms have
the whitest flower of any, the Flower de Luce, or
Lily.

If you demand, how, by white, nature would have
us understand joy and gladness? I answer, that the
analogy and uniformity is thus. For, as the white
doth outwardly disperse and scatter the rays of the
sight, whereby the optic spirits are manifestly
dissolved, according to the opinion of Aristotle in
his problems and perspective treatises; as you may
likewise perceive by experience when you pass over
mountains covered with snow, how you will complain
that you cannot see well; as Xenophon writes to
have happened to his men, and as Galen very largely
declareth, lib. 10, de usu partium : just so the heart
with excessive joy is inwardly dilated, and suffereth
a manifest resolution of the vital spirits, which may
go so far on, that it may thereby be deprived of its
nourishment, and by consequence of life itself, by
this pericharie or extremity of gladness, as Galen
saith, lib. 12, Method, lib. 5, de Locis Affectis, and
lib. 2, de Symptomatum Causis. And as it hath
come to pass in former times, witness Marcus
Tullius, lib. 1, Quæst. Tuscul. Verrius, Aristotle,
Titus Livius, in his relation of the battle of Cannæ,
Plinius, lib. 7, cap. 32 and 34, A. Gellius, lib. 3,
c. 15, and many other writers,—to Diagoras the
Rhodian, Chilon, Sophocles, Dionysius the tyrant of

[6] *Well-beloved.*—It should be well-disposed, as M. le Duchat
clearly proves Rabelais to have meant here; from the old word
bien-esmez.

Sicily, Philippides, Philemon, Polycrates,[7] Philistion,
M. Juventi,[8] and others who died with joy.   And as
Avicen speaketh, in 2 canon et lib. de virib. cordis,
of the saffron, that it doth so rejoice the heart, that,
if you take of it excessively, it will by a superfluous
resolution and dilation deprive it altogether of life.
Here peruse Alex. Aphrodiseus, lib. 1. Probl. cap.
19, and that for a cause.   But what?   It seems I
am entered further into this point than I intended
at the first.   Here, therefore, will I strike sail,
referring the rest to that book of mine, which
handleth this matter to the full.   Meanwhile, in a
word I will tell you, that blue doth certainly signify
heaven and heavenly things, by the very same tokens
and symbols that white signifieth joy and pleasure.[9]

CHAPTER XI

OF THE YOUTHFUL AGE OF GARGANTUA

GARGANTUA, from three years upwards unto five, was
brought up and instructed in all convenient discipline,
by the commandment of his father; and spent that
time like the other little children of the country,
that is, in drinking, eating, and sleeping : in eating,
sleeping, and drinking : and in sleeping, drinking,

[7] *Polycrates.*—Policrites it should be, for so is this woman
named by Parthenius and Plutarch, not Polycrates a man, as the
old edition of Aulus Gellius has it.

[8] *M. Juventi.*—M. Juventius Talva, Plin. l. 7, c. 53.   Val.
Max. l. 9, c. 12, where Pighius observes, from the Fasti Capito-
lini and MSS., that it should be written Thalma.

[9] [These and cognate matters are dealt with by Cornelius
Agrippa in his *Occult Philosophy*, an English translation of which,
by J. Freake, appeared in 1651.]

and eating. Still he wallowed and rolled himself
up and down in the mire and dirt: he blurred
and sullied his nose with filth; he blotted and
smutched his face with any kind of scurvy stuff;
he trod down his shoes in the heel; at the flies he
did often times yawn, and ran very heartily after
the butterflies, the empire whereof belonged to his
father. He pissed in his shoes, shit in his shirt, and
wiped his nose on his sleeve; he did let his snot and
snivel fall in his pottage, and dabbled, paddled
and slobbered everywhere; he would drink in his
slipper, and ordinarily rub his belly against a
pannier. He sharpened his teeth with a top,
washed his hands with his broth, and combed his
head with a bowl. He would sit down betwixt
two stools, and his arse to the ground; would cover
himself with a wet sack, and drink in eating of his
soup. He did eat his cake sometimes without
bread, would bite in laughing, and laugh in biting.
Oftentimes did he spit in the basin, and fart for fat-
ness, piss against the sun, and hide himself in the
water for fear of rain. He would strike out of the
cold iron, be often in the dumps, and frig and
wriggle it. He would flay the fox,[1] say the ape's
pater-noster, return to his sheep, and turn the hogs
to the hay. He would beat the dogs before the
lion, put the plough before the oxen, and claw
where it did not itch. He would pump one to draw
somewhat out of him, by griping all would hold fast
nothing, and always eat his white bread first. He
shoed the geese, tickled himself to make himself

[1] *Flay the Fox.—Escorcher le Regnard.* To cast up one's
accounts upon excessive drinking; either, says Cotgrave, because
in spewing one makes a noise like a fox that barks, or (from the
subject to the effect) because the flaying of so unsavoury a beast
will make any one spew.

laugh, and was cook-ruffin in the kitchen: made a
mock at the gods, could cause sing Magnificat at
matins, and found it very convenient so to do. He
would eat cabbage, and shite beets; knew flies in a
dish of milk, and would make them lose their feet.
He would scrape paper, blur parchment, then run
away as hard as he could. He would pull at the
kid's leather, or vomit up his dinner, then reckon
without his host. He would beat the bushes without catching the birds, thought the moon was made
of green cheese, and that bladders are lanterns.
Out of one sack he would take two moultures or
fees for grinding; would act the ass's part to get
some bran, and of his fist would make a mallet. He
took the cranes at the first leap, and would have the
mail-coats to be made link after link. He always
looked a gift horse in the mouth, leaped from the
cock to the ass, and put one ripe between two
green. By robbing Peter he paid Paul, he kept the
moon from the wolves, and hoped to catch larks if
ever the heavens should fall. He did make of
necessity virtue, of such bread such pottage, and
cared as little for the peeled as for the shaven.
Every morning he did cast up his gorge, and his
father's little dogs eat out of the dish with him, and
he with them. He would bite their ears, and they
would scratch his nose; he would blow in their
arses, and they would lick his chaps.

But harken, good fellows, the spigot ill betake
you, and whirl round your brains, if you do not give
ear! this little lecher was always groping his nurses
and governesses, upside down, arsiversy, topsiturvy,
harri bourriquet,[2] with a Yacco haick, hyck gio!

[2] *Harri, etc.*—In the original it is *harri bourriquet. Bourriquet*
is such a title for an ass, as jade for a horse; so *harri bourriquet,*
says Cotgrave, are words wherewith the millers, etc., in France

handling them very rudely in jumbling and tum-
bling them to keep them going; for he had already
begun to exercise the tools, and put his codpiece
in practice. Which codpiece, or braguette, his
governesses did every day deck up and adorn with
fair nosegays, curious rubies, sweet flowers, and fine
silken tufts, and very pleasantly would pass their
time in taking you know what between their fingers
and dandling it,³ till it did revive and creep up to
the bulk and stiffness of a suppository, or street
magdaleon, which is a hard-rolled-up salve spread
upon leather. Then did they burst out in laughing,
when they saw it lift up its ears, as if the sport had
liked them. One of them would call it her pillicock,⁴ her fiddle-diddle, her staff of love, her tickle-
gizzard, her gentle-titler. Another, her sugar-plum,
her kingo, her old rowley, her touch-trap, her flap
dowdle. Another again, her branch of coral, her
placket-racket, her Cyprian sceptre, her tit-bit, her
bob-lady. And some of the other women would
give these names, my Roger, my cockatoo, my

drive forward their asses. M. le Duchat says the same thing,
only he confines it to Languedoc; he also quotes the following
verse of Merlin Coccaie, in lib. 8, of his Macaronics—
'Non tibi fustigans asinum pronunciat *ari*.'
³ *Dandling it.*—Rabelais says, *Comme ung magdaleon d'entract*,
they moulded his cock like a roller of green salve. M. le Duchat
says, *Sorte d'onguent*. He goes on—Latin barbarous authors have
said, *magdaleones*; others more correct, *magdalia*, in the neuter
gender; the Greeks μαγδαλίαι, and μαγδαλίδες in the femi-
nine gender; the whole derived from μασσειν, to knead or
mould as dough, because this unguent is kneaded, as it were, to
give it the form of a cylinder. Extract or entrait, comes from
intractum, because it is drawn out, in order to lengthen it, and
withal give it a roundness.
⁴ *Pillicock.*—*Pine* or *pinne*: in the title 59 of the law of the
Germans, the word *pinne* seems to mean a probe; 'Pinna instru-
mentum chirugicum quo vulnera tentantur,' says Ducange, in
his Latin glossary at the word *pinna*.

nimble-wimble, bush-beater, claw-buttock, eves-
dropper, pick-lock, pioneer, bully-ruffin, smell-
smock, trouble-gusset, my lusty live sausage, my
crimson chitterlin, rump-splitter, shove-devil, down
right to it, stiff and stout, in and to, at her again,
my cony-burrow-ferret, wily-beguily, my pretty
rogue. It belongs to me, said one. It is mine, said
the other. What, quoth a third, shall I have no
share in it? By my faith, I will cut it then. Ha,
to cut it, said the other, would hurt him. Madam,
do you cut little children's things? Were his cut
off, he would be then Monsieur Sans-queue,[5] the
curtailed master. And that he might play and sport
himself after the manner of the other little children
of the country, they made him a fair weather whirl-
jack, of the wings of the windmill of Myrebalais.

CHAPTER XII

OF GARGANTUA'S WOODEN HORSES

AFTERWARDS, that he might be all his lifetime a good
rider, they made to him a fair great horse of wood,
which he did make leap, curvet, yerk out behind,
and skip forward, all at a time: to pace, trot, rack,
gallop, amble, to play the hobby, the hackney
gelding: go the gait of the camel, and of the wild
ass.[1] He made him also change his colour of hair,

5 *Monsieur Sans-queue.*—Strictly, Master without a tail, *i.e.*, one
that has no addition to his name, but only plain Mr Such-a-one.
Queue, besides its primary meaning, the tail of a beast, had several
secondary ones, such as the stalk of fruits, label of a deed, and
also label of mortality, or bauble of a man, etc.

1 *The Wild Ass.*—*L'onagrier*, a quick short step, like that of
a wild ass, whose Latin name, from the Greek, is *onager*.

as the Monks of Coultibo[2] (according to the variety
of their holidays) use to do their clothes, from bay
brown to sorrel, dapple-grey, mouse-dun, deer-colour,
roan, cow-colour, gin-gioline, skued colour, piebald,
and the colour of the savage elk.

Himself of a huge big post made a hunting nag,
and another for daily service of the beam of a wine-
press; and of a great oak made up a mule, with a
foot-cloth, for his chamber. Besides this, he had
ten or twelve spare horses, and seven horses for
post; and all these were lodged in his own
chamber, close by his bed-side. One day the Lord
of Breadinbag[3] came to visit his father in great
bravery, and with a gallant train: and at the same
time, to see him, came likewise the Duke of
Freemeale, and the Earl of Wetgullet. The house
truly for so many guests at once was somewhat
narrow, but especially the stables; whereupon the
steward and harbinger of the said Lord Breadinbag,
to know if there were any other empty stable in the
house, came to Gargantua, a little young lad, and
secretly asked him where the stables of the great

[2] *As the Monks of Coultibo.*—There are no such monks, nor any
such place. *Courtibaut*, for that is the word, is a monk's vest-
ment, so called from *curtum tibiale*, because it reaches but little
lower than the knee. The monks do, according to the festival,
change this *courtibaut*, as it is called in Berri, Saintonge, and
Touraine. It is a sort of tunic or ancient dalmatica; so that the
true translation of this place would be, Pantagruel made his horse
change the colour of his hair, as monks do their *coutibauts* (vestments) according to the variety of their holidays. Et lui faisoit
changer de poil, comme font les moynes de courtibaulx, selon les
festes.

[3] *Breadinbag.—Painensac.* (Bread-in-bag.) Of this name,
which at first sight looks as if it was fictitious, or rather
factitious, was the seneschal of Toulouse (le Sire de Pennensac)
in 1452. See the History of Charles VII., falsely ascribed to
Alan Chartier.

horses were, thinking that children would be ready
to tell all. Then he led them up along the stairs
of the castle, passing by the second hall unto a broad
great gallery, by which they entered into a large
tower, and as they were going up at another pair of
stairs, said the harbinger to the steward,—This child
deceives us, for the stables are never on the top of
the house. You may be mistaken, said the steward,
for I know some places at Lyons, at the Basmette,[4]
at Chaisnon,[5] and elsewhere, which have their
stables at the very tops of the houses; so it may be,
that behind the house there is a way to come to this
ascent.[6] But I will question him further. Then
said he to Gargantua, My pretty little boy, whither
do you lead us ? To the stable, said he, of my great
horses. We are almost come to it, we have but
these stairs to go up at. Then leading them along
another great hall, he brought them into his
chamber, and, closing the door, said unto them, This
is the stable you ask for, this is my gennet, this is

[4] *La Basmetta.*—It is a convent half a quarter of a league
below Angers, in the hollow of a mountain. René d'Anjou,
King of Sicily, Duke of Anjou, and Earl of Provence, founded it
in 1451, for the Cordeliers, on the model of the Sainte Baume
of Provence, called so from the Latin-barbarous Balmo. The
founder of this baumette called it so, as being but a diminutive of
the Sainte Baume, which the people of Provence do really believe
to have served Mary Magdalen for a place of retirement.
Anciently they called *basme,* that precious liquor which now is
called *baum,* from *balsamum,* which gave occasion to the change
that is made of the *baumette* of Anjou into *basmette.*
[5] *Chaisnon.*—This is *Chinon,* which Rabelais calls thus *de Caino,*
which is the name of this town, in Gregory of Tours. See
Adrian de Valois, under the word Caino.
[6] *There is a way to come to this ascent.*—It should be to the
mounting-block *au montcir.* Behind, as in all houses situated on
the side, or at the root of a hill ; there, beyond the stables, is an
easy way, leading to a place, where one may get on horseback,
and pursue one's way on level ground.

my gelding, this is my courser, and this is my
hackney, and laid on them with a great lever. I
will bestow upon you, said he, this Frizeland horse.
I had him from Francfort, yet will I give him you;
for he is a pretty little nag, and will go very well,
with a tessel of goshawks, half a dozen of spaniels,[7]
and a brace of grey-hounds; thus are you king of
the hares and partridges for all this winter. By St
John, said they, now we are paid, he hath gleeked
us to some purpose, bobbed we are now for ever. I
deny it, said he, he was not here above three days.
Judge you now, whether they had most cause, either
to hide their heads for shame, or to laugh at the jest.
As they were going down again thus amazed, he
asked them, Will you have a whimwham? What is
that? said they. It is, said he, five turds to make
you a muzzle. To-day, said the steward, though we
happen to be roasted, we shall not be burned, for
we are pretty well quipped and larded in my
opinion. O my jolly dapper boy, thou has given us
a gudgeon, I hope to see thee Pope[8] before I die.

[7] *Spaniels.*—Maturin Corderius tells us, this sort of dog has its
name from the country from whence the breed first came (Spain).
—Nay, the people of Spain were anciently called Spaniels, not
Spaniards; *Espaigneuls,* not *Espagnols,* which is a modern word
in comparison of the other.

[8] *Thou hast given us a gudgeon; I hope to see thee Pope.*—It
should be, Thou hast hay in thy horns, I shall see thee Pope
before I die. Fœnum habet in cornu, longè fuge. He has hay
in his horns, used to be the outcry at Rome against railers and
carping cynics; because when a bull or ox was vicious and
would run at people, the owner of him was obliged to fasten a
handful of hay to his horns, as a warning for people to keep out
of his way. The steward had the same idea of Gargantua, and
seeing him so full of waggery and witty roguery for one of his years,
says, he knows enough to be made a Pope in time. The vulgar
have always thought the Pope knows everything, from whence
they conclude that knowledge was the high road to the papacy.
The fable of Pope Joan, and the examples of some poor priests,

I think so, said he, myself; and then shall you be a
puppy, and this gentle popinjay a perfect papelard,
that is, dissembler. Well, well, said the harbinger.
But, said Gargantua, guess how many stitches there
are in my mother's smock. Sixteen, quoth the harbinger. You do not speak Gospel, said Gargantua,
for there is sent before, and sent behind,[9] and you
did reckon them ill, considering the two under
holes. When? said the harbinger. Even then, said
Gargantua, when they made a shovel of your nose
to take up a quarter of dirt,[10] and of your throat a
funnel, wherewith to put it into another vessel,
because the bottom of the old one was out.[11]
Cocksbod, said the steward, we have met with a
prater. Farewell, master tatler, God keep you, so
goodly are the words which you come out with, and
so fresh in your mouth, that it had need to be
salted.

Thus going down in great haste, under the arch

as well secular as regular, have helped forward this belief. Why,
I see you are a scholar, says Beroalde de Verville, in his Moyen
de Parvenir, you are in danger of being a Pope one of these days.
Thomas Naogeorgus was not in jest when he said in a satire
against John de la Casa, 'Quippe hoc sanctorum merita effecere
paparum ut vulgo insigne jam de nebulone feratur—
    'Tam malus est nequam, Christique inimicus, et osor,
        Ut fieri possit papa.'
    [9] *Sent before and sent behind.*—A pun upon the word cent (a
hundred) and *scent* (or smell), *sens*, the imperative of the verb
sentir.
    [10] *When they made a shovel of your nose to take up a quarter of
dirt, etc.*—The parallel here is half lost; Rabelais says, *Alors
qu'on feit de votre nez une dille pour tirer un muy de merde, etc.*—
i.e., When they made a faucet of your nose to draw off a hogs-
head of turd, and of your throat a funnel, etc.
    [11] *The bottom of the old one was out.*—By the bottom's being
out, or cracked, or ill-soldered, or badly caulked (as Rabelais
says elsewhere), Gargantua reproaches the steward's want of
sense.

of the stairs they let fall the great lever, which he had put upon their backs;[12] whereupon Gargantua said, What a devil ! you are, it seems, but bad horse-men, that suffer your bilder to fail you,[13] when you need him most. If you were to go from hence to Cahusac,[14] whether had you rather ride on a gosling, or lead a sow in a leash ? I had rather drink,[15] said the harbinger. With this they entered into the lower hall, where the company was, and relating to them this new story, they made them laugh like a swarm of flies.[16]

CHAPTER XIII

HOW GARGANTUA'S WONDERFUL UNDERSTANDING BE-
CAME KNOWN TO HIS FATHER GRANGOUSIER, BY
THE INVENTION OF A TORCHECUL OR WIPE-
BREECH.

ABOUT the end of the fifth year, Grangousier, return-ing from the conquest of the Canarians, went by the

[12] *The great lever which he had put upon their backs.—Le gros levier qu'il leur avoit chargé.* I fancy Rabelais means the great walking-staff he had put into their hands.

[13] *Suffer your bilder to fail you.*—I know not what bilder means. Taking it in the sense, as I said just now, of a walking-staff, then instead of bilder, it will be, Suffer your horse (which we often call one's walking-cane) to fail you. It is in French, *courtaut,* a crop-eared or bob-tail horse. *Judicet lector.* [A *bilder* is what is known in country districts as a *clodmell,* a heavy mallet with a long handle, used for breaking up clods of dry earth in the ploughed fields.]

[14] *Cahusac.*—An estate in the Agenois, then belonging to Louis, Baron d'Estissac. This *Cahusac* is again mentioned, l. 4, c. 52.

[15] *I had rather drink.*—The poor man having been so often catched by the young Gargantua, did not dare any more to make a direct answer.

[16] *Laugh like a swarm of flies.*— Confusedly, like the buzzing of flies.

way to see his son Gargantua. There was he filled
with joy, as such a father might be at the sight of
such a child of his : and whilst he kissed and embraced him, he asked many childish questions of him
about divers matters, and drank very freely with him
and with his governesses, of whom in great earnest
he asked, amongst other things, whether they had
been careful to keep him clean and sweet ? To this
Gargantua answered, that he had taken such a course
for that himself, that in all the country there was
not to be found a cleanlier boy than he. How is
that ? said Grangousier. I have, answered Gargantua,
by a long and curious experience, found out a means
to wipe my bum, the most lordly, the most excellent, and the most convenient that ever was seen.
What is that ? said Grangousier, how is it ? I will
tell you by and by, said Gargantua. Once I did
wipe me with a gentlewoman's velvet mask, and
found it to be good ; for the softness of the silk was
very voluptuous and pleasant to my fundament.
Another time with one of their hoods, and in like
manner that was comfortable. At another time with
a lady's neckkerchief, and after that I wiped me
with some earpieces of hers made of crimson satin,
but there was such a number of golden spangles in
them (turdy round things, a pox take them !) that
they fetched away all the skin off my tail with a
vengeance. Now I wish St Anthony's fire burn
the bum-gut of the goldsmith that made them, and
of her that wore them ! This hurt I cured by
wiping myself with a page's cap, garnished with a
feather after the Switzers' fashion.

   Afterwards, in dunging behind a bush, I found a
March-cat, and with it I wiped my breech, but her
claws were so sharp that they scratched and exul-
cerated all my perinee. Of this I recovered the

next morning thereafter, by wiping myself with my
mother's gloves, of a most excellent perfume and
scent of the Arabian benin.[1] After that I wiped me
with sage, with fennel, with anet, with marjorum,
with roses, with gourdleaves, with beets, with cole-
wort, with leaves of the vinetree, with mallows, wool-
blade,[2] which is a tail-scarlet, with lettuce, and with
spinage leaves. All this did very great good to my leg.
Then with mercury, with pursly,[2] with nettles, with
comfrey, but that gave me the bloody flux of Lombardy,
which I healed by wiping me with my braguette.
Then I wiped my tail in the sheets, in the coverlet,
in the curtains, with a cushion, with arras hangings,
with a green carpet, with a table-cloth, with a napkin,
with a handkerchief, with a combing-cloth; in all
which I found more pleasure than do the mangy
dogs when you rub them. Yea, but, said Grangousier,
which torchecul did you find to be the best ? I was
coming to it, said Gargantua, and by and by shall you
hear the *tu autem*, and know the whole mystery and
knot of the matter. I wiped myself with hay, with

---

[1] *Benin.*—The Arabian gum called beninne : so Cotgrave
renders Rabelais' word maujoin, which M. le Duchat says is
the same thing as benjoin, only called maujoin by way of
antiphrasis, or the rule of contrarieties.

[2] *Wool-blade.—Verbasce.* Its leaf, which is large and broad,
is covered with a prickly down, which makes Rabelais call it
tail-scarlet, because it inflames the place it touches, and makes
it look red.

[3] *Pursly.—Persiguiere* in the original, which signifies not
pursly, but what we English call arse-smart. This 1 have
often recommended to the country fellows for a wipe-brush, and
have been well diverted and not a little cursed for my advice.
This simple, says Duchat, is called in Latin, persicaria. Lobel,
in his Adversaria Nova, p. 134. 'Gallis culraige vocatum est
(he is speaking of the persicaria), ut cujus folia, quæ quis podici
(honor sit auribus) abstergendi causa affricuerit, inurant rabiem
clunibus, sive, ut loquuntur leguleii, culo.'

144

straw, with thatch-rushes, with flax, with wool, with
paper, but,

Who his foul tail with paper wipes,
Shall at his ballocks leave some chips.

What, said Grangousier, my little rogue, hast thou
been at the pot, that thou dost rhyme already? Yes,
yes, my lord the king, answered Gargantua, I can
rhyme gallantly, and rhyme till I become hoarse with
rheum.   Hark, what our privy says to the skiters :

Shittard
Squittard
Crakard
        Turdous,
Thy bung
Hath flung
Some dung
        On us :
Filthard
Cackard
Stinkard,
        St Anthony's fire seize
        on thy toane [boane ?]
If thy
Dirty
Dounby
        Thou do not wipe, ere
        thou be gone.

Will you have any more of it? Yes, yes, answered
Grangousier.   Then, said Gargantua,

A ROUNDELAY.

In shitting yesterday I did know
The cess I to my arse did owe :

The smell was such came from that slunk,
That I was with it all bestunk :
O had but then some brave Signor
Brought her to me I waited for,
　　In shitting !
I would have cleft her water-gap,
And join'd it close to my flip-flap,
Whilst she had with her fingers guarded
My foul nockandrow, all bemerded
　　In shitting.

Now say that I can do nothing ! By the Merdi,[4]
they are not of my making, but I heard them of this
good old grandam, that you see here, and ever since
have retained them in the budget of my memory.

Let us return to our purpose, said Grangousier.
What, said Gargantua, to skite ? No, said Grangousier,
but to wipe our tail. But, said Gargantua, will not
you be content to pay a puncheon of Breton wine,[5]
if I do not blank and gravel you in this matter, and
put you to a non-plus ? Yes truly, said Grangousier.

There is no need of wiping one's tail, said Gargantua, but when it is foul ; foul it cannot be, unless
one have been a skiting ; skite then we must, before
we wipe our tails. O my pretty little waggish boy,

[4] *Merdi.*—Instead of *mort Dieu*, Cotgrave says. The old
Dutch scholiast says it is equivalent to marmes, which Cotgrave
says is a rustical Languedoc oath for mon arme, or mon ame,
and to merdigues, which Cotgrave likewise interprets mother or
mercy of God, another rustical oath or interjection. Be all this
as it may, it is certain that par la merdé is a very proper allusion
to the subject of this chapter.

[5] *A puncheon of Breton wine.*—*Bussart de Vin Breton.* In
Anjou they call a bussart a half-pipe of wine ; and what they
call Breton wine is the best wine that grows in the whole peninsula formed about Chinon by the Loire and the Vienne. It has
this name belike from the Bretons (people of Bretagne) carrying
it all off, as they usually do, for their own drinking.

said Grangousier, what an excellent wit thou hast?
I will make thee very shortly proceed doctor in the
jovial quirks of gay learning and that, by God, for
thou hast more wit than age.   Now, I prythee, go
on in this torcheculatife, or wipe-bummatory discourse, and by my beard, I swear, for one puncheon,
thou shalt have threescore pipes, I mean of the good
Breton wine, not that which grows in Britain, but
in the good country of Verron.[6]   Afterwards I wiped
my bum, said Gargantua, with a kerchief, with a
pillow, with a pantoufle, with a pouch, with a
pannier, but that was a wicked and unpleasant
torchecul; then with a hat.   Of hats, note, that
some are shorn, and others shaggy, some velveted,
others covered with taffities, and others with satin.
The best of all these is the shaggy hat, for it makes
a very neat abstertion of the fecal matter.

Afterwards I wiped my tail with a hen, with a
cock, with a pullet, with a calf's skin, with a hare,
with a pigeon, with a cormorant, with an attorney's
bag, with a montero, with a coif, with a falconer's
lure.   But, to conclude, I say and maintain, that of
all torcheculs, arsewisps, bumfodders, tail napkins,
bunghole cleansers, and wipe-breeches, there is none

---

[6] *Not that which grows in Britain, but in the good country of*
Verron.—The Pais de Verron is all that peninsula from the confluence of the Loire and the Vienne, as far as the territory of
Chinon, inclusive; and is it indeed there that the good Breton
wine grows, and not in Bretagne; where, if what is related of
King Francis I. be no fable, it may be said, that the best grapes
are not worth a rush.   No, not in the neighbourhood of Rennes
itself, which is not the worst situated of any city of Bretagne.
The forementioned Francis I. related it as a matter of fact, that
a dog belonging to M. Ruzé, a councillor of Rennes, having
eaten but one bunch of grapes, near Rennes, fell that moment
to barking at the vinestock, by way of protesting that he would
revenge himself for the belly-ache, which the sourness of the
grapes had given him.   See last chapter of tales of Eutrapel.

in the world comparable to the neck of a goose, that
is well downed, if you hold her neck betwixt your
legs. And believe me therein upon mine honour,
for you will thereby feel in your knuckle a most
wonderful pleasure, both in regard of the softness
of the said down, and of the temperate heat of the
goose, which is easily communicated to the bum-gut,
and the rest of the inwards, in so far as to come even
to the regions of the heart and brains. And think not,
that the felicity of the heroes and demigods in the
Elysian fields consisteth either in their Asphodele,
Ambrosia, or Nectar, as our old women here used to
say; but in this, according to my judgment, that
they wipe their tails with the neck of a goose, holding her head betwixt their legs, and such is the
opinion of Master John of Scotland,[7] alias Scotus.

CHAPTER XIV

HOW GARGANTUA WAS TAUGHT LATIN BY A SOPHISTER

THE good man Grangousier having heard this discourse, was ravished with admiration, considering the
high reach and marvellous understanding of his son
Gargantua, and said to his governesses, Philip King
of Macedon knew the wit of his son Alexander, by
his skilful managing of a horse; for his horse Buce-

---

[7] *Master John of Scotland.*—Many have taken this subtile
doctor, John, to be a Scotchman, and that Duns was the name
of his family. Leland, from good authorities, and after him
Pitseus, say it is a vulgar error. John, according to them, was
born at Dunstan, vulgarly Dyns, a village about three English
miles from Alnwick, in Northumberland. His family name
was Scot, but his country was England.

phalus was so fierce and unruly, that none durst
adventure to ride him, after that he had given to his
riders such devilish falls, breaking the neck of this
man, the other man's leg, braining one, and putting
another out of his jaw-bone. This by Alexander
being considered, one day in the hippodrome (which
was a place appointed for the breaking and managing
of great-horses), he perceived that the fury of the
horse proceeded merely from the fear he had of his
own shadow, whereupon getting on his back, he run
him against the sun, so that the shadow fell behind,
and by that means tamed the horse, and brought him
to his hand. Whereby his father, knowing the
divine judgment that was in him, caused him most
carefully to be instructed by Aristotle, who at that
time was highly renowned above all the philosophers
of Greece. After the same manner I tell you, that
by this only discourse, which now I have here had
before you with my son Gargantua, I know that his
understanding doth participate of some divinity, and
that if he be well taught, and have that education
which is fitting, he will attain to a supreme degree
of wisdom. Therefore will I commit him to some
learned man to have him indoctrinated according to
his capacity, and will spare no cost. Presently they
appointed him a great sophister-doctor, called Master
Tubal Holophernes,[1] who taught him his A. B. C. so
well, that he could say it by heart backwards; and
about this he was five years and three months. Then
read he to him Donat,[2] le Facet,[3] Theodolet, and

[1] *Tubal Holophernes.*—Supposed by M. le Duchat to be a sham
name of Rabelais' own inventing.

[2] *Donat.*—*Ælii Donati de octo partibus Orationis Libellus.*

[3] *Le Facet, etc.*—These three treatises are part of the Auctores
octo morales, in Latin verse, printed with their Gloss. (also in
Latin) at Lyons (anno 1490), by John Fabri. The author of

Alanus in Parabolis. About this he was thirteen years, six months, and two weeks. But you must remark, that in the meantime he did learn to write in Gothic characters, and that he wrote all his books,—for the art of printing was not then in use,—and did ordinarily carry a great pen and ink-horn, weighing about seven thousand quintals (that is 700,000 pounds weight), the pencase whereof was as big and as long as the great pillar of Enay,[4] and the horn was hanging to it in great iron chains, it being of the wideness of a tun of merchant ware. After that he read unto him the book de Modis significandi,[5] with the commentaries of Hurtbise,[6] of Fasquin, of Tropdieux, of Gaulhaut, of John Calf, of Billonio, of Berlinguandus, and a rabble of others; and herein he spent more than eighteen years and eleven months, and was so well versed in it, that, to

Facetus, or of the book called Mr Merryman (if you will), was one Reinerus Allemannus, quoted by the vocabulist Hugutio, who died about the year 1212. See in Duchat a further account of these school-books, of which Alanus in Parabolis is the best. He died in 1189.

[4] *The great pillar of Enay.*—There are four such pillars. At Lyons, there is an abbey called Enay; or, as it should be written, Ainay, built on the ruins of the ancient Athenæum, or Temple of Augustus, at the point and mouth of the Rhone and Saone, famous for several antiquities still to be seen there; but there is nothing more remarkable than these pillars, which, because of their being spotted red and white, are reckoned by the people of Lyons to be an artificial made stone.

[5] *De modis significandi.*—One John de Garlandia, alias Garlandria, an Englishman, of the 11th century, wrote this book, which Erasmus speaks but contemptuously of in his Discourse de Colloquiorum Utilitate, printed after his Colloquies. See also Babelin's Opuscula.

[6] *Hurtbise, etc.*—Some of these names were forged by Rabelais, such as Hurtbise, quasi Heurter la bise, beating the air, as if he was such an impertinent writer, that the reading him would be throwing away one's time without any advantage, etc.

try masteries in school disputes with his condisciples,
he would recite it by heart backwards; and did sometimes prove on his finger ends to his mother, quod de
modis significandi non erat scientia. Then did he
read to him the Compost, for knowing the age of the
moon, the seasons of the year, and tides of the sea,
on which he spent sixteen years and two months, and
that justly at the time that his said preceptor died of
the French pox, which was in the year one thousand
four hundred and twenty.[7] Afterwards he got an old
coughing fellow to teach him, named Master Jobelin
Bridé, or muzzled dolt, who read unto him Hugutio,
Hebrard's *Grecisme*,[8] the Doctrinal, the Parts, the
Quid est, the Supplementum, Marmotret, De
Moribus in mensa servandis; Seneca de quatuor
Virtutibus cardinalibus; Passavantus cum commento,[9]

[7] *In the year one thousand etc.*—Thus given by Rabelais :—
        Et feut l'an mil quatre cens vingt   •
        De la verole qui luy vint.
  Two lines of Marot's, in his epitaph on the Cordelier Jean
Lévêque, of Orleans.
  [8] *Hugutio, Hebrard, etc.*—Ugutio, Bishop of Ferrara, author of
a grammar; Ebrard's (of Béthune) *Grecisme*, a work written in
1112, and still in use at the time of Erasmus; the *Doctrinal*, a
Latin grammar, written about 1242, by Alexander of Villedieu;
the *Parts*, instruction divided according to the eight parts of
speech; the *Quid est*, instruction in question and answer; the
Supplementum, Philippe de Bargame's *Supplementum Chronicorum*;
Marmotret, Marchesim's *Mammetractus, sive expositio in singulis
libris Bibliæ*; De Moribus in mensa servandis, a treatise of Jean
Sulpice, of Veroli, a writer of the 15th century; Seneca, a
pseudonym of Martin, Bishop of Brague, in 583.
  [9] *Passavantus cum commento.*—James Passavant, a celebrated
Jacobin of Florence, lived about the close of the 14th century.
He wrote the Specchio di Penitenza, so highly in esteem among
the Tuscans for the purity of its style. Rabelais, by jeu de mots,
in saying Passavantus instead of Passavantius, alludes to *pas savant*
(ignorant), and has ludicrously added *cum commento*, a way of
speaking usually in those days employed, when they had a mind
to say that a thing was well-conditioned, and nothing wanting.

and Dormi secure,[10] for the holidays, and some other
of such like meally stuff, by reading whereof he
became as wise as any we ever since baked in an
oven.[11]

CHAPTER XV

HOW GARGANTUA WAS PUT UNDER OTHER SCHOOL-MASTERS

AT the last his father perceived, that indeed he
studied hard, and that, although he spent all his time
in it, he did nevertheless profit nothing, but which
is worse, grew thereby foolish, simple, doted, and
blockish, whereof making .a heavy regret to Don
Philip of Marays, Viceroy or Depute King of Papeligosse,[1] he found that it were. better for him to learn

[10] *Dormi Securè, etc.*—The Sermons intituled Dormi Securè;
or, Sermones de Sanctis per Annum satis notabiles et utiles
omnibus Sacerdotibus, Pastoribus et Capellanis, qui Dormi
Securè; or, Dormi sine curâ sunt nuncupati, eò quod absque
magno studio faciliter possint incorporari et populo prædicari,
were printed in 1486, at Nuremberg, by Ant. Koberger ; at Paris,
in 1503, by John Petit; afterwards at Lyons, by John Vincle;
and lastly at Cologne, in 1612, and in 1615, by John Crithius,
with notes by Rodolph Clutius, a Jacobin. Luke Wading, de
Scriptoribus Ordinis Minoraticæ, informs us that Matthew Huss,
a Cordelier, and a German, wrote the Dormi Securè. [These
sermons were written for the use of inferior preachers, who were
thus enabled to sleep soundly, without care for the morrow's
homily, which was provided to their hand.]
[11] *He became as wise as any, etc.*—It means Gargantua, after
threescore and odd years' study, was no wiser, nor his bread
better baked (to use Rabelais's metaphor) than ours, who set in
but yesterday.
[1] *Papeligosse.*—An imaginary country, called Papeligosse, from
a supposition that the inhabitants of it dwell there in perfect
liberty, even to the ridiculing the Pope (se gauser du Pape) with
impunity.

nothing at all, than to be taught such like books,
under such schoolmasters; because their knowledge
was nothing but brutishness, and their wisdom but
blunt foppish toys, serving only to bastardise good
and noble spirits, and to corrupt all the flower of
youth. That it is so, take, said he, any young boy of
this time, who hath only studied two years; if he
have not a better judgment, a better discourse, and
that expressed in better terms than your son, with a
completer carriage and civility to all manner of
persons, account me for ever hereafter a very
clounch, and bacon-slicer of Brene.[2] This pleased
Grangousier very well, and he commanded that it
should be done. At night at supper the said Des
Marays brought in a young page of his of Ville-
gouges,[3] called Eudemon, so neat, so trim, so handsome in his apparel, so spruce, with his hair in so
good order, and so sweet and comely in his behaviour
that he had the resemblance of a little angel more
than of a human creature. Then he said to Grangousier, Do you see this young boy? He is not as
yet full twelve years old. Let us try, if it please
you, what difference there is betwixt the knowledge
of the doting Mateologians[4] of old time, and the
young lads that are now. The trial pleased Gran-

---

[2] *Bacon-slicer of Brene.—Taille-bacon de la Brene.* Bacon-slicer
is as much as to say, a worthless fellow, though strictly a brag-
gadochio, a vapourer, a beater of a fast-tied cow, a breaker-down
of open doors, such as trinc' amellos, a kernel-splitter, among
the people of Toulouse. [See Diction. de la Langue Toulousaine,
aux mots Amello et Trinca.] Bacon is as common a word, and
means the same thing, in the Lyonnois, Dauphiny, Poitou, and
Lorrain, as in England.—As for la Brene, mentioned above, it
is a small territory of Touraine, where is Mezieres, otherwise St
Michael, in Brene.

[3] *Ville-gouges.*—A parish of Berri, two leagues from the river
Indre.

[4] *Mateologians.*—A Greek word for vain discoursings.

gousier, and he commanded the page to begin. Then Eudemon, asking leave of the Viceroy his master so to do, with his cap in his hand, a clear and open countenance, beautiful and ruddy lips, his eyes steady, and his looks fixed upon Gargantua with a youthful modesty, standing up straight on his feet, began very gracefully to commend him; first, for his virtue and good manners; secondly, for his knowledge; thirdly, for his nobility; fourthly, for his bodily accomplishments: and in the fifth place, most sweetly exhorted him to reverence his father with all due observancy, who was so careful to have him well brought up. In the end he prayed him, that he would vouchsafe to admit of him amongst the least of his servants; for other favour at that time desired he none of heaven, but that he might do him some grateful and acceptable service. All this was by him delivered with such proper gestures, such distinct pronounciation, so pleasant a delivery, in such exquisite fine terms, and so good Latin, that he seemed rather a Gracchus, a Cicero, an Æmilius of the time past, than a youth of this age. But all the countenance that Gargantua kept was, that he fell to crying like a cow, and cast down his face, hiding it with his cap, nor could they possibly draw one word from him no more than a fart from a dead ass. Whereat his father was so grievously vexed, that he would have killed Master Jobelin, but the said Des Marays withheld him from it by fair persuasions, so that at length he pacified his wrath. Then Grangousier commanded he should be paid his wages, that they should whittle him up soundly like a sophister,[5]

5 *Whittle him up soundly like a sophister.*—It is in the original, *Qu'on le feist bien choppiner theologalement, i.e.,* Make him ply the pot theologically. The sottishness of the old regents of the college (schoolmasters) and of the Sorbonnists of past ages, had

with good drink, and then give him leave to go to all
the devils in hell. At least, said he, to-day shall it
not cost his host much, if by chance he should die
as drunk as an Englishman.[6] Master Jobelin being
gone out of the house, Grangousier consulted with
the viceroy what schoolmaster they should choose for
him, and it was betwixt them resolved that Ponocrates, the tutor of Eudemon, should have the charge,
and that they should go all together to Paris, to know
what was the study of the young men of France at
that time.

given occasion to this proverbial expression.   H. Stephens explains this tippling theologically, by drinking abundantly, and
that, too, of the very best wine.

[6] *Drunk as an Englishman.*—Rabelais says, *Saoul comme ung
Angloys.* The word *saoul* means as well glutted, cloyed, over-
charged with eating as well as drinking.   Saouler, to satiate,
give a gorge-full, etc.   The English soldiers, and ordinary people
are the fonder of wine, because there is none grows in their
country, says M. le Duchat.   That nation is moreover very
carnivorous (adds he), great flesh-eaters, and they had for a long
space ravaged France.   At that time, when the French burghers
could not, without extreme heart-breaking, behold the English
gorging themselves with their substance, it was customary (as
in the poet Cretins' epistle to King Francis I.) to call a rough,
harsh creditor, an Englishman; sometimes (as in Marot) an un-
relenting, hard-hearted bum-baily, living at discretion upon a
poor debtor, they would call un Anglois, an Englishman.   It is
to those times we are to refer this proverbial expression, which
Erasmus had before taken notice of in his Adages, and which is
also to be found in Rondeletius' Physical Works, c. 18, de
Sudoris excretione.

CHAPTER XVI

HOW GARGANTUA WAS SENT TO PARIS, AND OF THE
HUGE GREAT MARE THAT HE RODE ON; HOW SHE
DESTROYED THE OX-FLIES OF THE BEAUCE

IN the same season, Fayoles,[1] the fourth King of
Numidia, sent out of the country of Africa to Grangousier, the most hideous great mare that ever was
seen, and of the strangest form, for you know well
enough how it is said, that Africa always is productive
of some new thing. She was as big as six elephants,
and had her feet cloven into fingers, like Julius
Cæsar's horse, with slouch-hanging ears, like the
goats in Languedoc, and a little horn on her buttock.
She was of a burnt sorel hue, with a little mixture of
daple grey spots, but above all she had a horrible
tail; for it was little more or less, than every whit as
great as the steeple-pillar of St Mark,[2] besides
Langes : and squared as that is, with tuffs, and
ennicroches or hair-plaits wrought within one
another, no otherwise than as the beards are upon
the ears of corn.
If you wonder at this, wonder rather at the tails
of the Scythian rams, which weighed above thirty
pounds each, and of the Surian sheep, who need, if
Tenaud[3] say true, a little cart at their heels to

[1] *Fayoles.*—M. le Duchat declares he does not know who
this Fayoles is, unless he be of the house of Melet, of which there
was, in 1587, one Bertrand de Melet de Fayoles Sieur de Neuvy.

[2] *St Mark.*—Wrong. Read St Mars ; in Latin, Martius, and
sometimes Medardus. See Duchat further on this head.

[3] *Tenaud.*—It is said that the Abbot Guyet, by Tenaud, under-
stood the geographer, Stephanus, in which he was mistaken,
Stephanus, or Stephens, having related no such thing. It is
Herodotus, l. 3, 4, 113, speaking of the sheep of Arabia ; and

bear up their tail, it is so long and heavy. You female lechers in the plain countries have no such tails. And she was brought by sea in three carricks and a brigantine into the harbour of Olone in Thalmondois. When Grangousier saw her, 'Here is,' said he, 'what is fit to carry my son to Paris. So now, in the name of God, all will be well. He will in times coming be a great scholar. If it were not, my masters, for the beasts, we should live like clerks.[4] The next morning, after they drunk, you must understand, they took their journey; Gargantua, his pedagogue Ponocrates, and his train, and with them Eudemon the young page. And because the weather was fair and temperate, his father caused to be made for him a pair of dun boots; Babin calls them buskins. Thus did they merrily pass their time in travelling on their high way, always making good cheer, and were very pleasant till they came a little above Orleans, in which place there was a forest of five-and-thirty leagues long, and seventeen in breadth, or thereabouts. This forest was most

after him Ælian, c. 4, l. 10, of Animals. Aristotle 8, Animal. 28, speaking of the tails of the Scythian sheep, says they are a cubit wide; but that is all he says of them. Thus Rabelais' Tenaud is in all likelihood some modern, named Stephen, or Stephens. Suria, as Rabelais speaks, according to the custom of the age he lived in, perhaps from the Italian, Soria, is the ancient Syria.

[4] *If it were not for the beasts, we should live like clerks.*— Froissart, in ch. 173 of the 2d vol. of Verard's edition, frankly says, The temporal lords would not know how to live or behave, and would be no better than mere beasts, or idiots, were it not for the clergy. But here Rabelais, to let us see what his opinion was as to the capacity of the clergy of his time, affects to mistake Froissart's words, as it were, to make Grangousier say, since he resolved his son should be a student, that, after all, the world might do very well without such a clergy, whose example was the occasion that nobody cared a pin for instruction, or concerned themselves about what might tend thereto.

horribly fertile and copious in dorflies, hornets, and wasps, so that it was a very purgatory for the poor mares, asses, and horses. But Gargantua's mare did avenge herself handsomely of all the outrages therein committed upon beasts of her kind, and that by a trick whereof they had no suspicion. For as soon as ever they were entered into the said forest, and that the wasps had given the assault, she drew out and unsheathed her tail, and therewith skirmishing, did so sweep them, that she overthrew all the wood alongst and athwart, here and there, this way and that way, longwise and sidewise, over and under, and felled everywhere the wood with as much ease as the mower doth the grass, in such sort that never since hath there been there, neither wood, nor dorflies: 5 for all the country was thereby reduced to a plain champagne field. Which Gargantua took great pleasure to behold, and said to his company no more but this, ' Je trouve beau ce,' I find this pretty; whereupon that country hath been ever since that time called Beauce. But all the breakfast the mare got that day, was but a little yawning and gaping, in memory whereof the gentlemen of Beauce do as yet to this day break their fast with gaping,6 which

5 *Neither wood nor dorflies.*—The forest of Orleans is, however, still in being; but it had been newly felled at the time Rabelais speaks of, as they still continue from time to time to make great falls of timber and underwood, when it is too thick.

6 *Break their fast with gaping.*—Coquillart, in the Monologue of Perriwigs, speaking of certain people who dress out, and go very trim and jantée, though they want necessaries,

> Et desjeuner tous les matins
> Comme les escuïers de Beaulce.

> And every morning break their fast
> Like gentlemen of Beauce.

That is to say, they gape and spit, as it is usual in a morning when one has not broke one's fast.

they find to be very good, and do spit the better for
it. At last they came to Paris, where Gargantua
refreshed himself two or three days, making very
merry with his folks, and inquiring what men of
learning there were then in the city, and what wine
they drank there.

———

CHAPTER XVII

HOW GARGANTUA PAID HIS WELCOME TO THE PARISIANS, AND HOW HE TOOK AWAY THE GREAT BELLS OF OUR LADY'S CHURCH

SOME few days after that they had refreshed themselves, he went to see the city, and was beheld of
everybody there with great admiration; for the
people of Paris are so sottish, so badot, so foolish
and fond by nature, that a juggler, a carrier of
indulgences, a sumpter-horse, or mule with cymbals, or tinkling bells, a blind fiddler in the middle
of a cross lane, shall draw a greater confluence of
people together, than an Evangelical preacher.
And they pressed so hard upon him, that he was
constrained to rest himself upon the towers of
Our Lady's Church. At which place, seeing so
many about him, he said with a loud voice, I
believe that these buzzards will have me to pay
them here my welcome hither, and my Proficiat.
It is but good reason. I will now give them their
wine, but it shall be only in sport. Then smiling,
he untied his fair braguette, and drawing out his
mentul into the open air, he so bitterly all-to-be-

pissed them,[1] that he drowned two hundred and
sixty thousand four hundred and eighteen, besides
the women and little children. Some, nevertheless,
of the company escaped this piss-flood by mere speed
of foot, who, when they were at the higher end of
the university, sweating, coughing, spitting, and out
of breath, they began to swear and curse, some in
good hot earnest, and others in jest. Carimari,[2]
carimara : golynoly, golynolo. But my sweet Sanc-
tesse, we are washed in sport, a sport truly to
laugh at ;—in French, *Par ris*, for which that city
hath been ever since called Paris, whose name
formerly was Leucotia, as Strabo testifieth, lib.
quarto, from the Greek word λευχοτης, whiteness,
because of the white thighs of the ladies of that
place. And forasmuch as, at this imposition of a
new name, all the people that were there swore
every one by the Sancts of his parish, the Parisians,
which are patched up of all nations, and all pieces
of countries, are by nature both good jurors, and
good jurists, and somewhat overweening ; whereupon Joanninus de Barrauco, libro de copiositate

---

[1] *He so bitterly all-to-be-pissed them.*—King Francis I., if,
however, it be true that Rabelais did design him by the name
of Gargantua, had so many amiable qualities by nature, that
the French were transported with joy at having him for their
king; the Parisians, in particular, admired him. But soon
after his accession to the crown, that prince, who was unpro-
vided of the necessary funds for the war he was going to make
in Italy, having created several new imposts, and established the
venality of abundance of offices, all this together put a great
damp on the hopes the Parisians had conceived of the easiness
and mildness of his reign ; and in all probability it is this that
Rabelais means, in saying, he so bitterly all-to-be-pissed them,
soon after his arrival in their city ; that is to say he put such
hardships and affronts upon them, that they had much ado to
digest them.

[2] *Carimari.*—Confused, senseless sounds.

reverentiarum, thinks that they are called Parisians,
from the Greek word παρρησία, which signifies boldness and liberty of speech.[3]

This done, he considered the great bells, which
were in the said towers, and made them sound very
harmoniously. Which whilst he was doing, it came
into his mind, that they would serve very well for
tingling Tantans, and ringing Campanels, to hang
about his mare's neck, when she should be sent
back to his father, as he intended to do, loaded with
Brie cheese, and fresh herring. And indeed he
forthwith carried them to his lodging. In the
meanwhile there came a master beggar of the friars
of St Anthony, to demand in his canting way the
usual benevolence of some hoggish stuff, who, that
he might be heard afar off, and to make the bacon
he was in quest of shake in the very chimnies, made
account to filch them away privily. Nevertheless,
he left them behind very honestly, not for that they
were too hot, but that they were somewhat too heavy
for his carriage. This was not he of Bourg, for he
was too good a friend of mine.

All the city was risen up in sedition, they being,
as you know, upon any slight occasion, so ready to

---

[3] *Boldness and liberty of speech.*—This opinion, which is refuted
by Adrian de Valois, is one of those offered by Andrew du
Chesne, in ch. i. of his Antiquities of Paris, where it appears
that he whom Rabelais means by Joanninus de Barrauco, or
Barranco, as we read in Dolet's edition, must needs be William
le Breton, who, in Lib. i. of his Philippid, thus speaks of the
Parisians :—

> Finibus egressi patriis, per Gallica rura
> Sedem quærebant ponendis mœnibus aptam,
> Et se Parrhisios dixerunt nomine Græco,
> Quod sonat expositum nostris Audacia verbis,
> Erroris causâ vitandi, nomine solo
> A quibus extiterant Francis distare volentes.

uproars and insurrections, that foreign nations
wonder at the patience of the kings of France, who
do not by good justice restrain them from such
tumultuous courses, seeing the manifold inconveni-
ences which thence arise from day to day. Would
to God, I knew the shop wherein are forged these
divisions and factious combinations, that I might
bring them to light in the confraternities of my
parish ! Believe for a truth, that the place wherein
the people gathered together, were thus sulphured,
hopurymated, moiled, and be-pissed, was called
Nesle, where then was, but now is no more, the
Oracle of Leucetia.[4]   There was the case proposed,
and the inconvenience showed of the transporting
of the bells.   After they had well ergoted pro and
con, they concluded in baralipton, that they should
send the oldest and most sufficient of the faculty
unto Gargantua, to signify unto him the great and
horrible prejudice they sustained by the want of
those bells.   And notwithstanding the good reasons
given in by some of the university, why this charge
was fitter for an orator than a sophister, there was
chosen for this purpose our Master Janotus de
Bragmardo.[5]

[4] *Oracle of Leucetia.*—The goddess Isis is reckoned to have been
the tutelar deity of the Parisians, when they were in the state of
Paganism.   The idol which they had consecrated to her was still
subsisting, and in good condition, in the abbey of St Germain des
Prez, at the beginning of the 16th century; but in 1514 it was
taken away, by order of William Briconnet, Bishop of Meaux,
and Abbot of Saint Germain, who put up in the room of it a red
cross.   As for this idol, her statue, which was tall and erect,
rough, and discoloured with age, was placed against the wall, on
the north side, where the crucifix of the church stands, and it was
naked, except some drapery in a certain place or two.
[5] *Janotus de Bragmardo.*—Vallambert d'Avalon, physician and
poet, is the author of some Latin epigrams, among which are some
against one Janotus, a very tedious fatiguing orator.   The surname

CHAPTER XVIII

HOW JANOTUS DE BRAGMARDO WAS SENT TO GARGANTUA,
TO RECOVER THE GREAT BELLS

MASTER JANOTUS, with his hair cut round like a
dish à la Cæsarine, in his most antic accoutrement
liripipionated with a graduate's hood, and, having
sufficiently antidoted his stomach with oven marma-
lades, that is, bread and holy water of the cellar,
transported himself to the lodging of Gargantua,
driving before him three red-muzzled beadles, and
dragging after him five or six artless masters,[1] all
thoroughly bedraggled with the mire of the streets.
At their entry Ponocrates met them, who was
afraid, seeing them so disguised, and thought they
had been some maskers out of their wits, which
moved him to inquire of one of the said artless
masters of the company, what this mummery
meant? It was answered him, that they desired
to have their bells restored to them. As soon as
Ponocrates heard that, he ran in all haste to carry
the news unto Gargantua, that he might be ready
to answer them, and speedily resolve what was to
be done. Gargantua being advertised hereof, called
apart his schoolmaster Ponocrates, Philotimus steward
of his house, Gymnastes his esquire, and Eudemon,
and very summarily conferred with them, both of

of de Bragmardo puts me in mind of John le Cornu, to whom
the poet Villon, in his (little) Will and Testament, bequeaths his
Branc d'Acier (cutlass I take it), a word which Marot, in the
margin of his edition, renders Braquemard, and which Cotgrave
says, as I said before, is a sort of wood knife, hanger,|whineyard,
couteau.   *MOTLEY*

[1] *Artless Masters.*—Maistres Inerts, |as Rabelais ludicrously
calls them.

what he should do, and what answer he should give.
They were all of opinion that they should bring
them unto the goblet-office, which is the buttery,
and there make them drink like oysters, and line
their jackets soundly.   And that this cougher might
not be puft up with vain-glory, by thinking the
bells were restored at his request, they sent, whilst
he was chopining and plying the pot, for the major
of the city, the rector of the faculty, and the vicar
of the church, unto whom they resolved to deliver
the bells, before the sophister had propounded his
commission.   After that, in their hearing, he should
pronounce his gallant oration, which was done ; and
they being come, the sophister was brought in full
hall, and began as followeth, in coughing.

CHAPTER XIX

THE   ORATION   OF   MASTER   JANOTUS   DE   BRAGMARDO,
FOR   THE   RECOVERY   OF   THE   BELLS

HEM, hem, gud-day, sirs, gud-day.[1]   Et vobis, my
masters.   It were but reason that you should restore
to us our bells; for we have great need of them.
Hem, hem, aihfuhash.   We have often-times here-

---

[1] *Hem, hem, gud-day, sir, gud-day.*—In the original it runs,
Ehen, hen, hen, Mnadies, Monsieur, Mnadies.   On which M. le
Duchat observes, that what made Janotus cough thus, before he
began his speech, was neither the great age of that doctor, nor the
great quantity of bread he had eaten at home, or at Gargantua's.
It was a piece of premeditated affectation, to imitate the famous
preacher Oliver Maillard, who in his time was wont to cough at
the principal passages of his sermons.   The minister Faucheur,
p. 81, of the treatise of the action of an orator, mistakingly
ascribed by many to M. Gonrart, says, 'As for coughing, there

The oration of Master Janotus.

tofore refused good money for them of those of
London in Cahors,[2] yea and those of Bourdeaux in
Brie, who would have bought them for the sub-
stantific quality of the elementary complexion,
which is intronificated in the terrestreity of their
quidditative nature, to extraneize the blasting mists,
and whirlwinds upon our vines, indeed not ours, but
these round about us. For if we lose the piot and
liquor of the grape, we lose all, both sense and law.
If you restore them unto us at my request, I shall
gain by it six basketfuls of sausages, and a fine pair
of breeches, which will do my legs a great deal of
good, or else they will not keep their promise to
me. Ho by gob, Domine, a pair of breeches is
good, et vir sapiens non abhorrebit eam. Ha, ha, a
pair of breeches is not so easily got; I have experience of it myself. Consider, Domine, I have been

were heretofore preachers of so odd a fancy, as to cough in their
sermons without the least occasion, but only because they thought
it gave a grace and weight to their words; witness Oliver
Maillard, who, in a sermon preached at Bruges, 1500, marked the
places of his sermon where he designed a cough, by putting down
hem, hem, hen, as is still to be seen in the printed copies; which
gave occasion to the pretended Vigneul Marville, an inexact copier
of this place, to say, that had it not been for this example, people
would perhaps never have dreamed of such a thing as a coughing
eloquence.' But to proceed, 'As for the mnadies with which old
Janotus begins his oration, nothing can be better fancied, since
such an impertinent and senseless pronunciation of bona dies
equally shows the faltering of a drunkard, and the vicious and
barbarous way of speaking which prevailed in the schools before
the restitution of polite literature. Besides, could anything be
more sottish, than for this pedant to begin a speech to his prince
with a bona dies? (good day to you). And lastly, did it not
argue great want of sense, to revive the ridiculous custom of the
Menots and Maillards to speak sometimes French and sometimes
Latin in the same discourse?'

  [2] *London in Cahors, etc.—Londres en Cahors, etc.*, a wipe for those
who venture to speak of things beyond their understanding. They
make as many blunders as they speak words.

these eighteen days in matagrabolising[3] this brave
speech. Reddite quæ sunt Cæsaris, Cæsari, et quæ
sunt Dei, Deo. Ibi jacet lepus. By my faith,
Domine, if you will sup with me in cameris,[4] by
cox body, charitatis, nos faciemus bonum cherubin.[5]
Ego occidi unum porcum, et ego habet bonum
vino :[6] but of good wine we cannot make bad

[3] *Matagrabolising.*—A word forged at pleasure, and signifies
the studying or writing of vain things. When Rabelais coined
this word, says M. le Duchat, he had in his eye these three,
μάταιος ineptus, γράφω scribo, and βάλλω jacio, from whence
making ματαιογραφοβαλίζειν ineptas scriptiones mittere, he
afterwards formed his French matagraboliser.

[4] *Cameris, etc.*—The camera charitatis is the chamber where the
mendicants make good cheer with the tid-bits given them out of
charity.

[5] *Bonum cherubin.*—We shall make good cheer, and by banging
the bottle about shall make our faces cherubical.

[6] *Ego habet bonum vino.*—These are indeed Rabelais' words,
and it may be imagined by some, that he carried the railery too
far, or at least had only a view to the theologians, with respect to
that maxim, non debent verba cœlestis oraculi subesse regulis
Donati (St Gregory towards the close of the preface of his
morality). But there is no such thing; and it is most certainly
true, that abundance of doctors in all faculties did maintain, that
pronouns of the first person might, without incongruity, be joined
with the third person of a verb. 'Incredibile prope dictu est,' says
Freigius in Ramus' life, 'sed tamen verum, et editis libris
proditum, in Parisiensi Academia Doctores extitisse, qui mordicus
tuerentur ac defenderent, *Ego amat*, tam commodam orationem
esse, quàm, *Ego amo*, ad eamque pertinaciam comprimendam
consilio publico opus fuisse.' One would be at a loss to guess at
the grounds of these doctors' opinion, which was, however, at
length solemnly condemned by the Sorbonne, and by the divinity
faculty of Oxford, had not Agrippa informed us, that they built
this extravagant notion of theirs on the Hebrew text of two
passages of the old Testament, bringing in God speaking of
himself. (One in Isaiah, c. xxxviii. v. 5. Ecce *Ego addet* super
dies tuos, etc. Behold, I will add unto thy days, etc. For he
does not say, *addam*, but *addet*. The other in Malachi, c. i. v. 6.
If I be a master, where is my fear ? He does not say *Dominus ego*,
but *Domini ego*.) See more of this in Cornelius Agrippa, de
Vanitate Scientiarum, c. 3.

Latin.[7]   Well, de parte Dei date nobis bellas
nostras. Hold, I give you in the name of the
faculty a Sermones de Utino,[8] that utinam you will
give us our bells.   Vultis etiam pardonos ?   Per
diem [9] vos habebitis, et nihil payabitis.

[7] *But of good wine we cannot make bad Latin.*—*De bon vin, on ne
peult faire maulvais Latin.* It is certain, hating the falseness of
the concord, whether we say bonum vino, or bonus vina, as in
Dolet's edition, we understand that good wine is what is meant,
as easily as if we say bonum vinum.   Now, according to the
Canonists, it sufficeth if we be understood.   Ask them whether
it is a baptism to say, omine atris et ilii, etc., instead of nomine
patris et filii, etc.   They will tell you no, and that such a
diminution hinders it from being a baptism; for, say they, the
sense and meaning is removed and changed, for atris does not
signify father, nor ilii, son; ergò, such baptism is null.   But if
this diminution be at the end of the word, as if the *s* be taken
from patris, by saying patri, or the like, such diminution does not
hinder the baptism; for one and the same sense remains in the
words, but then the intention of saying them aright must go along
with them.   Of this we have an example in a decree de consecr.
dist. 4 cap. retulerunt: A priest ignorant in the Latin tongue,
baptizeth a child thus, In Nomina Patria et Filia Spitum Sancta,
amen.   In this decree the Pope says, the child was baptised;
considering the priest was a very devout man, and had an intention to speak aright, and only failed through ignorance and
inscience.

[8] *A Sermones de Utino, etc.*—Allusion of the word utinam to the
name Utinum or Udino, the chief city of Friuli, and the country
of a Dominican monk, who published a huge volume of sermons
under the title of 'Sermones aurei de Sanctis Fr. Leonardi de
Utino,' printed first in 1473, at Venice, reprinted in 1496, again
1503, at Lyons; then again here in 1517.   In order to understand this passage of Janotus' speech, we need but suppose, that
as these sermons were very much in vogue—the faculty, who
thought to please the prince's taste, being persuaded that Gargantua
might be prevailed on to restore the bells, if at the same time that
they besought him so to do, they presented him with a copy of
Utino's sermons—the pedant Janotus thought he could not more
properly tender his present, than by accompanying, with an
affectionate Utinam, the most humble petition which he made to
Gargantua to restore the bells of the church of Notre Dame.

[9] *Per diem.*—He swears per diem (by day) not daring to swear

O Sir, Domine, bellagivaminor[10] nobis; verily, est bonum urbis. They are useful to everybody. If they fit your mare well, so do they do our faculty; quæ comparata est jumentis insipientibus, et similis facta est eis, Psalmo nescio quo.[11] Yet did I quote it in my note-book, et est unum bonum Achilles,[12] a good defending argument. Hem, hem, hem, haikhash! For I prove unto you, that you should give me them. Ego sic argumentor. Omnis bella bellabilis in bellerio bellando, bellans bellativo, bellare facit, bellabiliter bellantes. Parisius habet bellas. Ergo gluc,[13] Ha, ha, ha. This is spoken to some purpose. It is in tertio primæ, in Darii, or elsewhere. By my soul, I have seen the time that I could play the devil in arguing, but now I am much failed, and henceforward want nothing but a cup of good wine, a good bed, my back to the fire,

per Deum; and Beza is still more facetious, when in swearing per diem in his Passavantius, he adds, sicut dicit David, as if that would save his oath, by favour of the 6th verse of the 121st Psalm. The sun shall not smite thee *by day, etc.*
[10] *Bellagivaminor.*—In the original, Clochidonnaminor nobis. [Let our bells (Cloches, in French) be given us.]
[11] *Psalmo nescio quo.*—A rare textuary, this Master Janotus! These words are in Psalm 49, ' Et homo cum in honore esset, non intellexit; comparatus est jumentis insipientibus et similis factus est illis.' His applying this passage to the university of Paris, is, because having abused their too great authority to the exciting several mutinies in preceding reigns, they were now somewhat curbed in comparison of what they were in those times.
[12] *Est unum bonum Achilles.*—He means that his argument, taken from the Psalm, was invincible, like a second Achilles.
[13] *Ergo gluc.*—M. le Duchat concludes that gluck is likewise a word used by the Germans, when they wish anyone well, as, that God would help them, etc. (from whence I suppose we have our word luck). In this sense it may be, that, after them, we have applied it to a timorous logician, and seeing him in convulsions at his ergo, we say to him gluck ! *i.e.*, cheer up, have a good heart, to encourage him to push home his argument.

my belly to the table, and a good deep dish. Hei,.
Domine, I beseech you, in nomine Patris, Filii, et
Spiritûs Sancti, Amen, to restore unto us our bells :
and God keep you from evil, and our Lady from·
health,[14] qui vivit et regnat per omnia secula
seculorum, Amen. Hem, hashchchhawksash, qzrch--
remhemhash.

Verum enim vero, quandoquidem, dubio procul..
Edepol, quoniam, ita certe, meus deus fidius; a
town without bells is like a blind man without a
staff, an ass without a crupper, and a cow without
cymbals. Therefore be assured, until you have
restored them unto us, we will never leave crying.
after you, like a blind man that hath lost his staff,.
braying like an ass without a crupper, and making
a noise like a cow without cymbals. A certain.
Latinisator, dwelling near the hospital, said once,.
producing the authority of one Taponus—I lie, it
was one Pontanus the secular poet [15]—who wished
those bells [16] had been made of feathers, and the

[14] *God keep you from evil and our Lady from health.*—This old·
dotard would have said, God, and our Lady of health, keep you
from evil ! Rabelais ridicules the vicious and careless ways of
speaking used by the old French, and too many of the moderns
too, especially among the vulgar.

[15] *Pontanus the secular poet.*—This is the famous John Jovian
Pontanus. Janotus calls him the secular poet by way of sneer;
for, under the notion of this nick-name, the Sorbonists generally.
comprehend all the good Greek and Latin authors both ancient
and modern, but particularly Reuchlin's friends, and others who·
then had renounced the empty titles of the schools, and the
barbarisms thereof, in order to bend their minds to the study of·
the languages, philosophy, and the belles lettres. Under the
pretence that Tully, Virgil, and such authors, had not taken
their doctor's degree at Paris or Cologne, they were, in these·
barbarian theologues' account, so many paltry secular poets.

[16] *Bells, etc.*—Pontanus did break a jest or two on bells in his:
dialogue, intituled Charon, which was indeed prohibited to be
read, not on that account, but because he made too free with:

clapper of a foxtail,[17] to the end that they might
have begot a chronicle [18] in the bowels of his brain,
when he was about the composing of his carmini-
formal lines. But nac [19] petetin petetac, tic, torche
lorgne, or rot kipipur kipipot put pantse malf, he
was declared an heretic. We make them as of
wax.[20] And no more saith the deponent. Valete
et plaudite.[21] Calepinus recensui.[22]

churchmen, but the author was never declared a heretic for either
one or the other.

[17] *A Fox-tail.*—This thought, which is repeated in ch. 27 of
l. 5, is to be met with in the book intituled the Ship of Fools, in
the chapter, advising, not to mind everybody's ill-natured or idle
discourse about us. All the calumnies that can be spread abroad
against an honest man, says that old book, ought no more to move
him than if they shook in his ears a bell with a fox-tail in it for
a clapper.

[18] *A Chronicle.*—Wrong ; *la chronique* is not a chronicle (or
history), but a chronical disorder, *i.e.*, Vertigo of the brain, etc.

[19] *Nac, etc.*—Janotus, in his dull way, rings the bells with his
voice and two arms, as if he was actually mocking poor Pontanus
and his bells.

[20] *We make them as of wax.*—We make heretics as we please,
to perfection, as if we cast them in a mould.

[21] *Valete et plaudite.*—Janotus having exhibited a comedy in
his own person, it was but just he should finish it, as Plautus
and Terence do most of theirs.

[22] *Calepinus recensui.*—The pedant concludes his speech like the
ancient grammarians, who used to put their names at the bottom
of their manuscripts, which they had revised and corrected; after
which, they were copied out. Thus Rabelais here gives to understand, that the vocabulist Calepin, who died about 1510, had
revised Janotus' speech, which this ignoramus had composed in
Latin yet worse than we see it in.

CHAPTER XX

HOW THE SOPHISTER CARRIED AWAY HIS CLOTH, AND
HOW HE HAD A SUIT IN LAW AGAINST THE
OTHER MASTERS

THE sophister had no sooner ended, but Ponocrates
and Eudemon burst out into a laughing so heartily,
that they had almost split with it, and given up the
ghost, in rendering their souls to God : even just as
Crassus did, seeing a lubberly ass eat thistles ; and
as Philemon,[1] who, for seeing an ass eat those figs
which were provided for his own dinner, died with
force of laughing. Together with them Master
Janotus fell a-laughing too as fast as he could, in
which mood of laughing they continued so long,
that their eyes did water by the vehement concus-
sion of the substance of the brain, by which these
lachrymal humidities, being prest out, glided through
the optic nerves, and so to the full represented
Democritus Heraclitising, and Heraclitus Demo-
critising.

When they had done laughing, Gargantua consulted with the prime of his retinue, what should
be done. There Ponocrates was of opinion, that
they should make this fair orator drink again; and
seeing he had showed them more pastime, and made
them laugh more than a natural fool[2] could have

[1] *Philemon.*—This is the same person whom (in l. 4, c. 17)
Rabelais calls Philomenes, to show he had also read Valerius
Maximus, in fol., Paris 1517, where he is called so, l. 9, c. 12.
This story is to be found in Lucian, l. 2, in the chapter treating
of the longevity of some persons.
[2] *A natural fool.*—*Songecreux* in French. Our author strikes
at Magister noster Songecrusius, whose character you have in
the catalogue of St Victor's library.

171

done, that they should give him ten baskets full of
sausages, mentioned in his pleasant speech, with a
pair of hose,[3] three hundred great billets of logwood,
five and twenty hogsheads of wine, a good large
down bed, and a deep capacious dish, which he said
were necessary for his old age. All this was done
as they did appoint : only Gargantua, doubting that
they could not quickly find out breeches fit for his
wearing, because he knew not what fashion would
best become the said orator, whether the martingal
fashion [4] of breeches, wherein is a spunghole with
a draw-bridge, for the more easy caguing : or the
fashion of the mariners,[5] for the greater solace and
comfort of his kidneys : or that of the Switzers,
which keeps warm the bedondaine or belly-tabret:
or round breeches with strait cannions, having in the
seat a piece like a cod's tail,[6] for fear of over-heating
his reins. All which considered, he caused to be
given him seven ells of white cloth for the linings.
The wood was carried by the porters, the masters of
arts carried the sausages and the dishes, and Master

[3] *A pair of hose.*—Une paire de chausses, means a pair of
breeches, not hose.
[4] *Martingal fashion.*—*A la martingale.* Beza, in his letter
under the name of Benedictus Passavantius, to the President
Liset, newly made Abbot of St Victor, acquaints us, that the said
President used to wear such breeches. 'Quamvis,' says he to
him, ' non plus faciat ad propositum quam si canendo Missam,
tu faceres totum (tu bene me intelligis) in caligis tuis ad
martingalam.' These martingal breeches, so called, as it is said
elsewhere, from the Martegaux people of Provence, were still in
fashion in 1579, among the court minions, who made them serve
for a quite different use than what they were at first invented for.
See note 114, bk. ii., ch. 7.
[5] *The fashion of the mariners.*—*A la mariniere.* Caligæ follicantes.
These breeches, different from those since called chausses à la
matelotte, were full of plaits and gathers both above and below,
and hardly reached to the knee.
[6] *Like a cod's tail.*—[This allusion is frequent in Rabelais].

Janotus himself would carry the cloth. One of the said masters, called Jousse Bandouille, showed him that it was not seemly nor decent for one of his condition to do so, and that therefore he should deliver it to one of them. Ha, said Janotus, Baudet, Baudet, or Blockhead, Blockhead, thou dost not conclude in modo et figura. For lo, to this end serve the Suppositions, and Parva Logicalia.[7] Pannus, pro quo supponit? Confusè, said Bandouille, et distributivè. I do not ask thee, said Janotus, blockhead, quomodo supponit, but pro quo? It is, blockhead, pro tibiis meis, and therefore I will carry it, Egomet, sicut suppositum portat appositum. So did he carry it away very close and covertly, as Patelin,[8] the

[7] *The Suppositions and Parva Logicalia.*—Agrippa, in his enumeration of the ridiculous and dangerous subtilties of the learning of the sophists or scholastics of his time, speaks thus of the book intituled ' Parva Logicalia,' where this pernicious doctrine was taught and treated to the bottom. ' The late Schools of Sophistry have made an addition of far greater and more monstrous prodigies. . . . vain and intolerable barbarisms which are thicksown in their Logical Systems (*Parva Logicalia*) whereby they endeavour to make all those things to appear truths which are in themselves absolutely false and impossible, and those things which are really true, like Furies breaking out of the Trojan Horse, they seek to ruin and destroy with the flames of their barbarous words.' —*Vanity of Arts and Sciences*, 1676, pp. 43-4. This false dialectic, which was set up in the 12th century, upon the crying down of the solid dialectic, taught by Aristotle, was some time after reduced into an art by Petrus Hispanus, of Lisbon, who lived to be Pope under the name of John XXII. This man was the author of the Parva Logicalia, consisting of eight particular treatises, to which were added two more in the re-impression which was made thereof in 8vo, with a large commentary, at Cologne, by H. Quintel, in 1500; and it was out of this fine work (highly valued by the old pedants) that the sophist Janotus had drawn the science he thought to get so much honour by with ·Gargantua, and those about him.

[8] *Patelin.*—See in Duchat an account at large of this old French farce, and of Reuchlin's supposed translation of it into

173

buffoon, did his cloth. The best was, that when
this cougher, in a full act or assembly held at the
Mathurins, had with great confidence required his
breeches and sausages, and that they were flatly
denied him, because he had them of Gargantua,
according to the informations thereupon made, he
showed them that this was gratis, and out of his
liberality, by which they were not in any sort quit
of their promises. Notwithstanding this, it was
answered him, that he should be content with
reason, without expectation of any other bribe there.
Reason ? said Janotus. We use none of it here.
Unlucky traitors, you are not worth the hanging.
The earth beareth not more arrant villains than you
are. I know it well enough; halt not before the
lame. I have practised wickedness with you. By
God's rattle I will inform the king of the enormous
abuses that are forged here and carried underhand
by you, and let me be a leper, if he do not burn you
alive like bougres, traitors, heretics,[9] and seducers,
enemies to God and virtue.

Latin, under the name of Alexander Connibertus, and intituled
' Veterator, alias Patelinus, etc.
   [9] *Bougres—Heretics*—Anciently, these two words, bougres,
and heretics, were terms convertible; two words for the same
thing, being joined immediately together, and most commonly
the second explaining the first.   Froissard, vol. i., chap. 227.
' Et fut (Don Pedro de Castile) en pleine Consistoire en Avignon,
et en la chambre des excommuniez publicquement declaré et
reputé pour bougre et incredule.'   And in ch. 7, vol. 4, one
Betisarch, treasurer to the Duke of Berri, is burnt alive at
Beziers, for having owned that he was a heretic, and held the
opinions of the Bougres; that is, in the language of that country,
denied the Trinity and Incarnation.   He had been only charged
with extortion, but he pretended to hold heretical opinions, in
hopes that being a cleric, he should be sent to the Pope, but the
Bailli of Beziers caused him to be executed on his own word.
In these two passages *Heretic* and *Bougre* are synonymous, and
mean the same thing; but here in Rabelais the case is somewhat

Upon these words they framed articles against him:
he on the other side warned them to appear. In
sum, the process was retained by the Court, and is
there as yet. Hereupon the magisters made a vow,
never to decrott themselves in rubbing off the dirt
of either their shoes or clothes : Master Janotus with
his adherents vowed never to blow or snuff their
noses, until judgment was given by a definitive
sentence.

By these vows do they continue unto this time
both dirty and snotty;[10] for the court hath not
garbled, sifted, and fully looked into all the pieces.
as yet. The judgment or decree shall be given out
and pronounced at the next Greek Calends,[11] that is,
never. As you know that they do more than nature,
and contrary to their own articles. The articles of
Paris maintain, that to God alone belongs infinity,
and nature produceth nothing that is immortal; for
she putteth an end and period to all things by her
engendered, according to the saying, Omnia orta
cadunt,[12] etc. But these thick-mist swallowers [13]

different, and I am apt to think Janotus accuses his brethren of
sodomy, treason, and heresy. Every man of reading knows
the proverb in the Confession of Sancy, l. 1, c. 2, ' In Francia
los Grandes y los Pedantes.'

[10] *Dirty and Snotty.*—Dirt, ordure, filth and vermin, were in a
manner inherent to the persons of Messieurs our Masters, particularly in Vives' time; who, speaking of the gowns of the
Sorbonists of Paris, tells us they wore them, ' crassas, detritas,
laceras, lutulentas, immundas, pediculosas.' He compares them
likewise to the ancient cynics, etc.

[11] *At the next Greek Calends.*—Never. The Greeks had no
Calends, *i.e.,* did not reckon by them.

[12] *Omnia orta cadunt.*—' Omniaque orta occident,' says Sallust, in
the beginning of his Bellum Jugurthinum.

[13] *Thick-mist swallowers.*—*Avalleurs de frimarts.* See elsewhere
why Rabelais calls the lawyers by this name, as *frimats* means a
thick mist; but there is another meaning in it, which is *frimat* for

make the suits in law depending before them both infinite and immortal. In doing whereof, they have given occasion to, and verified the saying of Chilo the Lacedæmonian, consecrated to the Oracle at Delphos, that misery is the inseparable companion of law-suits; and that suitors are miserable; for sooner shall they attain to the end of their lives, than to the final decision of their pretended rights.

CHAPTER XXI

THE STUDY OF GARGANTUA, ACCORDING TO THE DIS-CIPLINE OF HIS SCHOOLMASTERS AND SOPHISTERS

THE first day being thus spent, and the bells put up again in their own place, the citizens of Paris, in acknowledgment of this courtesy, offered to maintain and feed his mare as long as he pleased, which Gargantua took in good part, and they sent her to graze in the forest of Biere.[1] I think she is not there now.   This done, he with all his heart submitted his study to the discretion of Ponocrates; who for the beginning appointed that he should do as he was accustomed, to the end he might understand by what means, in so long time, his old masters had made him so sottish and ignorant.   He disposed therefore of his time in such fashion, that ordinarily he did awake between eight and nine o'clock, whether it was day or not, for so had his

fremart.   Now the word _ferme_ (a farm) used to be spelt _freme_, or _frime_, so then it will allude to their swallowing the farms of the poor widows and orphans, and the strong houses of the gentry.

[1] _Forest of Biere._—So called in old time.   It is near the village of Bievre, where rises the little river of Bievre, better known by the name of the Gobelins Brook.

ancient governors ordained, alleging that which
David saith, Vanum[2] est vobis ante lucem surgere.
Then did he tumble and toss, wag his legs, and
wallow in the bed some time, the better to stir up
and rouse his vital spirits, and apparelled himself
according to the season: but willingly he would
wear a great long gown of thick frieze,[3] furred with
fox skins. Afterwards he combed his head with an
Almain comb,[4] which is the four fingers and the
thumb. For his preceptor said, that to comb himself other ways, to wash and make himself neat, was
to lose time in this world. Then he dunged, pist,
spued, belched, cracked, yawned, spitted, coughed,
yexed, sneezed, and snotted himself[5] like an archdeacon, and to suppress the dew and bad air, went
to breakfast, having some good fried tripe, fair rashers
on the coals, excellent gammons of bacon, store of

[2] *Vanum, etc.*—Psalm cxxviii. v. 2. It is in vain for you to
rise up early.
[3] *Great long gown of thick frieze.*—This was a Bachelor or
Master of Arts gown, which by reason of its length was always
daggled. It was of a coarse thick stuff, like all the disciples or
scholars' habits in the university, as we learn from Vives. From
the length and width of these gowns of thick frieze (grosse frise)
the wits used to call the apartments or quarters of these gentry,
'le Pais de Frise,' the county of Freeze, or Freezeland.
[4] *Combed his hair with an Almain.*—'Se pygnoit du pygne de
Almaing.' Germans, of all the civilised nations of Europe, being
perhaps the last that came into the wear of periwigs, the French,
who are seldom seen without a comb in one hand, were apt to laugh
when they saw a German ever and anon all the day long using
both his to keep the hair on his forehead parted in two divisions,
as he had adjusted it with his comb in the morning.
[5] *Snotted himself, etc.*—'Se morvait en archidiacre.' Because
an archdeacon, having a much fatter prebend and a greater income
than the ordinary and undignified canons of his chapter, has
wherewithal to make better cheer, and so by faring better and
being fully fed, he must abound more with humours than the
others.

fine minced meat, and a great deal of sippet brewis, made up of the fat of the beef-pot, laid upon bread, cheese, and chopped parsley stewed together. Pono-crates showed him, that he ought not eat so soon after rising out of his bed, unless he had performed some exercise beforehand. Gargantua answered, What ! have not I sufficiently well exercised myself ? I have wallowed and rolled myself six or seven turns in my bed, before I rose. Is not that enough ? Pope Alexander did so,[6] by the advice of a Jew his physician, and lived till his dying day in despite of his enemies. My first masters have used me to it, saying that to breakfast made a good memory, and therefore they drank first. I am very well after it, and dine but the better. And Master Tubal, who was the first licenciate at Paris, told me, that it was not enough to run a pace, but to set forth betimes: so doth not the total welfare of our humanity depend upon perpetual drinking in a ribble rabble, like ducks, but on drinking early in the morning ; unde versus,

> To rise betimes is no good hour,
> To drink betimes is better sure.

After he had thoroughly broke his fast, he went to church and they carried him in a great basket, a huge impantoufled or thick covered breviary, weighing, what in grease, clasps, parchment, and cover, little more or less than eleven hundred and six pounds.

---

[6] *Pope Alexander did so.*—This must be meant of Pope Alexander V., a great crammer and as great a guzzler, says his historian Theodoric de Niem (l. 2, c. 33). I very well remem-ber to have read somewhere, that this Pontiff being unable so sit up (he was grown so corpulent and heavy), Marsilius of Parma, his physician, prescribed him a wench to frisk and gambol it together a-bed now and then by the way of exercise, and in this posture the holy father was one day surprised by company, who unexpectedly came to see him.

There he heard six and twenty or thirty masses. This while, to the same place came his orison-mutterer impaletocked, or lapped up about the chin, like a tufted whoop,[7] and his breath antidoted with the store of the vine-tree-sirup. With him he mumbled all his kiriels, and dunsicals breborions, which he so curiously thumbed and fingered, that there fell not so much as one grain to the ground. As he went from the church, they brought him, upon a dray drawn with oxen, a confused heap of pater-nosters and aves of Sanct Claude, every one of them being of the bigness of a hat-block; and thus walking through the cloisters, galleries or garden, he said more in turning them over, than sixteen hermits would have done. Then did he study some paltry half hour with his eyes fixed upon his book; but as the comic saith, his mind was in the kitchen. Pissing then a full urinal,[8] he sat down at table; and

[7] *Like a tufted whoop.*—Cotgrave says it is a sort of dunghill cock that loves to nestle in man's ordure, and hath a great crest or tuft of feathers on its head. M. le Duchat (quoting Belon, Of Birds) says, It is a silly bird, almost without any tongue, and, by its ill articulated voice, it resembles that of matin mumblers. [This bird is the Hoopoe, *La Huppe* in French (*upupa epops*), specimens of which are not uncommon in Devonshire and Cornwall, as well as in other parts of this country. Yarrell says, ' It utters a sound closely resembling the word hoop, hoop, hoop, but breathed out so softly but rapidly as to remind the hearer of the notes of the dove.']

[8] *Pissing then a full urinal.*—' Pissant donc plein official.' In all the editions except that of 1535, and that of Dolet, it is urinal instead of official, which inclines M. le Duchat to think that official, in the sense of urinal, is a word peculiar to the people of Lyons, where those two editions were printed. In c. 9, Rabelais laughs at those who call a chamber-pot an official; because in his time, some people, thinking to speak politely, would call that implement an official, under colour that it did the office of a wardrobe (garde-robe), so the French call a house of office, or close stool closet.

because he was naturally phlegmatic, he began his
meal with some dozens of gammons, dried neat's
tongues, hard roes of mullet, called botargos, an-
douilles, or sausages, and such other forerunners of
wine.   In the mean while, four of his folks did cast
into his mouth one after another continually mustard
by whole shovels full.   Immediately after that, he
drank a horrible draught of white-wine for the ease
of his kidneys.   When that was done, he ate according
to the season meat agreeable to his appetite, and then
left off eating when his belly began to strout, and
was like to crack for fulness.   As for his drinking,
he had neither end nor rule.   For he was wont to
say, that the limits and bounds of drinking were,
when the cork of the shoes of him that drinketh
swelleth up half a foot high.

CHAPTER XXII

THE GAMES OF GARGANTUA

THEN blockishly mumbling with a set-on countenance a piece of scurvy grace, he washed his hands in
fresh wine, picked his teeth with the foot of a hog,
and talked jovially with his attendants.   Then the
carpet being spread, they brought plenty of cards,
many dice, with great store and abundance of checkers
and chessboards.

There he played

At flusse	At trump
At primero	At the prick and spare
At the beast	not
At the rifle	At the hundred

At the peeny
At the unfortunate woman
At the fib
At the pass ten
At one and thirty
At post and pair, or even and sequence
At three hundred
At the unlucky man
At the last couple in hell
At the hock
At the surly
At the lanskenet
At the cuckoo
At puff, or let him speak that hath it
At take nothing and throw out
At the marriage
At the frolic or jack daw
At the opinion
At who doth the one, and doth the other
At the sequences
At the ivory bundles
At the tarots
At losing load him
At he's gulled and esto
At the torture
At the handruff
At the click
At honours
At love
At the chess
At Reynard the fox

At the squares
At the cowes
At the lottery
At the chance or mum-chance
At three dice or maniest bleaks
At the tables
At nivinivinack
At the lurch
At doublets or queen's game
At the failie
At the French trictrac
At the long tables or ferkeering
At feldown
At tods body
At needs must
At the dames or draughts
At bob and mow
At primus secundus
At mark-knife
At the keys
At span-counter
At even or odd
At cross or pile
At ball and huckle-bones
At ivory balls
At the billiards
At bob and hit
At the owl
At the charming of the hare
At pull yet a little
At trudgepig

At the magatipes
At the horn
At the flowered or shrov-
tide ox
At the madge-owlet
At pinch without laugh-
ing
At prickle me tickle me
At the unshoing of the
ass
At the cocksess
At hari hohi
At I set me down
At earlie beardie
At the old mode
At draw the spit
At put out
At gossip lend me your
sack
At the ramcod ball
At thrust out the harlot
At Marseil figs
At nicknamrie
At stick and hole
At boke or him, or flay-
ing the fox
At the branching it
At the cat selling
At trill madam, or
grapple my lady
At blow the coal
At the re-wedding
At the quick and dead
judge
At unoven the iron
At the false clown

At the flints, or at the
nine stones
At to the crutch hulch back
At the sanct is found
At hinch, pinch, and
laugh not
At the leek
At bumdockdousse
At the loose gig
At the hoop
At the sow
At belly to belly
At the dales or straths
At the twigs
At the quoits
At I'm for that
At tilt at weekie
At nine pins
At the cock quintin
At tip and hurle
At the flat bowles
At the veere and tourn
At rogue and ruffian
At bumbatch touch
At the mysterious trough
At the short bowls
At the dapple grey
At cock and crank it
At break pot
At my desire
At twirly whirlytril
At the rush bundles
At the short staff
At the whirling gigge
At hide and seek, or are
you all hid

At the picket
At the blank
At the pilferers
At the caveson
At prison bars
At have at the nuts
At cherry-pit
At rub and rice
At whip-top
At the casting top
At the hobgoblins
At the O wonderful
At the soilie smutchy
At fast and loose
At scutchbreech
At the broom-besom
At St Cosme I come to
    adore thee
At the lusty brown boy
At I take you napping
At fair and softly passeth
    Lent
At the forked oak
At truss
At the wolf's tail
At bum to buss or nose
    in breech
At Geordie give me my
    lance
At swaggy, waggy, or
    shoggyshou
At stook and rook, shear
    and threave
At the birch
At the musse
At the dilly dilly darling

At ox moudy
At purpose in purpose
At nine less
At blind-man-buff
At the fallen bridges
At bridled nick
At the white at buts
At thwack swinge him
At apple, pear, and plum
At mumgi
At the toad
At cricket
At the pounding stick
At jack and the box
At the queens
At the trades
At heads and points
At the vine-tree hug
At black be thy fall
At ho the distaffe
At Joanne Thomson
At the boulting cloth
At the oat's seed
At greedy glutton
At the moorish dance
At feebie
At the whole frisk and
    gambole
At battabum, or riding
    the wild mare
At Hinde the Plowman
At the good mawkin
At the dead beast
At climb the ladder
    Billy
At the dying hog

At the salt doup
At the pretty pigeon
At barley break
At the bavine
At the bush leap
At crossing
At bo-peep
At the hardit arsepursey
At the harrowers nest
At forward hey
At the fig
At gunshot crack
At mustard peel

At the gome
At the relapse
At jog breech, or prick
   him forward
At knockpate
At the Cornish chough
At the crane dance
At slash and cut
At bobbing, or flirt on
   the nose
At the larks
At filipping

After he had thus well played, revelled, past and spent his time, it was thought fit to drink a little, and that was eleven glassfuls the man, and, immediately after making good cheer again, he would stretch himself upon a fair bench, or a good large bed, and there sleep two or three hours together, without thinking or speaking any hurt. After he was awakened he would shake his ears a little. In the mean time they brought him fresh wine. Then he drank better than ever. Ponocrates showed him, that it was an ill diet to drink so after sleeping. It is, answered Gargantua, the very life of the patriarchs and holy fathers ;[1] for naturally I sleep salt, and my

---

[1] *The very life of the patriarchs and holy fathers.*—There is no patriarchs in the original, only fathers. This thought of Gargantua's alludes to the 42d chapter of the rule of St Benedict, which directs the monks of that order ' mox ut surrexerint à cœna (from dinner) sedeant omnes in unum et legat unus collationes, vel vitas patrum: aut certè aliquid quod ædificet audientes.' It is founded upon this; after such reading, the monks are used to go and drink a cup in the refectory. Now Gargantua thought himself privileged to drink like them at the hour of vespers, because, though indeed he slept while those monks got thirsty by reading

sleep hath been to me instead of so many gammons of bacon. Then began he to study a little, and out came the patenotres or rosary of beads, which the better and more formally to despatch, he got up on an old mule, which had served nine kings, and so mumbling with his mouth, nodding and doddling his head, would go see a coney ferreted or caught in a gin. At his return he went into the kitchen, to know what roast meat was on the spit, and what otherwise was to be drest for supper. And supped very well upon my conscience, and commonly did invite some of his neighbours that were good drinkers, with whom carousing and drinking merrily, they told stories of all sorts from the old to the new. Amongst others, he had for domestics the Lords of Fou, of Gourville,[2] of Griniot, and of Marigny. After supper were brought in upon the place the fair wooden gospels, and the books of the four kings, that is to say, many pairs of tables and cards; or the fair flusse, one, two, three; or all to make short work; or else they went to see the wenches thereabouts, with little small banquets, intermixed with collations and rear-suppers. Then did he sleep without unbridling, until eight o'clock in the next morning.

the Lives of the Fathers, and the Collations and Conferences of Cassian, his nature being, he said, to sleep salt, he found himself at that hour no less athirst than they were.

   [2] *Lords of Fou, of Gourville, etc.*—These were worthy gentlemen of Poitou. In the neighbourhood of Poitiers, there is a seat or castle called Du Fou.

CHAPTER XXIII

HOW GARGANTUA WAS INSTRUCTED BY PONOCRATES,
AND IN SUCH SORT DISCIPLINATED, THAT HE
LOST NOT ONE HOUR OF THE DAY

WHEN Ponocrates knew Gargantua's vicious manner
of living, he resolved to bring him up in another
kind; but for a while he bore with him, considering
that nature cannot endure such a change, without
great violence. Therefore to begin his work the
better, he requested a learned physician of that time,
called Master Theodorus,[1] seriously to perpend, if
it were possible, how to bring Gargantua unto a
better course. The said physician purged him
canonically with Anticyrian hellebore,[2] by which
medicine he cleansed all the alteration and perverse habitude of his brain. By this means also
Ponocrates made him forget all that he had learned
under his ancient preceptors, as Timotheus did to
his disciples,[3] who had been instructed under other

---

[1] *Master Theodorus.*—Theodorus, *i.e.*, God's Gift. By the
Greek name of this physician, Rabelais would give us to understand, that it was through the especial favour and gift of God,
that Gargantua was at last put into the hands of other-guise
masters than those who till then had been spoiling his head and
corrupting his heart.

[2] *Anticyrian hellebore.*—Hellebore was made use of to purge the
brain, in order to fit it the better for study. Pliny, l. 25, c. 25.
Aulus Gellius, l. 17, c. 15.

[3] *As Timotheus did to his disciples.*—Quintilian, l. 2, c. 3,
relates that such as had a mind to learn music of that excellent
master, were obliged to give him a double salary, in case they
had before received any tincture of that art from other hands;
because he was to take double the pains with them. First to
unteach them what they had been taught amiss, and then to instruct them aright. All the old editions have Thimotus, by

musicians. To do this better, they brought him
into the company of learned men, which were there,
in whose imitation he had a great desire and affection
to study otherwise, and to improve his parts. Afterwards he put himself into such a road and way of
studying that he lost not any one hour in the day,
but employed all his time in learning and honest
knowledge. Gargantua awaked, then, about four
o'clock in the morning. Whilst they were in rubbing of him, there was read unto him some chapter
of the Holy Scripture aloud and clearly, with a
pronunciation fit for the matter, and hereunto was
appointed a young page born in Basché, named
Anagnostes. According to the purpose and argument of that lesson, he oftentimes gave himself to
worship, adore, pray, and send up his supplications
to that good God, whose word did show his majesty
and marvellous judgment. Then went he into
the secret places to make excretion of his natural
digestions. There his master repeated what had
been read, expounding unto him the most obscure
and difficult points. In returning, they considered
the face of the sky, if it was such as they had
observed it the night before, and into what signs
the sun was entering, as also the mood for that day.
This done, he was apparelled, combed, curled,
trimmed, and perfumed, during which time they
repeated to him the lessons of the day before. He
himself said them by heart, and upon them would
ground some practical cases concerning the estate
of man, which he would prosecute sometimes two
or three hours, but ordinarily they ceased as soon

following bad editions of Quintilian, as hath been already noted
in the case of Polycrates (ch. 10), by following an old copy of
Aulus Gellius, printed at Paris, 1508.

as he was fully clothed. Then for three good hours
he had a lecture read unto him. This done, they
went forth, still conferring of the substance of the
lecture, either unto a field[4] near the university
called the Brack, or unto the meadows where they
played at the ball, the long-tennis, and at the pile
trigone,[5] most gallantly exercising their bodies, as
formerly they had done their minds. All their play
was but in liberty, for they left off when they
pleased, and that was commonly when they did
sweat over all their body, or were otherwise weary.
Then were they very well wiped and rubbed,
shifted their shirts, and walking soberly, went to see
if dinner was ready. Whilst they stayed for that,
they did clearly and eloquently pronounce some
sentences that they had retained of the lecture.
In the meantime Master Appetite came, and then
very orderly sat they down at table. At the
beginning of the meal, there was read some pleasant
history of the warlike actions of former times, until
he had taken a glass of wine. Then, if they thought
good, they continued reading, or began to discourse
merrily together ; speaking first of the virtue, pro-
priety, efficacy, and nature of all that was served in
at that table; of bread, of wine, of water, of salt,
of fleshes, fishes, fruits, herbs, roots, and of their
dressing. By means whereof, he learned in a little
time all the passages competent for this, that were

[4] *A field, etc.*—Read a Tennis Court, in the suburb of St
Marcellus, at the sign of the Bracque, a short-tailed spotted setting dog.
 [5] *Pile trigone.*—Read, A la Pile Trigone. Duchat says, It is
an ancient game at tennis, wherein three persons, placed at the
corners of a triangle, strike the ball reciprocally from one to the
other. Martial, Epig. 19, l. 4. ' Seu lentum ceroma teris,
tepidumve trigona.'

to be found in Pliny, Athenæus, Dioscorides, Julius
Pollux, Galen, Porphyrius, Oppian, Polybius, Helio-
dorus, Aristotle, Ælian, and others. Whilst they
talked of these things, many times, to be the more
certain, they caused the very books to be brought
to the table, and so well and perfectly did he in
his memory retain the things above said, that in
that time there was not a physician that knew half
so much as he did. Afterwards they conferred of
the lessons read in the morning, and ending their
repast with some conserve or marmalade of quinces,
he picked his teeth with mastic tooth-pickers,[6]
washed his hands and eyes with fair fresh water,
and gave thanks unto God in some fine canticks,
made in praise of the divine bounty and munificence.
This done, they brought in cards, not to play, but
to learn a thousand pretty tricks and new inventions,
which were all grounded upon arithmetic. By this
means he fell in love with that numerical science,
and every day after dinner and supper he passed his
time in it as pleasantly as he was wont to do at
cards and dice ; so that at last he understood so well
both the theory and practical part thereof, that
Tunstal the Englishman,[7] who had written very
largely of that purpose, confessed that verily in

[6] *He picked his teeth with mastic tooth-pickers.*—*S'escuroit les
dens avecques ung trou de lentisce.* In the ancientest editions we
find *trou* instead of *tronc*, by changing the *n* into a *u*, as in couvent
instead of convent (Covent-garden instead of Convent-garden).
Trou de lentisque therefore means the stem or stalk of the lentisk
tree; the stalks of this tree, from whence drops the mastic, were
used by the Romans for tooth-pickers, preferable to quills.
Martial, Epig. 22, l. 24.

> ' Lentiscum melius: sed si tibi frondea cuspis
>   Defuerit, dentes, penna, levare potes.'

[7] *Tunstal the Englishman.*—Cuthbert Tonstal, Bishop of Durham,
in England.

189

comparison of him he had no skill at all. And not only in that, but in the other mathematical sciences, as geometry, astronomy, music, etc. For in waiting on the concoction, and attending the digestion of his food, they made a thousand pretty instruments and geometrical figures, and did in some measure practise the astronomical canons.

After this they recreated themselves with singing musically, in four or five parts, or upon a set theme or ground at random, as it best pleased them. In matter of musical instruments, he learned to play upon the lute, the virginals, the harp, the Almain flute with nine holes, the violin, and the sackbut. This hour thus spent, and digestion finished, he did purge his body of natural excrements, then betook himself to his principal study for three hours together, or more, as well to repeat his matutinal lectures, as to proceed in the book wherein he was, as also to write handsomely, to draw and form the antique and Roman letters. This being done, they went out of their house, and with them a young gentleman of Touraine, named the Esquire Gymnast, who taught him the art of riding. Changing then his clothes, he rode a Naples courser, Dutch roussin, a Spanish gennet, a barbed or trapped steed, then a light fleet horse, unto whom he gave a hundred carieres, made him go the high saults, bounding in the air, free a ditch with a skip, leap over a stile or pale, turn short in a ring both to the right and left hand. There he broke not his lance; for it is the greatest foolery in the world to say, I have broken ten lances at tilts or in fight. A carpenter can do even as much. But it is a glorious and praiseworthy action, with one lance to break and overthrow ten enemies. Therefore with a sharp, stiff, strong, and well-steeled lance, would he usually force up a door,

pierce a harness, beat down a tree, carry away the
ring, lift up a cuirassier saddle, with the mail-coat
and gauntlet. All this he did in complete arms
from head to foot. As for the prancing flourishes,
and smacking popisms, for the better cherishing of
the horse, commonly used in riding, none did them
better than he. The voltiger of Ferrara was but as
an ape compared to him. He was singularly skilful
in leaping nimbly from one horse to another without
putting foot to ground, and these horses were called
desultories. He could likewise from either side,
with a lance in his hand, leap on horseback without
stirrups, and rule the horse at his pleasure without
a bridle, for such things are useful in military en-
gagements. Another day he exercised the battle-
axe, which he so dexterously wielded, both in the
nimble, strong, and smooth management of that
weapon, and that in all the feats practiceable by it,
that he passed knight of arms in the field, and at
all essays.

Then tossed he the pike, played with the two-
handed sword, with the back sword, with the
Spanish tuck, the dagger, poniard, armed, unarmed,
with a buckler, with a cloak, with a target. Then
would he hunt the hart, the roebuck, the bear, the
fallow deer, the wild boar, the hare, the pheasant,
the partridge, and the bustard. He played at the
balloon, and made it bound in the air, both with
fist and foot. He wrestled, ran, jumped, not at
three steps and a leap, called the hops, nor at
clochepied, called the hare's leap, nor yet at the
Almain's; for, said Gymnast, these jumps are for
the wars altogether unprofitable, and of no use;
but at one leap he would skip over a ditch, spring
over a hedge, mount six paces upon a wall, ramp and
grapple after this fashion up against a window, of

the full height of a lance. He did swim in deep
waters on his belly, on his back, sideways, with all
his body, with his feet only, with one hand in the
air, wherein he held a book, crossing thus the
breadth of the River Seine, without wetting, and
dragging along his cloak with his teeth, as did
Julius Cæsar; then with the help of one hand he
entered forcibly into a boat, from whence he cast
himself again headlong into the water, sounded the
depths, hollowed the rocks, and plunged into the
pits and gulfs. Then turned he the boat about,
governed it, led it swiftly or slowly with the stream
and against the stream, stopped it in his course,
guided it with one hand, and with the other laid
hard about him with a huge great oar, hoisted the
sail, hied up along the mast by the shrouds, ran
upon the edge of the decks, set the compass in
order, tackled the bowlines, and steered the helm.
Coming out of the water, he ran furiously up against
a hill, and with the same alacrity and swiftness ran
down again. He climbed up trees like a cat,
leaped from the one to the other like a squirrel.
He did pull down the great boughs and branches,
like another Milo; then with two sharp well-
steeled daggers, and two tried bodkins, would he
run up by the wall to the very top of a house like
a rat; then suddenly come down from the top to
the bottom, with such an even composition of
members, that by the fall he would catch no
harm.

He did cast the dart, throw the bar, put the
stone, practise the javelin, the boar spear or partisan,
and the halbert. He broke the strongest bows in
drawing, bended against his breast the greatest cross-
bows of steel, took his aim by the eye with the
hand-gun, and shot well, traversed and planted the

cannon, shot at butt-marks, at the papgay from
below upwards, or to a height from above downwards, or to a descent; then before him, sidewise,
and behind him, like the Parthians. They tied a
cable-rope to the top of a high tower, by one end
whereof hanging near the ground he wrought himself with his hands to the very top; then upon the
same tract came down so sturdily and firm that you
could not on a plain meadow have run with more
assurance. They set up a great pole fixed upon
two trees. There would he hang by his hands, and
with them alone, his feet touching at nothing, would
go back and fore along the aforesaid rope with so
great swiftness, that hardly could one overtake him
with running; and then, to exercise his breast and
lungs, he would shout like all the devils in hell.
I heard him once call ' Eudemon ! ' from St Victor's
gate to Montmartre. Stentor never had such a voice
at the siege of Troy. Then for the strengthening
of his nerves or sinews, they made him two great
sows of lead,[8] each of them weighing eight thousand
and seven hundred quintals, which they called
Alteres.[9] Those he took up from the ground, in
each hand one, then lifted them up over his head,
and held them so without stirring three quarters of
an hour or more, which was an inimitable force.

---

[8] *Sows of Lead.*—So we English call them. The French call
them *salmons*, not *sows* of lead, because of their resembling that fish,
both in shape and size. The reader will forgive the digression
I am going to make. In Derbyshire there is a living worth
£500 or £600 a-year in tithe pigs. It is Wirksworth. (Pigs of
lead.)

[9] *Alteres.*—A poise of iron, stone, but chiefly lead, which
tumblers, and dancers on ropes, hold in their hands for a
counterpoise, also a piece of lead, etc., to lift up with both hands
for exercise. In Latin, or rather Greek, Halter, eris, ἀλτήρ, ἀπὸ
τοῦ ἅλλεσθαι, a saliendo. Dumb-bells in English.

He fought at barriers with the stoutest and most
vigorous champions; and when it came to the cope,
he stood so sturdily on his feet, that he abandoned
himself unto the strongest, in case they could
remove him from his place, as Milo was wont to do
of old. In whose imitation likewise he held a
pomegranate in his hand, to give it unto him that
could take it from him. The time being thus
bestowed, and himself rubbed, cleansed, wiped, and
refreshed with other clothes, he returned fair and
softly; and passing through certain meadows, or
other grassy places, beheld the trees and plants,
comparing them with what is written of them in
the books of the ancients, such as Theophrast,
Dioscorides, Marinus, Pliny, Nicander, Macer, and
Galen, and carried home to the house great hand-
fuls of them, whereof a young page called Rizotomos
had charge; together with little mattocks, pickaxes,
grubbing hooks, cabbies, pruning knives, and other
instruments requisite for herborising. Being come
to their lodging, whilst supper was making ready,
they repeated certain passages of that which had
been read, and then sat down at table. Here
remark, that his dinner was sober and thrifty, for he
did then eat only to prevent the gnawings of his
stomach, but his supper was copious and large; for
he took then as much as was fit to maintain and
nourish him; which indeed is the true diet
prescribed by the art of good and sound physic,
although a rabble of loggerheaded physicians muzzled
in the brabbling shop of sophisters,[10] counsel the

---

[10] *Sophisters.*—By these Sophisters, or Arabians, as Dolet's
edition has it, Rabelais means Avicenna and his followers; and
by those of the good and sound opinion, Galen and his disciples.
It is certain, the Goths first brought in the custom of set dinners
and suppers, that is, of eating two full meals a day; whereas the

contrary. During that repast was continued the lesson read at dinner as long as they thought good : the rest was spent in good discourse, learned and profitable. After that they had given thanks, he set himself to sing vocally, and play upon harmonious instruments, or otherwise passed his time at some pretty sports, made with cards and dice, or in practising the feats of legerdemain, with cups and balls. There they staid some nights in frolicking thus, and making themselves merry till it was time to go to bed; and on other nights they would go make visits unto learned men, or to such as had been travellers in strange and remote countries. When it was full night before they retired themselves, they went unto the most open place of the house to see the face of the sky, and there beheld the comets, if any were, as likewise the figures, situations, aspects, oppositions and conjunctions of both the fixed stars and planets.

Then with his master did he briefly recapitulate, after the manner of the Pythagoreans, that which he had read, seen, learned, done and understood in the whole course of that day.

Then prayed they unto God the Creator, in falling down before him, and strengthening their faith towards him, and glorifying him for his boundless bounty; and, giving thanks unto him for the time that was past, they recommended themselves to his divine clemency for the future. Which being done, they went to bed, and betook themselves to their repose and rest.

ancients used to make a light dinner, but at supper they would eat their fill.

CHAPTER XXIV

HOW GARGANTUA SPENT HIS TIME IN RAINY WEATHER

IF it happened that the weather were anything
cloudy, foul, and rainy, all the forenoon was employed, as before specified, according to custom,
with this difference only, that they had a good clear
fire lighted, to correct the distempers of the air.
But after dinner, instead of their wonted exercitations, they did abide within, and, by way of
Apotherapie,[1] did recreate themselves in bottling
up of hay, in cleaving and sawing of wood, and in
threshing sheaves of corn at the barn. Then they
studied the art of painting or carving; or brought
into use the antique play of tables,[2] as Leonicus
hath written of it, and as our good friend Lascaris
playeth at it. In .playing they examined the
passages of ancient authors, wherein the said play
is mentioned, or any metaphor drawn from it. They
went likewise to see the drawing of metals, or the

[1] *Apotherapie.*—The new editions have it *Apotherapic*, with a
c, which is no word at all. The Dutch editor says ἀποθεραπεία
means, the issue and end of exercise. I like Robertson's defini-
tion better, 'Cura post remedia vehementiora, vel curatio post
exercitationem exhibita.' Anglicè, a healer after hard drinking,
as one may say in mirth, from ἀπὸ et θεραπέιω.

[2] *Tables.*—Read instead of Tables, Talus, or Tali. Talus is
a bone to play with like a die. Ludus Talarius, in Latin. All
the editions, except this of Duchat, have it Tables, but it should
be Tales, *i.e.*, Tali, as above, and as in l. 4, c. 7. Leonicus,
who is mentioned by Rabelais, in the same breath, wrote a
Treatise by way of Dialogue, de Lude Talario, intituled Sannutus
(not Samnutus, as in Gryphius' Edition, both in title and text.
The game of the Tali (τῶν ἀστραγάλων) is certainly of great
antiquity, especially if it be true that the Lydians used it, even
before the Trojan war; nor did it cease to be in vogue in Italy,
under the name of *Parelles*, till about 1484.

casting of great ordnance: how the lapidaries did
work, as also the goldsmiths and cutters of precious
stones. Nor did they omit to visit the alchymists,
money-coiners, upholsterers, weavers, velvet-workers,
watchmakers, looking-glass framers, printers, organists,
and other such kind of artificers, and everywhere
giving them somewhat to drink, did learn and consider the industry and invention of the trades. They
went also to hear the public lectures, the solemn
commencements, the repetitions, the acclamations,
the pleadings of the gentle lawyers, and sermons of
Evangelical preachers. He went through the halls
and places appointed for fencing, and there played
against the masters themselves at all weapons, and
showed them by experience, that he knew as much
in it as, yea more than they. And, instead of herborising, they visited the shops of druggists, herbalists
and apothecaries, and diligently considered the fruits,
roots, leaves, gums, seeds, the grease and ointments
of some foreign parts,[3] as also how they did adulterate
them.[4] He went to see jugglers, tumblers, mounte-
banks and quacksalvers, and considered their cun-

[3] *Grease and ointments of some foreign parts.—Axunges peregrines.*
Axunge signifies grease, properly of swine, says Cotgrave, also
ointment made thereof. Duchat says, the softest and most
humid fat, or grease of beasts. Boyer says, *Axonge*, man's
grease prepared with herbs, and good against cold humours.
The authors of Camb. Dict., 'Axungia ab unguendo plaustri
axe, ad faciliorem circumactum rotarum.' Grease or unguent,
for an axle-tree, whence its name *axungia*, swine's grease; also
the fat, froth, or cream of any other thing.

[4] *Adulterate them.*—It is indeed *adulterer* in French; but here
it means to compound, make up, mingle together, as you will
find adultero in the Camb. Dict. sometimes to signify. Duchat
confirms me in this opinion: 'Adulterer, la maniere dont on
faisoit des remedes composez de toutes ces Drogues.' In this
sense it is an apothecary's business to adulterate, and not any
objection to him for doing so.

ning, their shifts, their summer-saults and smooth
tongues, especially of those of Chauny in Picardy,
who are naturally great praters, and brave givers of
fibs, in matter of green apes.

At their return they did eat more soberly at
supper than at other times, and meats more dessica-
tive and extenuating; to the end that the in-
temperate moisture of the air, communicated to the
body by a necessary confinity, might by this means
be corrected, and that they might not receive any
prejudice for want of their ordinary bodily exercise.
Thus was Gargantua governed, and kept on in this
course of education, from day to day profiting, as
you may understand such a young man of his age 5
may, of a pregnant judgment, with good discipline
well continued. Which, although at the beginning
it seemed difficult, became a little after so sweet,
so easy, and so delightful, that it seemed rather the
recreation of a king than the study of a scholar.
Nevertheless Ponocrates, to divert him from this
vehement intension of the spirits, thought fit, once
in a month, upon some fair and clear day to go out
of the city betimes in the morning, either towards
Gentilly, or Boulogne, or to Montrouge, or Charan-
ton-bridge, or to Vanves, or St Clou, and there

5 *Of his age.*—It appears before, in chap. 14, that Gargantua,
in 1420, had spent in study fifty-three years, ten months and
two weeks. He was at least five years old when Master Thubal
gave him his first lesson; but let us reckon no more than fifty-
eight years. He is made to read, since 1420, the Supplimentum
Chronicorum, which came out sixty-five years after, viz., in
1485. Add these sixty-five to the other fifty-eight, and you
will find that this young man Gargantua was at least a hundred
and twenty-three years old, even before he put himself under
the discipline of Ponocrates. But this is, because Gargantua's
adolescency ought to be in proportion to the duration of his
life; now his life was of a very great length, since l. 2, c. 2, he
was 524 years old when he begot Pantagruel.

spend all the day long in making the greatest cheer
that could be devised, sporting, making merry,
drinking healths, playing, singing, dancing, tum-
bling, in some fair meadow, unnestling of sparrows,
taking of quails, and fishing for frogs and crabs.
But although that day was past without books or
lecture, yet was it not spent without profit; for
in the said meadows they usually repeated certain
pleasant verses of Virgil's agriculture, of Hesiod,
and of Politian's husbandry; would set a-broach
some witty Latin epigrams, then immediately turned
them into roundelays and songs for dancing in the
French language.   In their feasting, they would
sometimes separate the water from the wine that
was therewith mixed, as Cato teacheth, De Re
Rustica, and Pliny with an ivy cup[6] would wash the
wine in a basin full of water, then take it out again
with a funnel as pure as ever.   They made the
water go from one glass to another, and contrived
a thousand little automatory engines,[7] that is to say,
moving of themselves.

· [6] *With an ivy cup.*—Pliny, l. 16, c. 35, after Cato, c. De Re
Rust.
    [7] *Automatory engines.*—The reader may upon this satisfy him-
self further, by having recourse to Leonicus, l. 1, c. 7, of his
' De Varia Historia.'

CHAPTER XXV

HOW THERE WAS A GREAT STRIFE AND DEBATE RAISED
BETWIXT THE CAKE-BAKERS OF LERNÉ, AND THOSE
OF GARGANTUA'S COUNTRY, WHEREUPON WERE
WAGED GREAT WARS

AT that time, which was the season of vintage, in the
beginning of harvest,[1] when the country shepherds
were set to keep the vines, and hinder the starlings
from eating up the grapes, as some cake-bakers of
Lerné[2] happened to pass along in the broad highway,
driving into the city ten or twelve horses loaded with
cakes, the said shepherds courteously entreated them
to give them some for their money, as the price then
ruled in the market.   For here it is to be remarked,
that it is a celestial food to eat for breakfast, hot fresh
cakes with grapes, especially the frail clusters, the
great red grapes, the muscadine, the verjuice grape,
and the luskard, for those that are costive in their
belly; because it will make them gush out, and squirt
the length of a hunter's staff, like the very tap of a
barrel; and oftentimes, thinking to let a squib, they
did all-to-besquatter and conskite themselves, where-

[1] *Harvest.*—Autumn, Rabelais says.
[2] *Lerné.*—Lerné or Lerney, as Bernier spells it, is a parish in
Poitou, where they make a kind of Galette (wreathed cake, says
Cotgrave, a broad thin cake, says Boyer, with whom I concur).
Be that as it will, it was a large sort of brown cake, or a bun,
hastily baked on a hot hearth (Focus in Latin, from whence I
suppose the people of Perigord, Languedoc, etc., call it Fouace),
with hot embers laid on it, and burning coals over it.   In
France, the people that make and sell the fouace cake, are they
whom Rabelais calls *foüaciers*: cake-bakers or cake-venders of
Lerné.

upon they are commonly called the vintage thinkers.[3]
The bunsellers or cake-makers were in nothing in-
clinable to their request; but (which was worse) did
injure them most outrageously, calling them prattling
gabblers, licorous gluttons, freckled bittors, mangy
rascals, shite-a-bed scoundrels, drunken roysters, sly
knaves, drowsy loiterers, slapsauce fellows, slabber-
degullion druggels, lubbardly louts, cozening foxes,
ruffian rogues, paltry customers, sycophant-varlets,
drawlatch hoydons, flouting milksops, jeering companions, staring clowns, forlorn snakes, ninny lob-
cocks, scurvy sneaksbies, fondling fops, base loons,
saucy coxcombs, idle lusks, scoffing braggards, noddy
meacocks, blockish grutnols, doddipol joltheads,
jobbernol goosecaps, foolish loggerheads, flutch calf-
lollies, grouthead gnat-snappers, lob-dotterels, gaping
changelings, codshead loobies, woodcock slangams,
ninnie-hammer flycatchers, noddiepeak simpletons,
turdy-gut, shitten shepherds, and other such like
defamatory epithets; saying further that it was not

3 *Vintage thinkers.*—An Englishman will be apt to stare at
this word, and imagine it should be vintage drinkers. But no,
it is rightly translated ; *Cuideurs de vendanges* are Rabelais'
words; and since, as the French proverb says, a filthy tale
seldom wants filthy auditors, 'à cul de foirard toujours abonde
merde,' I will even explain these words. There is you must
know an ancient home-spun French saying, ' Je cuidois seulement
peter, et je me suis embrene.' I thought (mind that word, for
it explains thinkers)—I thought to have only farted and have
all beshit myself. This piece of loose wit is grounded on the
laxative quality of the white grape, called for that very reason
foirard (squitterer): of which when a man, and the same with
a woman, I suppose, has eaten too freely, and thinks to ease
him (or her) self by farting, they are very apt to do something
more. Thus when Rabelais, ch. 9 of his Pantagruelian Prognostication, says, that in Autumn the cuidez will be in season,
he means that in time of vintage, people will often have occasion
to say *Je cuidois, etc.* I thought, etc. He says many a one
will let a brewer's fizzle, *i.e.*, grains and all.

for them to eat of these dainty cakes, but might very
well content themselves with the coarse unraunged
bread,[4] or to eat of the great brown household loaf.
To which provoking words, one amongst them,
called Forgier, an honest fellow of his person, and a
notable springal, made answer very calmly thus.
How long is it since you have got horns, that you
are become so proud? Indeed formerly you were
wont to give us some freely, and will you not now
let us have any for our money? This is not the part
of good neighbours, neither do we serve you thus,
when you come hither to buy our good corn, whereof
you make your cakes and buns. Besides that, we

[4] *Coarse unraunged bread, etc.*—*Gros pain ballé, et de tourte.*
Ballé is the chaff or coat that holds the grains of wheat or other
corn. So pain ballé is chaff bread. This bread, coarse with a
witness, which in Poitou is given only to country servants, consists
of several sorts of corn, as oats, barley, and the great and small
plâtre (a sort of rye, if I do not mistake M. le Duchat's petit blé),
the ear of which is very long, and the grain placed two and two
in a husk, which is flat and very hard. Now, as no great care is
taken at the mill to separate this husk nor even the chaff (ballé
above mentioned) from the meal, this makes the chaff bread (pain
ballé) so despicable. As for the other word Rabelais uses, viz.,
tourte, Cotgrave, from whom Sir T. U. takes it, says, it is a loaf
of household (or brown) bread, called so in Lionnois and Dauphiné.
But M. le Duchat being more particular, I shall translate what
he says of this same tourte. It is bread made of rye, peculiar to
the peasants of certain provinces, chiefly to the poor inhabitants
of the mountains of the country of Foretz, the Lyonnois, Savoy,
Auvergne, and the Bourbonnois. This bread, which is made into
loaves, almost as big as a Parmesan cheese, and muchwhat of the
same form, will keep several months; nay, it is said, that tourte
is more savoury for being stale, and that age gives it a yellow
colour, like that of wax, if due care be taken to pile these huge
loaves one upon another as soon as they come out of the oven,
and some very heavy weight be set upon them. Upon the whole,
this sort of bread it very undigestive, and agrees with none but
ploughmen, porters, quarry-men, masons, bricklayers, ano black-
smiths. See Jerom. Mercurialis, Var. Lect. l. 2, c. 5. Bruyerin
de re Cibaria, l. 1. c. 9.

Strife between the Cake--Bakers.

would have given you to the bargain some of our
grapes, but, by his zounds, you may chance to repent
it, and possibly have need of us at another time,
when we shall use you after the like manner, and
therefore remember it.   Then Marquet, a prime
man in the confraternity of the cake-bakers, said
unto him, Yea, sir, thou art pretty well crest-risen
this morning, thou didst eat yesternight too much
millet and bolymong.[5]   Come hither, sirrah, come
hither, I will give thee some cakes.   Whereupon
Forgier, dreading no harm, in all simplicity went
towards him, and drew a sixpence out of his leather
satchel, thinking that Marquet would have sold him
some of his cakes.   But instead of cakes, he gave him
with his whip such a rude lash overthwart the legs,
the marks of the whipcord knots were apparent in
them, then would have fled away; but Forgier cried
out as loud as he could, O murder, murder, help,
help, help ! and in the meantime threw a great
cudgel after him, which he carried under his arm,
wherewith he hit him in the coronal joint of his
head, upon the crotaphic artery of the right side
thereof, so forcibly, that Marquet fell down from
his mare, more like a dead than a living man.
Meanwhile the farmers and country swains that
were watching their walnuts near to that place,
came running with their great poles and long staves,
and laid such load on these cake-bakers, as if they
had been to thrash upon green rye.   The other
shepherds and shepherdesses, hearing the lamentable
shout of Forgier, came with their slings and slackies [6]

5 *Bolymong.*—Mingled corn.   This is not in the original; it
says only millet, which if you feed a cock with over night, he
will be the stouter and bolder for it the next day.
   6 *Slackies.*—I know not what slacky means; I suppose it may
be a Scotch word for something like a sling; for that is what

following them, and throwing great stones at them,
as thick as if it had been hail. At last they overtook them, and took from them about four or five
dozen of their cakes. Nevertheless they paid for
them the ordinary price, and gave them over and
above one hundred eggs,[7] and three baskets full of
mulberries.[8] Then did the cake-bakers help to get
up to his mare, Marquet, who was most shrewdly
wounded, and forthwith returned to Lerné, changing
the resolution they had to go to Pareille, threatening
very sharp and boisterously the cowherds, shepherds,
and farmers, of Sevillé and Sinays. This done, the
shepherds and shepherdesses made merry with these
cakes and fine grapes, and sported themselves together
at the sound of the pretty small pipe, scoffing and
laughing at those vain glorious cake-bakers, who had
that day met with a mischief for want of crossing
themselves with a good hand in the morning. Nor
did they forget to apply to Forgier's leg some fair
great red medicinal grapes,[9] and so handsomely
dressed it and bound it up, that he was quickly
cured.

Rabelais means by the word brassier.—*Cotgrave*. [See, however,
p. 226, *post*, where a 'slacky' is made equivalent to 'a short
cudgel.']

[7] *One hundred eggs.*—Rabelais does not say eggs, but shelled
nuts, for that's the meaning of *quecas*, Cotgrave says, and M. le
Duchat too. Un cent de noix, etc., says Duchat, a hundred
walnuts, which Grangousier's tenants had just been shelling for
themselves.

[8] *Mulberries.*—*Francs aubiers* means, according to M. le Duchat,
a sort of white grapes, the pulp whereof is very firm. The word
comes from albus, white.

[9] *Great red medicinal grapes.*—*Gros raisins chenins;* a kind of
great red grape, fitter for medicines than for meat.—*Cotgrave*.

CHAPTER XXVI

HOW THE INHABITANTS OF LERNÉ, BY THE COMMAND--
MENT OF PICROCHOLE, THEIR KING, ASSAULTED
THE SHEPHERDS OF GARGANTUA UNEXPECTEDLY
AND ON A SUDDEN

THE cake-bakers, being returned to Lerné, went
presently, before they did either eat or drink, to the
capitol,[1] and there before their King, called Picro--
chole,[2] the third of that name,[3] made their complaint,
showing their panniers broken, their caps all
crumbled, their coats torn, their cakes taken away,
but, above all, Marquet most enormously wounded,
saying, that all that mischief was done by the
shepherds and herdsmen of Grangousier, near the
broad highway beyond Sevillé. Picrochole incon--
tinent grew angry and furious ; and, without asking

[1] *Capitol.—Capitoly* in French. In some provinces of France
they call the session-house and court of judicature, the capitol,
and at Thoulouse the echevins (magistrates not unlike the English
sheriffs), are called capitouls. It is in this sense, we are to·
understand the country gibberidge capitoly, since it is said the
cake-bakers went thither to carry their complaints, and supplicate
their king for justice, who, according to ancient custom, dispensed·
it to his subjects personally and instantly.
[2] *Picrochole.—*Bitter bile, Greek; *i.e.,* a choleric man.
[3] *The third of that name.—*M. le Duchat takes this to mean,.
that he was still more choleric than his two predecessors of the
same name. To call one Simpleton the third, Codshead the
third, is the same as to call him a complete simpleton, a finished
fool, a codshead in the superlative degree. In this sense it is,
that ch. 27, l. 5, our author, speaking of King Benius, founder of
the order of Semiquaver Friars, says he was the third of the name
of Benius, as much as to say he was a greater Tony (Benest in
French) than his predecessors, who had impoverished themselves
to enrich other orders which they had likewise founded. See·
ch. 6 and 27, Rabelais, l. 5.

205

.any further what, how, why or wherefore, commanded the ban and arriere-ban to be sounded
throughout all his country, that all his vassals of
what condition soever should, upon pain of the
halter,[4] come in the best arms they could, unto the
great place before the castle, at the hour of noon,[5]
and the better to strengthen his design, he caused
the drum to be beat about the town. Himself,
whilst his dinner was making ready, went to see his
artillery mounted upon* the carriage, to display his
colours, and set up the great royal standard, and
loaded wains with store of ammunition both for the
field and the belly, arms and victuals. At dinner he
despatched his commissions, and by his express edict
my Lord Shagrag[6] was appointed to command the
vanguard, wherein were numbered sixteen thousand
and fourteen harquebussiers or firelocks, together
with thirty thousand and eleven volunteer adventurers. The great Torquedillon, master of the
horse, had the charge of the ordnance, wherein were
reckoned nine hundred and fourteen brazen pieces,
in cannons, double cannons, basilisks, serpentines,
culverins, bombards or murtherers, falcons, bases or
passevolans, spiroles and other sorts of great guns.
The rearguard was committed to the Duke of
Scrapegood. In the main battle was the king, and
the princes of his kingdom. Thus being hastily
furnished, before they would set forward, they sent
three hundred light horsemen under the conduct of

---

[4] *Halter.—Sur peine de la hart.* *Hart* properly means a green
withy, with which in old time malefactors were hanged, and still
are, says Cotgrave, in some barbarous countries.
[5] *At the hour of noon.*—Rabelais could not have pitched upon a
properer hour for this choleric prince to do a hot-headed thing,
than at high noon.
[6] *Shagrag.—Trepelu.* Pilosissimus, in Latin.

Captain Swillwind, to discover the country, clear
the avenues, and see whether there was any ambush
laid for them. But, after they had made diligent
search, they found all the land round about in peace
and quiet, without any meeting or convention at all;
which Picrochole understanding commanded that
everyone should march speedily under his colours.
Then immediately in all disorder, without keeping
either rank or file, they took the fields one amongst
another, wasting, spoiling, destroying and making
havoc of all wherever they went, not sparing poor nor
rich, privileged nor unprivileged places, church nor
laity, drove away oxen and cows, bulls, calfs, heifers,
wethers, ewes, lambs, goats, kids, hens, capons,
chickens, geese, ganders, goslings, hogs, swine, pigs
and such like; beating down the walnuts, plucking
the grapes, tearing the hedges, shaking the fruit-trees,
and committing such incomparable abuses, that the
like abomination was never heard of. Nevertheless,
they met with none to resist them, for everyone
submitted to their mercy, beseeching them, that they
might be dealt with courteously, in regard that they
had always carried themselves as became good and
loving neighbours; and that they had never been
guilty of any wrong or outrage done unto them, to
be thus suddenly surprised, troubled and disquieted,
and that if they would not desist, God would punish
them very shortly. To which expostulations and
remonstrances no other answer was made, but that
they would teach them to eat cakes.

***

CHAPTER XXVII

HOW A MONK OF SEVILLÉ SAVED THE CLOSE OF THE
ABBEY FROM BEING RANSACKED BY THE ENEMY

So much they did, and so far they went pillaging
and stealing, that at last they came to Sevillé, where
they robbed both men and women, and took all they
could catch: nothing was either too hot or too heavy
for them. Although the plague was there in the
most part of all their houses, they nevertheless
entered everywhere, then plundered and carried
away all that was within, and yet for all this not one
of them took any hurt, which is a most wonderful
case. For the curates, vicars, preachers, physicians,
chirurgeons and apothecaries, who went to visit, to
dress, to cure, to heal, to preach unto, and admonish
those that were sick, were all dead with the infection;
and these devilish robbers and murderers caught
never any harm at all. Whence comes this to pass,
my masters? I beseech you think upon it. The
town being thus pillaged, they went unto the abbey
with a horrible noise and tumult, but they found it
shut and made fast against them. Whereupon the
body of the army marched forward towards a pass or
ford called the Gué de Véde, except seven companies
of foot, and two hundred lancers, who, staying there,
broke down the walls of the close, to waste, spoil and
make havoc of all the vines and vintage within that
place. The monks (poor devils) knew not in that
extremity to which of all their sancts they should
vow themselves. Nevertheless, at all adventures,
they rang the bells *ad capitulum capitulantes.*[1] There

---

[1] *Ad capitulum capitulantes.*—All such as had a vote in the

it was decreed, but they should make a fair procession, stuffed with good lectures, prayers, and litanies *contra hostium insidias*, and jolly responses *pro pace*.[2]

There was then in the abbey a claustral monk, called Friar John of the funnels and gobbets, in French, des Entommeures, young, gallant, frisk, lusty, nimble, quick, active, bold, adventurous, resolute, tall, lean, wide-mouthed, long-nosed, a fair despatcher of morning prayers, unbridler of masses, and runner over vigils; and, to conclude summarily in a word, a right monk, if ever there was any, since the monking world monked a monkery: for the rest, a clerk even to the teeth[3] in matter of breviary. This monk, hearing the noise that the enemy made within the inclosure of the vineyard, went out to see what they were doing; and perceiving that they were cutting and gathering the grapes, whereon was grounded the foundation of all their next year's wine, returned unto the quire of the church where the other monks were, all amazed and astonished like so many bell-melters. Whom when he heard sing, im,[4] im, pe, ne, ne, ne, ne, nene, tum, ne num, num, ini, i mi, co, o, no, o, o, neno, ne, no, no, no, rum, nenum, num: It is well shit, well sung, said he. By the virtue of God, why do not you sing, Panniers farewell,

chaper. This is come by ringing a certain little bell. Neither the service nor converts are at all concerned to meet at this call.

[2] *Responses, etc.*—Prayers of the gradual. Part of the mass reviewed by Pope Celestine, A. 1770.

[3] *Clerk even to the teeth.*—A proverbial expression, used in speaking of a debauched priest or monk, who has, as it were, devoured his mass-book; well-read in his porringer; as excellent clerk as a cook's clog.

[4] *Im, etc.*—Read it thus, for so Rabelais writ it, Im, im, pe, e, ne, ne, tum, tum, in, i, ni, i, mi, co, e, o, o, o, o, rum, tum. These syllables belong to an anthem, or some response, and they form the words impetum inimicorum, of which they represent the plain song.

vintage is done? The devil snatch me, if they be
not already within the middle of our close, and cut
so well both vines and grapes that, by God's body,
there will not be found for these four years to come
so much as a gleaning in it. By the belly of Sanct
James, what shall we poor devils drink the while?
Lord God! da mihi potum. Then said the prior of
the convent;—What should this drunken fellow do
here? let him be carried to prison for troubling the
divine service. Nay, said the monk, the wine
service, let us behave ourselves so, that it be not
troubled; for you, yourself, my lord prior, love to
drink of the best, and so doth every honest man.
Never yet did a man of worth dislike good wine, it
is a monastical apophthegm. But these responses
that you chant here, by God, are not in season.
Wherefore is it, that our devotions were instituted
to be short in the time of harvest and vintage, and
long in the advent and all the winter? The late
friar, Macé Pelosse, of good memory, a true zealous
man (or else I give myself to the devil), of our
religion, told me, and I remember it well, how the
reason was, that in this season we might press and
make the wine, and in winter whiff it up. Hark
you, my masters, you that love the wine, Cop's body,
follow me; for Sanct Anthony burn me as freely as
a faggot, if they get leave to taste one drop of the
liquor, that will not now come and fight for relief of
the vine. Hog's belly, the goods of the church!
Ha, no, no. What the devil [5] Sanct Thomas of
England was well content to die for them; if I died
in the same cause, should not I be a sanct likewise?
Yes. Yet shall not I die there for all this, for it is

[5] *What the devil, etc.*—Read, *Oons,* St. Thomas of England
would gladly have laid down his life for them. He means
Thomas à Becket.

I that must do it to others and send them a pack-
ing.

As he spake this, he threw off his great monk's
habit, and laid hold upon the staff of the cross,
which was made of the heart of a sorb-apple tree, it
being of the length of a lance, round, of a full gripe,
and a little powdered with lilies called flower de
luce,[6] the workmanship whereof was almost all
defaced and worn out. Thus went he out in a
fair long-skirted jacket, putting his frock scarfwise
athwart his breast, and in this equipage, with his
staff, shaft, or truncheon of the cross, laid on so
lustily, brisk, and fiercely upon his enemies, who
without any order, or ensign, or trumpet, or drum,
were busied in gathering the grapes of the vineyard.
For the cornets, guidons, and ensign-bearers had
laid down their standards, banners, and colours by
the wallsides: the drummers had knocked out the
heads of their drums on one end, to fill them with
grapes: the trumpeters were loaded with great
bundles of bunches, and huge knots of clusters: in
sum, every one of them was out of array, and all in
disorder. He hurried, therefore, upon them so
rudely, without crying gare or beware, that he
overthrew them like hogs, tumbled them over like
swine, striking athwart and alongst, and by one
means or other laid so about him, after the old
fashion of fencing, that to some he beat out their

[6] *Flower-de-luces almost all defaced.*—Many will have the moral
sense of the words, and of this action of Friar John to be, that
the Kings of France having thought fit to give, in their kingdom, a
very great authority to ecclesiastics, these latter have often made
use of it to oppress their enemies, without taking any, or very
little notice of the power and sovereignty of their benefactors.
But might there not be some other mystery in what Rabelais
adds, that Friar John's staff was of the sorb-apple tree, the
hardest of all woods ?

brains, to others he crushed their arms, battered
their legs, and bethwacked their sides till their
ribs cracked with it. To others again he unjointed
the spondyles or knuckles of the neck, disfigured
their chaps, gashed their faces, made their cheeks
hang flapping on their chin, and so swinged and
belammed them, that they fell down before him
like hay before a mower. To some others he
spoiled the frame of their kidneys, marred their
backs, broke their thigh-bones, pushed in their noses,
poached out their eyes, cleft their mandibules, tore
their jaws, dashed in their teeth into their throat,
shook asunder their omoplates or shoulder blades,
sphacelated their shins, mortified their shanks, in-
flamed their ankles, heaved-off-of-the-hinges their
ishies, their sciatica or hip-gout,[7] dislocated the joints
of their knees, squattered into pieces the boughts or
pestles of their thighs, and so thumped, mauled and
belaboured them everywhere, that never was corn so
thick and threefold thrashed upon by ploughmen's
flails, as were the pitifully disjoined members of
their mangled bodies, under the merciless baton of
the cross. If any offered to hide himself amongst
the thickest of the vines, he laid him squat as a
flounder, bruised the ridge of his back, and dashed
his reins like a dog. If any thought by flight to
escape, he made his head to fly in pieces by the
lambdoidal commissure, which is a seam in the
hinder part of the skull. If anyone did scramble up

[7] *Heaved-off-of-the-hinges their ishies, their sciatica or hip-gout.*—
It is *desgoudoit les ischies*, heaved off the hinges, the huckle-bones;
for I take ischies to be ischia, the plural of ischium, the huckle-
bone, the hip. Sir T. U. finding in Cotgrave that Rabelais'
word ischie means the sciatica or hip-gout, sets it down so without considering the absurdity of such a construction, or the
erroneousness of Cotgrave in that respect. *Ischias* is indeed the
hip-gout, but not *ischium*.

into a tree, thinking there to be safe, he rent up his
perineum and impaled him in at the fundament.
If any of his old acquaintance happened to cry out,
Ha, Friar John, my friend, Friar John, quarter,
quarter, I yield myself to you, to you I render
myself! So thou shalt, said he, and must, whether
thou wouldst or no, and withal render and yield up
thy soul to all the devils in hell, then suddenly gave
them *dronos*, that is, so many knocks, thumps, raps,
dints, thwacks and bangs, as sufficed to warn Pluto
of their coming, and despatch them a going. If any
was so rash and full of temerity as to resist him to
his face, then was it he did show the strength of his
muscles, for without more ado he did transpierce
him, by running him in at the breast, through the
mediastine and the heart. Others, again, he so
quashed and bebumped, that, with a sound bounce
under the hollow of their short ribs, he overturned
their stomachs so that they died immediately. To
some, with a smart souse on the epigaster, he would
make their midriff swag, then, redoubling the blow,
gave them such a home-push on the navel, that he
made their puddings to gush out. To others through
their ballocks he pierced their bum-gut, and left not
bowel, tripe, nor entrail in their body, that had not
felt the impetuosity, fierceness, and fury of his
violence. Believe, that it was the most horrible
spectacle that ever one saw. Some cried unto Sanct
Barbe, others to St George. O the holy Lady
Nytouch, said one, the good Sanctess! O our
Lady of Succours, said another, help, help! Others
cried, Our Lady of Cunaut,[8] of Loretto, of Good
Tidings,[9] on the other side of the water St Mary

---

[8] *Cunaut.*—A fat priory in Anjou.
[9] *Good tidings.*—A royal abbey near Orleans.

Over.[10] Some vowed a pilgrimage to St James, and others to the holy handkerchief at Chamberry, which three months after that burnt so well in the fire, that they could not get one thread of it saved. Others sent up their vows to St Cadouin,[11] others to St John d'Angly, and to St Eutropius of Xaintes. Others again invoked St Mesmes of Chinon, St Martin of Candes, St Clouaud of Sinays, the holy relics of Laurezay, with a thousand other jolly little saints and saintrels. Some died without speaking, others spoke without dying; some died in speaking, others spoke in dying. Others shouted as loud as they could, Confession, Confession! Confiteor! Miserere! In manus! So great was the cry of the wounded, that the Prior of the Abbey with all his monks came forth, who, when they saw these poor wretches so slain amongst the vines, and wounded to death, confessed some of them. But whilst the priests were busied in confessing them, the little monkitos ran all to the place where Friar John was, and asked him, wherein he would be pleased to require their assistance! To which he answered, that they should cut the throats of those he had thrown down upon the ground. They presently, leaving their outer habits and cowls upon the rails, began to throttle and make an end of those whom he had already crushed. Can you tell with what instruments they did it? With fair gullies,[12]

[10] On the other side of the water St Mary Over.—Read, by our Lady Lenou, of Riviere. The first whereof is a parish of Touraine, between Chinon and Richelieu. The other not far from it.

[11] Others sent up their vows to St Cadouin.—See all these explained at large in M. le Duchat's notes.

[12] Gullies.—Goucts, a little cut-purse knife. [The Scotch call the large knives with which the Highlanders were armed during 'the '45,' gullies. The rebel troops were accused of practices very similar to those described above.]

214

which are little haulch-backed demi-knives, the iron
tool whereof is two inches long, and the wooden
handle one inch thick, and three inches in length,
wherewith the little boys in our country cut
ripe walnuts ·in two, while they are yet in the
shell, and pick out the kernel, and they found them
very fit for the expediting of wezand-slitting exploits.
In the meantime Friar John, with his formidable
baton of the cross, got to the breach which the
enemies had made, and there stood to snatch up
those that endeavoured to escape.　Some of the
monkitos carried the standards, banners, ensigns,
guidons, and colours into their cells and chambers,
to make garters of them.　But when those that had
been shriven would have gone out at the gap of the
said breach, the sturdy monk quashed and felled
them down with blows, saying, These men have had
confession and are penitent souls, they have got
their absolution and gained the pardons: they go
into paradise as straight as a sickle, or as the way is
to Faye,[13] (like Crooked-lane at Eastcheap).　Thus
by his prowess and valour were discomfited all those
of the army that entered into the close of the abbey
unto the number of thirteen thousand six hundred
twenty and two, besides the women and little
children, which is always to be understood.　Never
did Maugis the Hermit bear himself more valiantly
with his bourdon or pilgrim's staff against the
Saracens, of whom is written in the Acts of the
four sons of Haymon, than did this monk against his
enemies with the staff of the cross.[14]

[13] *The way to Faye.*—*Faie-la-vineuse*, a little village situated on
so steep an eminence, that there is no getting at it but by winding
round the mountain.
[14] *Maugis the Hermit.*—Cousin to the four sons of Aymon.　In
this ludicrous account of the exploits of Friar John, Rabelais

Rabelais' Works [Book i.

CHAPTER XXVIII

HOW PICROCHOLE STORMED AND TOOK BY ASSAULT
THE ROCK CLERMOND, AND OF GRANGOUSIER'S
UNWILLINGNESS AND AVERSION FROM THE UNDER-
TAKING OF WAR

WHILST the monk did thus skirmish, as we have said,
against those which were entered within the close,
Picrochole in great haste passed the ford of Védé,—
a very especial pass,—with all his soldiery, and set
upon the rock Clermond, where there was made him
no resistance at all: and, because it was already
night, he resolved to quarter himself and his army
in that town, and to refresh himself of his pugnative
choler.[1] In the morning he stormed and took the
bulwarks and castle, which afterwards he fortified
with rampiers, and furnished with all ammunition
requisite, intending to make his retreat there, if he
should happen to be otherwise worsted; for it was a
strong place, both by art and nature, in regard of the
stance and situation of it. But let us leave them
there, and return to our good Gargantua, who is at
Paris very assiduous and earnest at the study of good

designed to ridicule the grave and circumstantial narrations given
in the writings of Trouvères, of the prodigious slaughter of giants
and misbelieving Paynims, achieved by the Knights and Paladins
of Arthur and Charlemagne, in their innumerable adventures, and
effected by an astonishing anatomical variety of wounds, all of
which are faithfully detailed in these romances, so popular during
the middle ages.
  [1] *Pugnative choler.*—It should be *pungitive*, as being not only so
in the best editions of Rabelais, but a word often used by the
physicians of the lower ages in the sense of 'pungendi vim
habens.'

216

letters, and athletical exercitations, and to the good
old man Grangousier his father, who after supper
warmeth his ballocks by a good, clear, great fire, and,
waiting upon the broiling of some chestnuts, is very
serious in drawing scratches on the hearth, with a
stick burnt at the one end, wherewith they did stir
up the fire, telling to his wife and the rest of the
family pleasant old stories and tales of former times.
    Whilst he was thus employed, one of the shepherds
which did keep the vines, named Pillot, came
towards him, and to the full related the enormous
abuses which were committed, and the excessive
spoil that was made by Picrochole, King of Lerné,
upon his lands and territories, and how he had
pillaged, wasted, and ransacked all the country, except the inclosure at Sevillé, which Friar John des
Entonneures, to his great honour, had preserved;
and that at the same present time the said king was
in the rock Clermond, and there, with great industry
and circumspection, was strengthening himself and
his whole army. Halas! Halas! Alas! said Grangousier, what is this, good people? Do I dream, or
is it true that they tell me? Picrochole, my ancient
friend of old time, of my own kindred and alliance,
comes he to invade me? What moves him? What
provokes him? What sets him on? What drives
him to it? Who hath given him this counsel?
Ho, ho, ho, ho, ho! my God, my Saviour, help me,
inspire me, and advise me what I shall do! I
protest, I swear before thee, so be thou favourable to
me, if ever I did him or his subjects any damage or
displeasure, or committed any the least robbery in
his country; but, on the contrary, I have succoured
and supplied him with men, money, friendship, and
counsel, upon any occasion, wherein I could be
steadable for the improvement of his good. That

he hath therefore at this nick of time so outraged
and wronged me, it cannot be but by the malevolent
and wicked spirit. Good God, thou knowest my
courage, for nothing can be hidden from thee! If
perhaps he be grown mad, and that thou hast sent
him hither to me for the better recovery and re-
establishment of his brain, grant me power and
wisdom to bring him to the yoke of thy holy will by
good discipline. Ho, ho, ho, ho! my good people,
my friends, and my faithful servants, must I hinder
you from helping me? Alas, my old age required
henceforward nothing else but rest, and all the days
of my life I have laboured for nothing so much as
peace;[2] but now I must, I see it well, load with
arms my poor, weary and feeble shoulders, and take
in my trembling hand the lance and horseman's
mace, to succour and protect my honest subjects.
Reason will have it so; for by their labour am I
entertained, and with their sweat am I nourished, I,
my children and my family. This notwithstanding,
I will not undertake war, until I have first tried all
the ways and means of peace: that I resolve upon.

Then assembled he his council, and proposed the
matter as it was indeed. Whereupon it was concluded, that they should send some discreet man
unto Picrochole, to know wherefore he had thus
suddenly broken the peace, and invaded those lands
unto which he had no right nor title. Furthermore,
that they should send for Gargantua, and those under
his command, for the preservation of the country,

---

[2] *And all the days of my life I have laboured for nothing so much
as peace.*—A true picture of the good King Louis XII., of whom
Mezeray says, that he had so great an aversion to war, lest his
subjects should suffer by it, that he rather chose to lose his duchy
of Milan, than seek to recover it by a war, which he could not
carry on without loading his subjects with new taxes.

and defence thereof now at need. All this pleased
Grangousier very well, and he commanded that so it
should be done. Presently therefore he sent Basque
his lackey, to fetch Gargantua with all diligence, and
wrote to him as followeth.

CHAPTER XXIX

THE TENOR OF THE LETTER WHICH GRANGOUSIER
WROTE TO HIS SON GARGANTUA

THE fervency of thy studies did require, that I
should not in a long time recall thee from that
philosophical rest thou now enjoyest, if the confidence reposed in our friends and ancient confederates had not at this present disappointed the
assurance of my old age. But seeing such is my
fatal destiny, that I should be now disquieted by
those in whom I trusted most, I am forced to call
thee back to help the people and goods, which by
the right of nature belong unto thee. For even as
arms are weak abroad, if there be not counsel at
home, so is that study vain, and counsel unprofitable,
which in a due and convenient time is not by virtue
executed and put in effect. My deliberation is not
to provoke, but to appease—not to assault, but to
defend—not to conquer, but to preserve my faithful
subjects and hereditary dominions, into which Picrochole is entered in a hostile manner without any
ground or cause, and from day to day pursueth his
furious enterprise with that height of insolence that
is intolerable to free-born spirits. I have endeavoured
to moderate his tyrannical choler, offering him all
that which I thought might give him satisfaction;

and oftentimes have I sent lovingly unto him, to understand wherein, by whom, and how he found himself to be wronged. But of him could I obtain no other answer, but a mere defiance, and that in my lands he did pretend only to the right of a civil correspondency and good behaviour,[1] whereby I knew that the eternal God hath left him to the disposure of his own free will and sensual appetite—which cannot choose but be wicked, if by divine grace it be not continually guided—and to contain him within his duty, and to bring him to know himself, hath sent him hither to me by a grievous token. Therefore, my beloved son, as soon as thou canst, upon sight of these letters, repair hither with all diligence, to succour not me so much, which nevertheless by natural piety thou oughtest to do, as thine own people, which by reason thou mayest save and preserve. The exploit shall be done with as little effusion of blood as may be. And, if possible, by means far more expedient, such as military policy, devices and stratagems of war, we shall save all the souls, and send them home as merry as crickets unto their own houses. My dearest son, the peace of Jesus Christ our Redeemer be with thee. Salute from me Ponocrates, Gymnastes, and Eudemon. The twentieth of September.

Thy Father Grangousier.

---

[1] *And that in my lands he did pretend only to the right of a civil correspondency and good behaviour.*—Instead of all which, read, And that my lands lay fit for him; for that is the meaning of the word bienseante. Old Louis XIV. used that very word in one of his declarations of war against the Dutch, That Flanders, etc., stood convenient for him, and assigned no other reason for attacking them.

CHAPTER XXX

HOW ULRICH GALLET WAS SENT UNTO PICROCHOLE

THE letters being dictated, signed, and sealed, Grangousier ordained that Ulrich Gallet,[1] Master of the
Requests, a very wise and discreet man, of whose
prudence and sound judgment he had made trial in
several difficult and debateful matters, [should] go
unto Picrochole, to show what had been decreed
amongst them. At the same hour departed the
good man Gallet, and, having passed the ford, asked
at the miller that dwelt there, in what condition
Picrochole was : who answered him, that his soldiers
had left neither cock nor hen, that they were retired[2]
and shut up into the rock Clermond, and that he
would not advise him to go any further for fear of
the scouts, because they were enormously furious.
Which he easily believed, and therefore lodged that
night with the miller.

The next morning he went with a trumpeter to
the gate of the castle, and required of the guards he
might be admitted to speak with the king of somewhat that concerned him. These words being told
unto the king, he would by no means consent that
they should open the gate; but, getting upon the

---

[1] *Ulrich Gallet.*—Menage, under the word Gallet, says, It is
not long since there was at Chinon a family of that name.
Gallet, the gamester, who built at Paris the Hôtel de Sulli, was
of this family, and Ulrich, or Hurly Gallet, Master of Requests
to Grangousier, was so too, as we are informed by Menage, who
had it from Gallet, the gamester's own mouth.

[2] *Retired, etc.*—Read, They had taken up their quarters in La
Roche-Clermauld. (It is a parish within the territory of
Chinon.)

top of the bulwark, said unto the ambassador, What
is the news, what have you to say ? Then the ambassador began to speak as followeth.

CHAPTER XXXI

THE SPEECH MADE BY GALLET TO PICROCHOLE

THERE cannot arise amongst men a juster cause of
grief, than when they receive hurt and damage,
where they may justly expect for favour and good
will; and not without cause, though without reason,
have many, after they had fallen into such a cala-
mitous accident, esteemed this indignity less support-
able than the loss of their own lives, in such sort,
that, if they have not been able by force of arms,
nor any other means, by reach of wit or subtility, to
correct it, they have fallen into desperation, and
utterly deprived themselves of this light. It is
therefore no wonder if King Grangousier, my master,
be full of high displeasure, and much disquieted in
mind upon thy outrageous and hostile coming : but
truly it would be a marvel, if he were not sensible
of, and moved with the incomparable abuses and
injuries perpetrated by thee and thine upon those
of his country, towards whom there hath been no
example of inhumanity omitted. Which in itself is
to him so grievous, for the cordial affection wherewith he hath always cherished his subjects, that
more it cannot be to any mortal man; yet in this,
above human apprehension, is it to him the more
grievous, that these wrongs and sad offences hath
been committed by thee and thine, who, time out of
mind, from all antiquity, thou and thy predecessors,

have been in a continual league and amity with him,
and all his ancestors; which, even until this time,
you have, as sacred, together inviolably preserved,
kept, and entertained, so well that not he and his
only, but the very barbarous nations of the Poic-
tevins, Bretons, Manceaux, and those that dwell
beyond the isles of the Canaries, and that of Isabella,
have thought it as easy to pull down the firmament,
and to set up the depths above the clouds, as to
make a breach in your alliance ; and have been so
afraid of it in their enterprises, that they have never
dared to provoke, incense, or indamage the one for
fear of the other.   Nay, which is more, this sacred
league hath so filled the world, that there are few
nations at this day inhabiting throughout all the
continent and isles of the ocean, who have not
ambitiously aspired to be received into it, upon your
own covenants and conditions, holding your joint
confederacy in as high esteem as their own territories
and dominions, in such sort, that from the memory
of man, there hath not been either prince or league
so wild and proud, that durst have offered to invade,
I say not your countries, but not so much as those
of your confederates.   And if, by rash and heady
counsel, they have attempted any new design against
them, as soon as they heard the name and title of
your alliance, they have suddenly desisted from their
enterprises.   What rage and madness, therefore, doth
now incite thee, all old alliance infringed, all amity
trod under foot, and all right violated, thus in a
hostile manner to invade his country, without having
been by him or his in any thing prejudiced, wronged,
or provoked.   Where is faith ?   Where is law ?
Where is reason ?   Where is humanity ?   Where
is the fear of God ?   Dost thou think that these
atrocious abuses are hidden from the Eternal Spirit,

and the supreme God, who is the just rewarder of all
our undertakings? If thou so think, thou deceivest
thyself; for all things shall come to pass, as in his
incomprehensible judgment he hath appointed. Is
it thy fatal destiny, or influences of the stars, that
would put an end to thy so long enjoyed ease and
rest? For that all things have their end and period,
so as that when they are come to the superlative
point of their greatest height, they are in a trice
tumbled down again, as not being able to abide long
in that state. This is the conclusion and end of
those who cannot by reason and temperance moderate
their fortunes and prosperities. But if it be pre-
destinated that thy happiness and ease must now
come to an end, must it needs be by wronging my
king—him by whom thou wert established? If thy
house must come to ruin, should it therefore in its
fall crush the heels of him that set it up? The
matter is so unreasonable, and so dissonant from
common sense, that hardly can it be conceived by
human understanding, and [it will remain] altogether
incredible unto strangers till by the certain and un-
doubted effects thereof it be made apparent, that
nothing is either sacred or holy to those, who having
emancipated themselves from God and reason, do
merely follow the perverse affections of their own
depraved nature. If any wrong had been done by
us to thy subjects and dominions—if we had favoured
thy ill-willers—if we had not assisted thee in thy
need—if thy name and reputation had been wounded
by us—or, to speak more truly, if the calumniating
spirit, tempting to induce thee to evil, had, by false
illusions and deceitful fantasies, put into thy conceit
the impression of a thought, that we had done unto
thee any thing unworthy of our ancient correspondence and friendship, thou oughtest first to have

inquired out the truth, and afterwards by a season-
able warning to admonish us thereof ; and we should
have so satisfied thee, according to thine own heart's
desire, that thou shouldest have had occasion to be
contented. But, O eternal God, what is thy enterprise ? Wouldest thou, like a perfidious tyrant, thus
spoil and lay waste my master's kingdom ? Hast
thou found him so silly and blockish, that he would
not, or so destitute of men and money, of counsel
and skill in military discipline, that he cannot with-
stand thy unjust invasion ? March hence presently,
and to-morrow, some time of the day, retreat into
thine own country, without doing any kind of violence or disorderly act by the way ; and pay withal
a thousand besants of gold [1] (which, in English
money, amounted to five thousand pounds), for reparation of the damages thou hast done in his
country. Half thou shalt pay to-morrow, and the
other half at the ides of May next coming, leaving
with us in the meantime, for hostages, the Dukes of
Turnbank, Lowbuttock and Smalltrash, together with
the Prince of Itches (Scrubbado), and Viscount of
Snatchbit.[2]

[1] *And pay withal a thousand besants of gold.*—Ulrich Gallet
maintains his master's dignity, by imposing this sum on
Picrochole; at the same time as he offers him peace. The
besant was an ancient piece of money, coined at Constantinople
(Byzantium).

[2] *Prince of Scrubbado and Viscount Snatchbit.*—Names fitted to
the uneasy troublesome humour of these two men, whom Ulrich
Gallet insists upon having for hostages that he might put them
out of a condition to influence their master to disturb the repose
of his neighbours.

CHAPTER XXXII

HOW GRANGOUSIER, TO BUY PEACE, CAUSED THE CAKES
TO BE RESTORED

WITH that the good man Gallet held his peace, but
Picrochole to all his discourse answered nothing but,
'Come and fetch them; come and.fetch them; they
have [1] ballocks fair and soft; they will knead and
provide some cakes for you.' Then returned he to
Grangousier, whom he found upon his knees, bare-
headed, crouching in a little corner of his cabinet,
and humbly praying unto God, that he would vouchsafe to assuage the choler of Picrochole, and bring
him to the rule of reason without proceeding by
force. When the good man came back, he asked
him, Ha, my friend, my friend, what news do you
bring me? There is neither hope nor remedy, said
Gallet : the man is quite out of his wits, and forsaken of God. Yea, but, said Grangousier, my
friend, what cause doth he pretend for his outrages?
He did not show me any cause at all, said Gallet,
only that in a great anger he spoke some words of
cakes. I cannot tell, if they have done any wrong
to his cake-bakers. I will know, said Grangousier,
the matter thoroughly, before I resolve any more
upon what is to be done. Then sent he to learn
concerning that business, and found by true information, that his men had taken violently some
cakes from Picrochole's people, and that Marquet's
head was broken with a slacky or short cudgel : that,
nevertheless, all was well paid, and that the said

They have, etc.—'Ils ont belle couille et moulle.' A Poitevin
expression for, You will see whether they are cullions (cowards
in one sense) or no.

226

Marquet had first hurt Forgier with a stroke of his whip athwart the legs. And it seemed good to his whole council, that he should defend himself with all his might. Notwithstanding all this, said Grangousier, seeing the question is but about a few cakes, I will labour to content him; for I am very unwilling to wage war against him. He inquired then what quantity of cakes they had taken away, and understanding, that it was but some four or five dozen, he commanded five cart-loads of them to be baked that same night; and that there should be one full of cakes made with fine butter, fine yolks of eggs, fine saffron, and fine spice, to be bestowed upon Marquet, unto whom likewise he directed to be given seven hundred thousand and three Philips [2] (that is, at three shillings the piece, one hundred and five thousand pounds, nine shillings of English money), for reparation of his losses and hindrances, and for satisfaction of the chirurgeon that had dressed his wound; and furthermore settled upon him and his for ever in freehold, the apple orchard [3] called La Pomardiere. For the conveyance and passing of all which was sent Gallet, who by the way as they went, made them gather near the willow-trees, great store of boughs, canes, and reeds, wherewith all the carriers were enjoined to garnish and deck their carts, and each of them to carry one in his hand, as himself likewise did, thereby to give all men to understand, that they demanded but peace, and that they came to buy it.

Being come to the gate, they required to speak with Picrochole from Grangousier. Picrochole

<hr />

[2] *Philips.*—A coin so called from King Philip, of the house of Valois.

[3] *Apple Orchard, etc., La Mestairie, etc.*—The farm de la Pomardiere. The apple farm if you will.

would not so much as let them in, nor go to
speak with them, but sent them word that he was
busy, and that they should deliver their mind to
Captain Touquedillon, who was then planting a
piece of ordnance upon the wall. Then said the
good man unto him, My Lord, to ease you of all
this labour, and to take away all excuses why you
may not return unto our former alliance, we do here
presently restore unto you the cakes upon which the
quarrel arose. Five dozen did our people take away :
they were well paid for : we love peace so well that
we restore unto you five cart-loads, of which this cart
shall be for Marquet, who doth most complain.
Besides, to content him entirely, here are seven
hundred thousand and three Philips, which I deliver
to him, and, for the losses he may pretend to have
sustained, I resign for ever the farm of the Pomardiere, to be possessed in fee-simple by him and
his, for ever, without the payment of any duty, or
acknowledgment of homage, fealty, fine, or service
whatsoever, and here is the tenor of the deed. And,
for God's sake, let us live henceforward in peace,
and withdraw yourselves merrily into your own
country from within this place, unto which you have
no right at all, as yourselves must needs confess, and
let us be good friends as before. Touquedillon
related all this to Picrochole, and more and more
exasperated his courage, saying to him : These
clowns are afraid to some purpose. By God, Grangousier conskites himself for fear, the poor drinker.
He is not skilled in warfare, nor hath he any stomach
for it. He knows better how to empty the flagons
—that is his art. I am of opinion, that it is fit we
send back [4] the carts and the money, and for the

---

[4] *We send back.*—No, it should be *retain*, and not *send back* the

rest, that very speedily we fortify ourselves here, then prosecute our fortune. But what! Do they think to have to do with a ninny-whoop, to feed you thus with cakes? You may see what it is. The good usage, and great familiarity which you have had with them heretofore, hath made you contemptible in their eyes. Ungenton purget pungentom rustius unget.[5]

Ça, ça, ça, said Picrochole, by St James you have given a true character of them. One thing I will advise you, said Touquedillon. We are here but badly victualled, and furnished with mouth-harness very slenderly. If Grangousier should come to besiege us I would go presently, and pluck out of all your soldiers' heads and mine own all the teeth, except three to each of us, and with them alone we should make an end of our provision but too soon. We shall have, said Picrochole, but too much sustenance and feeding stuff. Came we hither to eat or to fight? To fight, indeed, said Touquedillon; yet from the paunch comes the dance, and where famine rules, force is exiled. Leave off your prating, said Picrochole, and forthwith seize upon what

carts and money; *retenons*, not *retournons*. And, indeed, it appears presently, they kept the carts and money.

[5] *Ungenton, etc.*—Rabelais' words are only—Oignez vilain, il vous poindra. Poignez vilain, il vous oindra.

In plain English—
A base, unthankful, clownish brood
Return bad offices for good;
But use them ill, they're the reverse,
And would be glad to kiss your arse.

As for the Ungenton purget purgentom rustius unget, Sir T. U. spells it wrong on purpose, to ridicule the speaker. The true reading should be—

Ungentem pungit, pungentum rusticus ungit.

they have brought. Then took they money and cakes, oxen and carts, and sent them away without speaking one word, only that they would come no more so near, for a reason that they would give them the morrow after. Thus without doing anything returned they to Grangousier, and related the whole matter unto him, subjoining that there was no hope left to draw them to peace, but by sharp and fierce wars.

CHAPTER XXXIII

HOW SOME STATESMEN OF PICROCHOLE, BY HAIRBRAINED COUNSEL, PUT HIM IN EXTREME DANGER

THE carts being unloaded, and the money and cakes secured, there came before Picrochole the Duke of Smalltrash, the Earl of Swashbuckler, and Captain Durtaille, who said unto him, Sir,[1] this day we make you the happiest, the most warlike and chivalrous prince that ever was, since the death of Alexander of Macedonia. Be covered, be covered, said Picrochole. Grammercie, said they, we do but our duty. The manner is thus. You shall leave some captain here to have the charge of this garrison, with a party competent for keeping of the place, which, besides its natural strength, is made stronger by the rampiers and fortresses of your devising. Your army you are to divide into two parts, as you know very well how to do. One part thereof shall fall upon Grangousier and his forces. By it shall he be easily at the very first shock routed, and then shall you get money by

___
[1] *Sir.*—Rabelais has it Cyre, because he derives it from Κύριος, Dominus. Sire comes from Senior.

heaps, for the clown hath store of ready coin. Clown we call him, because a noble and generous prince hath never a penny,[2] and that to hoard up treasure is but a clownish trick. The other part of the army in the meantime shall draw towards Onys, Xaintonge, Angoumois and Gascony. Then march to Perigourt, Medos, and Elanes,[3] taking wherever you come, without resistance, towns, castles, and forts : afterwards to Bayonne, St John de Luz, to Fuentarabia, where you shall seize upon all the ships, and coasting along Gallicia and Portugal, shall pillage all the maritime places, even unto Lisbon, where you shall be supplied with all necessaries befitting a conqueror. By copsodie, Spain will yield, for they are but a race of loobies. Then are you to pass by the Straits of Gibraltar, where you shall erect two pillars more stately than those of Hercules, to the perpetual

[2] *A noble and generous prince hath never a penny.*—There is an old French proverb:

> Un noble prince, un gentil roy,
> N'a jamais ne pile, ne croix.
> A gallant monarch never rich is,
> Nor cross, nor pile, has in his breeches.

Yet there is a remedy for this, though there is none against death nor taxes. The French say, 'Que je sois officier, au moins d'un moulin.' Let me be an officer though it be but of a mill. Make the king an officer (a placeman), and he will soon grow rich; quoth an old preacher in our Edward VI.'s time.

Before I dismiss this article, I would know why, in a piece of money, the opposite side to the cross is called the pile side. Cotgrave says the under-iron of the stamp, wherein money is stamped, is called pile. If so, I am satisfied; if not, I must go further a-field.

[*Cross-and-pile*, a term derived from the money of the second race of the French kings, on the reverse of which was a peristyle (or columns, called *pilæ*), vid. Ducange s. v. *crux*.]

[3] *Medos and Elanes.*—Read Medoc and les Landes. See further in Duchat.

memory of your name, and the narrow entrance there shall be called the Picrocholinal sea.

Having passed the Picrocholinal sea, behold, Barbarossa yields himself your slave. I will, said Picrochole, give him fair quarter and spare his life. Yea, said they, so that he be content to be christened.[4] And you shall conquer the kingdoms of Tunis, of Hippo,[5] Argier, Bomine,[6] Corone,[7] yea all Barbary. Furthermore, you shall take into your hands Majorca, Minorca, Sardinia, Corsica, with the other islands of the Ligustic and Balearian seas. Going along on the left hand, you shall rule all Gallia Narbonensis, Provence, the Allobrogians, Genua, Florence, Lucca, and then God b'w'ye Rome. [Our poor Monsieur the Pope dies now for fear.] By my faith, said Picrochole, I will not then kiss his pantofle.

Italy being thus taken, behold Naples, Calabria, Apulia, and Sicily all ransacked, and Malta too. I wish the pleasant knights heretofore of Rhodes would but come to resist you, that we might see their urine. I would, said Picrochole, very willingly go to Loretto. No, no, said they, that shall be at our return. From thence we will sail eastwards and take Candia, Cyprus, Rhodes, and the Cyclade Islands, and set

---

[4] *So that he be content to be christened.*—In imitation of the worthies and champions of old time, who are represented in the romances as never giving quarter to a Saracen, before he promised to be baptised.

[5] *Hippo.*—The Hippo-Diarrythus of the ancients, now Biserta.

[6] *Bomine.*—Read Bona; it is the Hippo-Regius of the ancients (whence Silius 'delectus Regibus Hippon') here St Austin was born: a strong city under the government of Algiers. This and the preceding are both on the sea-coast. Both the Hippos are here called kingdoms, because Strabo, l. 17, speaking of them, says ἄμφω βασιλεία.

[7] *Corone.*—It is the ancient Cyrene; its modern name is Corene. Rabelais has preferred Corone, a name of the same signification, and moreover peculiar to our old romances.

upon the Morea. It is ours, by St Trenian.[8] The
Lord preserve Jerusalem; for the great Soldan is not
comparable to you in power. I will then, said he,
cause Solomon's Temple to be built. No, said they,
not yet, have a little patience, stay a while, be never
too sudden in your enterprises. Can you tell what
Octavian Augustus said? Festina lentè. It is requisite that you first have the Lesser Asia, Caria,
Lycia, Pamphylia, Cilicia, Lydia, Phrygia, Mysia,
Bithynia, Carazia, Satalia, Samagaria, Castamena,
Luga, Savasta, even unto Euphrates.[9] Shall we see,
said Picrochole, Babylon and Mount Sinai? There
is no need, said they, at this time. Have we not
hurried up and down, travelled and toiled enough, in
having transfreted and past over the Hircanian sea,
marched along the two Armenias, and the three
Arabias? Ay, by my faith, said he, we have played
the fools, and are undone. Ha, poor souls ! What's
the matter? said they. What shall we have, said he,
to drink in these deserts? For Julian Augustus with
his whole army died there for thirst, as they say.
We have already, said they, given order for that. In
the Syriac sea you have nine thousand and fourteen
great ships laden with the best wines in the world.
They arrived at Port Joppa. There they found two
and twenty thousand camels, and sixteen hundred
elephants, which you shall have taken at one hunting
about Sigelmes, when you entered into Lybia; and,

----

[8] *St Trenian.*—He is called by Bede, Ninias; by the succeeding
writers, Ninianus, from whence corruptly Trignan and Trenian.
He was the first preacher of Christianity in Scotland, where he
was Bishop of Whithern, in Latin, Candida Casa, which many
call by the saint's name. He died there 16 Sept. 432.

[9] *Bithynia, etc.*—On this M. le Duchat says, that Rabelais, to
render Picrochole's ministers more ridiculous, designedly makes
them speak like ignoramuses in geography, who take the different
names of one and the same place for so many different places.

besides this, you had all the Mecca caravan. Did
not they furnish you sufficiently with wine? Yes,
but, said he, we did not drink it fresh. By the virtue,
said they, not of a fish, a valiant man, a conqueror,
who pretends and aspires to the monarchy of the
world, cannot always have his ease. God be thanked,
that you and your men are come safe and sound unto
the banks of the River Tigris. But, said he, what
doth that part of our army in the meantime, which
overthrows that unworthy swill-pot Grangousier?
They are not idle, said they. We shall meet with
them by and by. They shall have won you Brittany,
Normandy, Flanders, Hainhault, Brabant, Artois,
Holland, Zealand; they have passed the Rhine over
the bellies of the Switzers and Lanskenets, and a
party of these hath subdued Luxemburg, Lorrain,
Champagne, and Savoy, even to Lyons, in which
place they have met with your forces returning from
the naval conquests of the Mediterranean Sea; and
have rallied again in Bohemia, after they had
plundered and sacked Suevia, Wirtemberg, Bavaria,
Austria, Moravia, and Styria. Then they set fiercely
together upon Lubeck, Norway, Swedeland, Rie,[10]
Denmark,[11] Gitland,[12] Greenland, the Sterlins,[13]
even unto the Frozen Sea. This done, they conquered the isles of Orkney, and subdued Scotland,
England and Ireland. From thence sailing through
the sandy sea, and by the Sarmates, they have vanquished and overcome Prussia, Poland, Lithuania,
Russia, Wallachia, Transylvania, Hungary, Bulgaria,
Turquieland, and are now at Constantinople. Come,

[10] *Rie.*—Rich, in Rabelais. It means either Riga in Livonia,
or the Isle of Rugen.
[11] *Denmark.*—Dacia, in Rabelais. It means Denmark.
[12] *Gitland.*—Gothia, in Rabelais.
[13] *Sterlins.*—Estrelins, in Rabelais.

said Picrochole, let us go join with them quickly, for
I will be Emperor of Trebezonde also. Shall we
not kill all these dogs, Turks and Mahometans?
What a devil should we do else? said they. And
you shall give their goods and lands to such as shall
have served you honestly. Reason, said he, will have
it so, that is but just. I give unto you Caramania,
Suria, and all Palestine. Ha, sir, said they, it is out
of your goodness; grammercie, we thank you. God
grant you may always prosper. There was there
present at that time an old gentleman well experienced in the wars, a stern soldier, and who had been
in many great hazards, named Echephron, who, hearing this discourse, said, I do greatly doubt that all
this enterprise will be like the tale or interlude of
the pitcher full of milk, wherewith a shoemaker made
himself rich in conceit: but, when the pitcher was
broken, he had not whereupon to dine. What do
you pretend by these large conquests? What shall
be the end of so many labours and crosses? Thus
it shall be, said Picrochole, that when we are returned we shall sit down, rest, and be merry. But,
said Echephron, if by chance you should never come
back, for the voyage is long and dangerous, were it
not better for us to take our rest now, than unneces-
sarily to expose ourselves to so many dangers? O,
said Swashbuckler, by God, here is a good dotard,
come, go hide ourselves in the corner of a chimney,
and there let us spend the whole time of our life
amongst ladies, in threading of pearls, or spinning
like Sardanapalus. He, that nothing ventures, hath
neither horse nor mule, says Solomon. He, who
adventureth too much, said Echephron, loseth both
horse and mule, as answered Malchon. Enough,
said Picrochole, go forward. I fear nothing but
that these devilish legions of Grangousier, whilst we

are in Mesopotamia, will come on our backs, and charge up our rear. What course shall we then take? What shall be our remedy? A very good one, said Durtaille; a pretty little commission, which you must send unto the Muscovites, shall bring you into the field in an instant four hundred and fifty thousand choice men of war. Oh that you would but make me your Lieutenant-General, I should for the lightest faults of any inflict great punishments. I fret! I charge! I strike! I take! I kill! I slay! I play the devil! On, on, said Picrochole, make haste, my lads, and let him that loves me follow me!

CHAPTER XXXIV

HOW GARGANTUA LEFT THE CITY OF PARIS, TO SUCCOUR HIS COUNTRY, AND HOW GYMNAST EN-COUNTERED WITH THE ENEMY

In this same very hour Gargantua, who was gone out of Paris as soon as he had read his father's letters, coming upon his great mare, had already passed the Nunnery-bridge,[1] himself, Ponocrates, Gymnast, and Eudemon, who all three, the better to enable them to go along with him, took post-horses. The rest of his train came after him by even journeys at a slower pace, bringing with them all his books and philosophical instruments. As soon as he had alighted at Parillé, he was informed by a farmer of Gouguet, how Picrochole had fortified himself within the rock

[1] *Nunnery bridge.*—Read Nun's-bridge; so they call the large stone bridges about Chinon. They are half a league long, stand upon irregular arches, and have abundance of crosses on them.

Clermond,[2] and had sent Captain Tripet[3] with a
great army to set upon the wood of Vede and Vaugaudry, and that they had already plundered the
whole country, not leaving cock nor hen, even as
far as to the wine-press of Billard. These strange
and almost incredible news of the enormous abuses,
thus committed over all the land, so affrighted Gargantua, that he knew not what to say nor do. But
Ponocrates counselled to go unto the Lord of
Vauguyon,[4] who at all times had been their friend
and confederate, and that by him they should be
better advised in their business. Which they did
incontinently, and found him very willing and fully
resolved to assist them, and therefore was of opinion
that they should send some one of his company, to
scout along and discover the country, to learn in
what condition and posture the enemy was, that they
might take counsel, and proceed according to the
present occasion. Gymnast offered himself to go.
Whereupon it was concluded, that for his safety,
and the better expedition, he should have with him
some one that knew the ways, avenues, turnings,
windings, and rivers thereabout. Then away went
he and Prelingot, the equerry or gentleman of
Vauguyon's horse, who scouted and espied as
narrowly as they could upon all quarters without
any fear. In the meantime Gargantua took a little
refreshment, ate somewhat himself, the like did
those who were with him, and caused to give to his
mare a picotine of oats, that is, threescore and fourteen quarters and three bushels. Gymnast and his
comrade rode so long, that at last they met with

[2] *Within the rock Clermond.*—Read, at la Roche Clermauld.
[3] *Captain Tripet.*—Captain Paunch, Captain Tripe-all.
[4] *Lord of Vauguyon.*—See M. le Duchat's conjecture who this
might be.

the enemy's forces, all scattered and out of order,
plundering, stealing, robbing and pillaging all they
could lay their hands on. And, as far off as they
could perceive him, they ran thronging upon the
back of one another in all haste towards him, to
unload him of his money, and untruss his portman-
teaus. Then cried he out unto them, My masters, I
am a poor devil, I desire you to spare me. I have
yet one crown [5] left. Come, we must drink it, for
it is aurum potabile, and this horse here shall be sold
to pay my welcome. Afterwards take me for one of
your own, for never yet was there any man that
knew better how to take, lard, roast and dress, yea,
by God, to tear asunder and devour a hen, than I
that am here: and for my *proficiat* I drink to all
good fellows. With that he unscrewed his borracho
(which was a great Dutch leathern bottle), and without putting in his nose drank very honestly. The
marroufle rogues looked upon him, opening their
throats a foot wide, and putting out their tongues
like greyhounds, in hopes to drink after him; but
Captain Tripet, in the very nick of that their
expectation, came running to him to see who it was.
To him Gymnast offered his bottle, saying, Hold,
captain, drink boldly and spare not; I have been thy
taster, it is wine of La Faye Monjau.[6] What ! said
Tripet, this fellow gibes and flouts us ? Who art
thou ? said Tripet. I am, said Gymnast, a poor devil
(*pauvre diable*). Ha, said Tripet, seeing thou art a

[5] *Crown.*—In those days when they spoke of crowns, they
meant crowns of gold.
[6] *La Faye Monjau.*—Read *La Faie Moniau;* it is a parish in the
jurisdiction of Niort. It produces excellent good wine, called by
Ch. Stephens, in his Prædium Rusticum, Vina Faymongiana;
but this very thing proves he was ignorant of the origin of the
names of these wines, since the priory of the place is called
Faya-mona-chalis. Baudrand has it Moniau, and so it ought to be.

poor devil, it is reason that thou shouldest be permitted to go whithersoever thou wilt, for all poor
devils pass everywhere without toll or tax. But it is
not the custom of poor devils to be so well mounted;
therefore, Sir Devil, come down, and let me have
your horse, and if he do not carry me well, you,
Master Devil, must do it;[7] for I love a-life[8] that
such a devil as you should carry me away.

CHAPTER XXXV

HOW GYMNAST VERY SOUPLY AND CUNNINGLY KILLED CAPTAIN TRIPET, AND OTHERS OF PICROCHOLE'S MEN

WHEN they heard these words, some amongst them
began to be afraid, and blest themselves with both
hands, thinking indeed that he had been a devil disguised, insomuch that one of them, named Good
John, captain of the trained bands of the country
bumpkins, took his psalter out of his codpiece, and
cried out aloud, Hagios ho Theos.[1] If thou be of

[7] *You, master devil, must do it.*—'Is, *qualis sit equus, me vehet,
aut ego illum,*' says proverbially in Vives, a young fellow who was
jeered about the weakness of his horse.

[8] *I love a-life.*—I suppose Sir T. U. means, I love as my life.
It is the same in both editions of the English, and so are all the
other unintelligibles already taken notice of. [Sir T. U. trans-
lates it correctly. The original reads, 'Car j'ayme fort qu'ung
diable tel m'emporte.']

[1] *Hagios ho Theos.*—The first words of the Trisagion of the
Greeks, Ἅγιος ὁ Θεὸς, ἅγιος ἰσχυρὸς, ἅγιος ἀθανατος, ἐλέησον
ἡμας, 'O Holy God, O Mighty Holy One, Immortal
Holy One, have mercy on us!' These words are sung both in
Greek and Latin in the Roman Church at mass on Good Friday.
Now as such words which are least understood are thought to
have most efficacy, this of Hagios, especially thrice repeated, has
made people believe it to have great virtue in invocations.

God, speak, if thou be of the other spirit, avoid
hence, and get thee going. Yet he went not away :
which words being heard by all the soldiers that were
there, divers of them being a little inwardly terrified
departed from the place. All this did Gymnast very
well remark and consider, and therefore making as if
he would have alighted from off his horse, as he was
poising himself on the mounting side, he most nimbly
with his short sword by his thigh, shifting his foot in
the stirrup, performed the stirrup-leather feat, whereby, after the inclining of his body downwards, he
forthwith launched himself aloft in the air, and
placed both his feet together on the saddle, standing
upright with his back turned towards the horse's
head. Now, said he, my case goes backward. Then
suddenly, in the same very posture wherein he was,
he fetched a gambol upon one foot, and, turning to
the left hand, failed not to carry his body perfectly
round, just into its former stance, without missing
one jot. Ha, said Tripet, I will not do that at this
time, and not without cause. Well, said Gymnast,
I have failed, I will undo this leap. Then, with a
marvellous strength and agility, turning towards the
right hand, he fetched another frisking gambol, as
before, which done, he set his right hand thumb
upon the hind bow of the saddle, raised himself up,
and sprung in the air; poising and upholding his
whole body upon the muscle and nerve of the said
thumb, and so turned and whirled himself about
three times. At the fourth, reversing his body, and
overturning it upside down, and foreside back, without touching anything, he brought himself betwixt
the horse's two ears, springing with all his body into
the air, upon the thumb of his left hand, and in that
posture, turning like a windmill, did most actively
do that trick which is called the miller's pass. After

Gymnast vaults on his horse.

this, clapping his right hand flat upon the middle of
the saddle, he gave himself such a jerking swing,
that he thereby seated himself upon the crupper,
after the manner of gentlewomen sitting on horseback. This done, he easily past his right leg over
the saddle, and placed himself like one that rides in
croup. But, said he, it were better for me to get
into the saddle; then putting the thumbs of both
hands upon the crupper before him, and thereupon
leaning himself, as upon the only supporters of his
body, he incontinently turned heels over head in the
air, and straight found himself betwixt the bows of
the saddle in a good settlement. Then with a
summer-sault springing into the air again, he fell to
stand with both his feet close together upon the
saddle, and there made above a hundred frisks, turns,
and demi-pommads, with his arms held out across,
and in so doing cried out aloud, I rage ! I rage !
Devils, I am stark mad ! Devils ! I am mad ! hold
me, Devils ! hold me ! hold, Devils, hold, hold !

Whilst he was thus vaulting, the rogues in great
astonishment said to one another, By cock's death !
he is a goblin or a devil thus disguised,—*Ab hoste
maligno libera nos, Domine*,—and ran away in a full
flight, as if they had been routed, looking now and
then behind them, like a dog that carrieth away a
goose-wing in his mouth. Then Gymnast, spying
his advantage, alighted from his horse, drew his
sword, and laid on great blows upon the thickest,
and highest-crested among them, and overthrew
them in great heaps, hurt, wounded, and bruised,
being resisted by nobody, they thinking he had been
a starved devil, as well in regard of his wonderful
feats in vaulting, which they had seen, as for the
talk Tripet had with him, calling him poor devil.
Only Tripet would have traitorously cleft his head

with his horseman's sword, or lansquenet fauchion; but he was well armed, and felt nothing of the blow, but the weight of the stroke. Whereupon turning suddenly about, he gave Tripet a home-thrust, and upon the back of that, whilst he was about to ward his head from a slash, he ran him in at the breast with a hit, which at once cut his stomach, the fifth gut called the colon, and the half of his liver, wherewith he fell to the ground, and in falling gushed forth above four pottles of pottage, and his soul mingled with the pottage.

This done, Gymnast withdrew himself, very wisely considering that a case of great adventure and hazard should not be pursued unto its utmost period, and that it becomes all cavaliers modestly to use their good fortune, without troubling or stretching it too far. Wherefore, getting to horse, he gave him the spur, taking the right way unto Vauguyon, and Prelingot with him.

CHAPTER XXXVI

HOW GARGANTUA DEMOLISHED THE CASTLE AT THE FORD OF VEDE, AND HOW THEY PASSED THE FORD

As soon as he came, he related the estate and condition wherein they had found the enemy, and the stratagem which he alone had used against all their multitude, affirming that they were but rascally rogues, plunderers, thieves, and robbers, ignorant of all military discipline, and that they might boldly set forward unto the field; it being an easy matter to fell and strike them down like beasts. Then Gargantua mounted his great mare, accompanied as

we have said before, and finding in his way a high
and great tree, which commonly was called by the
name of St Martin's tree, because heretofore St
Martin planted a pilgrim's staff there, which in
tract of time grew to that height and greatness, said,
This is that which I lacked : this tree shall serve
me both for a staff and lance.   With that he pulled
it up easily, plucked off the boughs, and trimmed it
at his pleasure.   In the meantime his mare pissed
to ease her belly, but it was in such abundance, that
it did overflow the country seven leagues, and all the
piss of that urinal flood ran glib away towards the
ford of Vede, wherewith the water was so swollen,
that all the forces the enemy had there were with
great horror drowned, except some who had taken
the way on the left hand towards the hills.   Gargantua, being come to the place of the wood of
Vede, was informed by Eudemon, that there was
some remainder of the enemy within the castle,
which to know, Gargantua cried out as loud as he
was able, Are you there, or are you not there ?   If
you be there, be there no more; and if you are not
there, I have no more to say.   But a ruffian gunner,
whose charge was to attend the portcullis over the
gate, let fly a cannon-ball at him, and hit him with
that shot most furiously on the right temple of his
head, yet did him no more hurt than if he had but
cast a prune or kernel of a wine-grape at him.
What is this ? said Gargantua ; do you throw at us
grape-kernels here ?   The vintage shall cost you
dear ; thinking indeed that the bullet had been the
kernel of a grape, or raisin-kernel.

Those who were within the castle, being till then
busy at the pillage, when they heard this noise, ran
to the towers and fortresses, from whence they shot
at him above nine thousand and five-and-twenty

falcon-shot and harquebusades, aiming all at his
head, and so thick did they shoot at him, that he
cried out, Ponocrates, my friend, these flies here are
like to put out mine eyes; give me a branch of those
willow-trees to drive them away, thinking that the
bullets and stones[1] shot out of the great ordnance
had been but dun-flies. Ponocrates looked and saw
that there were no other flies, but great shot which
they had shot from the castle. Then was it that he
rushed with his great tree against the castle, and
with mighty blows overthrew both towers and fortresses, and laid all level with the ground, by which
means all that were within were slain and broken in
pieces. Going from thence, they came to the bridge
at the mill, where they found all the ford covered
with dead bodies so thick that they had choked up
the mill, and stopped the current of its water, and
these were those that were destroyed in the urinal
deluge of the mare. There they were at a stand,
consulting how they might pass without hindrance
by these dead carcasses. But Gymnast said, If the
devils have passed there, I will pass well enough.
The devils have passed there, said Eudemon, to carry
away the damned souls. By St Rhenian![2] said

---

[1] *Bullets and stones.*—*Plumbées et pierres d'artilleries : plombées*,
leaden balls or pellets; *glans plumbata*, says Nicot. In old time,
plumbée was a club studded with lead to make it give the heavier
blow. The stones of the great ordnance, or artillery stones, to
which iron shot succeeded, were huge stones, rounded, with which
certain heavy cannon were charged, and these cannon were
called *pedereroes* (from *pierre* or rather *piedra*, a stone). The
French were the first that left off the use of these *pedereroes*,
and stone bullets; and when in the reign of Charles VIII. they
carried the war into Italy, it was amazing to see the havock made
by their numerous and well-served train of artillery of large brass
ordnance, drawn by stout horses.

[2] *St Rhenian.*—Read St Treignan. An account of this Scotch
saint see a little before.

Ponocrates, then by necessary consequence he shall
pass there. Yes, yes, said Gymnast, or I shall
stick in the way. Then, setting spurs to his horse,
he passed through freely, his horse not fearing, nor
being anything affrighted at the sight of the dead
bodies ; for he had accustomed him, according to
the doctrine of Ælian, not to fear armour, nor the
carcasses of dead men; and that not by killing men
as Diomedes did the Thracians, or as Ulysses did in
throwing the corpses of his enemies at his horse's
feet, as Homer saith, but by putting a Jack-a-lent
amongst his hay, and making him go over it ordinarily, when he gave him his oats. The other three
followed him very close, except Eudemon only,
whose horse's foreright or far forefoot sank up to
the knee in the paunch of a great fat chuff, who
lay there upon his back drowned, and could not
get it out. There was he pestered, until Gargantua,
with the end of his staff, thrust down the rest of the
villain's tripes into the water, whilst the horse pulled
out his foot; and, which is a wonderful thing in
hippiatrie, the said horse was thoroughly cured of
a ring-bone which he had in that foot, by this touch
of the burst guts of that great looby.

CHAPTER XXXVII

HOW GARGANTUA, IN COMBING HIS HEAD, MADE THE
GREAT CANNON-BALLS FALL OUT OF HIS HAIR

BEING come out of the river of Vede, they came
very shortly after to Grangousier's castle, who waited
for them with great longing. At their coming they
were entertained with many congies, and cherished

with embraces. Never was seen a more joyful company, for Supplementum Supplementi Chronicorum
saith, that Gargamelle died there with joy; for my
part, truly, I cannot tell, neither do I care very
much for her, nor for anybody else. The truth was,
that Gargantua, in shifting his clothes, and combing
his head with a comb, which was nine hundred feet
long of the Jewish cane measure, and whereof the
teeth were great tusks of elephants, whole and
entire, he made fall at every rake about seven balls
of bullets, at a dozen the ball, that stuck in his hair,
at the razing of the castle of the wood of Vede.
Which his father Grangousier seeing, thought they
had been lice, and said unto him, What, my dear
son, hast thou brought us this far some short-winged
hawks of the college of Montague? I did not mean
that thou shouldest reside there. Then answered
Ponocrates, My sovereign lord, think not that I have
placed him in that lousy college,[1] which they call
Montague; I had rather have put him amongst the
grave-diggers of Sanct Innocent, so enormous is the
cruelty and villainy that I have known there: for
the galley-slaves are far better used amongst the
Moors and Tartars, the murderers in the criminal
dungeons, yea, the very dogs in your house, than
are the poor wretched students in the aforesaid
college. And if I were King of Paris, the devil
take me if I would not set it on fire, and burn both
principal and regents, for suffering this inhumanity
to be exercised before their eyes. Then, taking up
one of these bullets, he said, These are cannon-shot,
which your son Gargantua hath lately received by

---

[1] *Lousy college.*—Erasmus fell sick there by being lodged in an
unwholesome room, where they gave him nothing to eat but
rotten eggs; see his colloquy, entitled ' *Le Repas du poisson.*'

the treachery of your enemies, as he was passing before the wood of Vede.

But they have been so rewarded, that they are all destroyed in the ruin of the castle, as were the Philistines by the policy of Samson, and those whom the tower of Silohim[2] slew, as it is written in the thirteenth of Luke. My opinion is, that we pursue them whilst the luck is on our side; for occasion hath all her hair on her forehead; when she is past, you may not recall her—she hath no tuft whereby you can lay hold on her, for she is bald in the hinder part of her head, and never returneth again. Truly, said Grangousier, it shall not be at this time; for I will make you a feast this night, and bid you welcome.

This said, they made ready supper, and, of extra-ordinary, besides his daily fare, were roasted sixteen oxen, three heifers, two and thirty calves, three score and three fat kids, four score and fifteen wethers, three hundred farrow pigs souced in sweet wine or musk, eleven score partridges, seven hundred snipes and woodcocks, four hundred Loudun and Cornwall[3] capons, six thousand pullets, and as many pigeons, six hundred crammed hens, fourteen hundred leverets, or young hares and rabbits, three hundred and three buzzards, and one thousand and seven hundred cockerels. For venison, they could not so suddenly come by it, only eleven wild boars, which the Abbot of Turpenay[4] sent, and eighteen fallow deer, which the Lord of Gramount bestowed; together with

[2] *Silohim.*—Read Siloam.

[3] *Cornwall.*—Not Cornwall in England, but Cornoüaille in France.

[4] *Turpenay.*—The Abbey of Tourpenay *(Turpiniacum)* and the Manor of Grammont are adjoining to the Forest of Chinon. So it was no hard matter for the Abbot of Turpenay and the Lord of Grammont to procure venison.

247

seven score pheasants, which were sent by the Lord
of Essars ; and some dozens of queests, cushats, ring-
doves, and woodculvers ; river fowl, teals, and aw-
teals, bitterns, courtes, plovers, francolins, briganders,
tyrasons, young lapwings, tame ducks, shovelers,
woodlanders, herons, moor hens, criels, storks, cane-
petiers, oronges, flamans, which are phænicopters,
or crimson-winged sea-fowls, terrigoles, turkeys,
arbens, coots, solan-geese, curlews, termagants, and
water-wagtails, with a great deal of cream, curds,
and fresh cheese, and store of soup, pottages, and
brewis with great variety. Without doubt there
was meat enough, and it was handsomely dressed
by Snapsauce, Hotchpot, and Brayverjuice, Grangousier's cooks. Jenkin Trudg-apace and Clean-
glass were very careful to fill them drink.

CHAPTER XXXVIII

HOW GARGANTUA DID EAT UP SIX PILGRIMS IN A SALLAD

THE story requireth, that we relate that which happened unto six pilgrims, who came from Sebastian[1]
near to Nantes : and who for shelter that night,
being afraid of the enemy, had hid themselves in the
garden upon the chichling peas, among the cabbages
and lettuces. Gargantua finding himself somewhat
dry, asked whether they could get any lettuce to
make him a sallad ; and hearing that there were the
greatest and fairest in the country, for they were as
great as plum-trees, or as walnut-trees, he would go

[1] Read St Sebastian.

248

thither himself, and brought thence in his hand what
he thought good, and withal carried away the six
pilgrims, who were in so great fear, that they did not
dare to speak nor cough. Washing them, therefore,
first at the fountain, the pilgrims said one to another
softly, What shall we do ? We are almost drowned
here amongst these lettuce, shall we speak ? But if
we speak he will kill us for spies. And, as they
were thus deliberating what to do, Gargantua put
them with the lettuce into a platter of the house, as
large as the huge tun[2] of the White Friars of the
Cistertian order; which done, with oil, vinegar, and
salt, he ate them up, to refresh himself a little before
supper, and had already swallowed up five of the
pilgrims, the sixth being in the platter, totally hid
under a lettuce, except his bourdon or staff that appeared, and nothing else. Which Grangousier seeing,
said to Gargantua, I think that is the horn of a shell
snail, do not eat it. Why not, said Gargantua, they
are good all this month : which he no sooner said,
but, drawing up the staff, and therewith taking up
the pilgrim, he ate him very well, then drank a
terrible draught of excellent white wine. The

[2] *The huge tun of the Cistertians.*—Robert Cenault says, that it
held near 300 hogsheads, and this other ship of the Argonauts
abundantly out-measured the tun of Erpach, between Heidelberg
and Francfort, which Althamar, a German author, represents in
the following verse rather as a vast sea than a vessel for wine.

> The world's eighth wonder Erpach boasts: a tun
> Of such dimensions that the rolling sun
> Its like ne'er saw; a sea of wine it shows.
> And night and day with Bacchus' nectar flows.
> Call, Bernard, the Cistertians all around :
> Among them, let *thy* order too be found!
> This vessel shall their annual stores supply,
> Nor danger run of ever being dry.
> Swill Erpach's monks! make Bacchanalian cheer!
> This BACBUC safe, no thirst you need not fear.

pilgrims, thus devoured, made shift to save themselves as well as they could, by drawing their bodies
out of the reach of the grinders of his teeth, but
could not escape from thinking they had been put in
the lowest dungeon of a prison. And when Gargantua whiffed the great draught, they thought to
have drowned in his mouth, and the flood of wine
had almost carried them away into the gulf of his
stomach. Nevertheless, skipping with their bour-
dons, as St Michael's [3] palmers use to do, they
sheltered themselves from the danger of that in-
undation under the banks of his teeth. But one of
them by chance, groping or sounding the country
with his staff, to try whether they were in safety or
no, struck hard against the cleft of a hollow tooth,
and hit the mandibulary sinew or nerve of the jaw,
which put Gargantua to very great pain, so that he
began to cry for the rage that he felt. To ease himself therefore of his smarting ache, he called for his
tooth-picker, and rubbing towards a young walnut-
tree, where they lay skulking, unnestled you my
gentlemen pilgrims.

For he caught one by the legs, another by the
scrip, another by the pocket, another by the scarf,
another by the band of the breeches, and the poor
fellow that had hurt him with the bourdon, him he
hooked to him by the codpiece, which snatch
nevertheless did him a great deal of good, for it
pierced unto him a pocky botch he had in the groin,
which had grievously tormented him ever since they
were past Ancenis. The pilgrims thus dislodged,

---

[3] *St Michael's palmers.*—*Miquelots* in French. These miquelots
are little boys that go in pilgrimage to St Michael on the sea,
almost over against England, and who take that occasion to beg.
Thence comes a saying in France, 'None but great beggars go to
St James in Gallicia, and little ones to St Michael.'

ran away athwart the plain a pretty fast pace, and
the pain ceased, even just at the time when by
Eudemon he was called to supper, for all was ready.
I will go then, said he, and piss away my misfortune,[4] which he did do in such a copious measure,
that, the urine taking away the feet from the
pilgrims, they were carried along with the stream
unto the bank of a tuft of trees. Upon which, as
soon as they had taken footing, and that for their
self-preservation they had run a little out of the
road, they on a sudden fell all six, except Fourniller,
into a trap that had been made to take wolves by a
train,[5] out of which, nevertheless, they escaped by
the industry of the said Fourniller, who broke all the
snares and ropes. Being gone from thence, they lay
all the rest of that night in a lodge near unto
Goudray, where they were comforted in their
miseries by the gracious words of one of their
company, called Swear-to-go, who showed them,
that this adventure had been foretold by the Prophet
David, in the Psalms—*Quum exsurgerent homines in
nos, fortè vivos deglutissent nos;* when we were eaten
in the sallad, with salt, oil, and vinegar. *Quum iras-
ceretur furor eorum in nos, forsitan aqua absorbuisset
nos;* when he drank the great draught. *Torrentem
pertransivit anima nostra;* when the stream of his
water carried us to the thicket. *Forsitan pertransisset
anima nostra aquam intolerabilem:* that is, the water of
his urine, the flood whereof cutting our way, took
our feet from us. *Benedictus Dominus, qui non dedit*

---

[4] *Piss away my misfortune.—Pisser mon malheur:* strictly this is
said of those who have got a clap, or have lost at gaming; when
they go to make water, people laugh, and say, 'He is gone to
piss away his misfortune.'

[5] *Train.*—They trail a dead horse, or other carrion along the
ground to a place where it is almost impossible for the wolves
not to fall into a trap laid for them.

nos in captionem dentibus eorum. Anima nostra sicut passer, erepta est de laqueo venantium; when we fell into the trap. *Laqueus contritus est,* by Fourniller, *et nos liberati sumus. Adjutorium nostrum, etc.*

CHAPTER XXXIX

HOW THE MONK WAS FEASTED BY GARGANTUA, AND OF THE JOVIAL DISCOURSE THEY HAD AT SUPPER

WHEN Gargantua was set down at table, after all of them had somewhat stayed their stomachs by a snatch or two of the first bits eaten heartily, Grangousier began to relate the source and cause of the war, raised between him and Picrochole; and came to tell, how Friar John of the Funnels had triumphed at the defence of the close of the abbey, and extolled him for his valour above Camillus, Scipio, Pompey, Cæsar, and Themistocles. Then Gargantua desired that he might be presently sent for, to the end that with him they might consult of what was to be done. Whereupon, by a joint consent, his steward went for him, and brought him along merrily, with his staff of the cross, upon Grangousier's mule. When he was come, a thousand huggings, a thousand embracements, a thousand good days were given. Ha, Friar John, my friend, Friar John, my brave cousin, Friar John from the devil! Let me clip thee, my heart, about the neck; to me an armsful. I must gripe thee, my ballock, till thy back crack with it. Come, my cod, let me coll thee till I kill thee. And Friar John, the gladdest man in the world, never was man made welcomer, never was any more courteously and graciously received than Friar John. Come, come,

said Gargantua, a stool here close by me at this end.
I am content, said the monk, seeing you will have it
so. Some water, page; fill, my boy, fill, it is to
refresh my liver. Give me some, child, to gargle my
throat withal. *Deposita cappà*, said Gymnast, let us
pull off this frock. Ho, by God, gentlemen, said
the monk, there is a chapter in Statutis Ordinis,
which opposeth my laying of it down. Pish! said
Gymnast, a fig for your chapter! This frock breaks
both your shoulders, put it off. My friend, said the
monk, let me alone with it; for, by God, I'll drink
the better that it is on. It makes all my body
jocund. If I should lay it aside, the waggish pages
would cut to themselves garters out of it as I was
once served at Coulaines. And, which is worse, I
shall lose my appetite. But if in this habit I sit
down at table, I will drink, by God, both to thee
and to thy horse, and so, courage, frolic, God save
the company! I have already supped, yet will I eat
never a whit the less for that: for I have a paved
stomach, as hollow as a butt of malvoisie, or St
Benedictus' boot,[1] and always open like a lawyer's
pouch. Of all fishes but the tench[2] take the wing

[1] *St Benet's boots.*—Lower, in l. 4, c. 16, by St Benet's sacred
boot. This is wrongly translated in both places. It should be
by St Benet's holy butt (of wine), not boot. *Par la sacre botte de
St Benoist.* Botte sometimes means a boot, but here a butt; as
it does, and is translated in l. 4, c. 43. This butt of St Benet is
still to be seen at the Benedictines, of Bologna on the sea, right
over against England, and is a vessel or tun not much less than
that of Clervaux. See Menage, at the word bouteille, Βούτις,
Cupa. See likewise, in Duchat, three or four curious distinctions
about the word botte, when made of wood, glass, or leather, to
put wine in, not the legs as Sir T. U. imagined.
[2] *Of all fishes but the tench, etc.*—Take the back and leave the
paunch. *De tous poissons, forsque la tenche, prenez le dos, laissez
la panche.* This is really the proverb which H. Stephens affirms
to be a proverb of Picardy (Precell. du Lang. Fr., etc., p. 139), and

Rabelais' Works [Book i.

of a partridge, or the thigh of a nun. Doth not he die like a good fellow that dies with a stiff catso?[3] Our prior loves exceedingly the white of a capon. In that, said Gymnast, he doth not resemble the foxes: for of the capons, hens, and pullets, which they carry away, they never eat the white. Why? said the monk. Because, said Gymnast, they have no cooks to dress them; and, if they be not competently made ready, they remain red and not white; the redness of meats being a token that they have not got enough of the fire, whether by boiling, roasting, or otherwise, except shrimps, lobsters, crabs, and cray-fishes, which are cardinalised with boiling. By God's feast-gazers, said the monk, the porter of our abbey, then, hath not his head well boiled, for his eyes are as red as a mazer made of an alder-tree.

which is here, by Friar John, accommodated to the design of playing the wag.

[3] *Doth he not die like a good fellow, that dies with a stiff catso?*— *N'est ce falotement mourir quand on meurt le caiche roidde?* The adverb *falotement* is very energetic here. It equivocates both to the word *falot, i.e.,* good fellow, and to a lanthorn fixed at the end of a long pole, which, when the light is spent, or otherwise put out, the staff still continues in statu quo, rigid as it was before. It is easy to apply the comparison to such as die in the condition Friar John speaks of. It is held, by way of a merry tradition, that erection after death happens to such as have enjoyed a nun, which has given occasion to this verse, 'Qui monachâ potitur, virgâ tendente moritur,' reported first by Joannes Vincentius Metulinus, etc. See farther in M. le Duchat himself, who says, *falot* may likewise allude to the Greek Φαλλὸς, which see in Cham. Dict., synonymous to the Italian *cazzo,* or, as they pronounce it themselves, *catso,* and means what our merry translator calls sometimes the carnal trapstick (though the ladies call it their sugar-stick). Rabelais' Caiche above, comes from *cazzo,* and so does Cazzoni, the famous singer's name, though it means a larger sort of catzo, an eleven-inch sugar-stick, etc., etc., etc. In the second Scaligerana, *cats* is interpreted braguette, a codpiece, taking the *continens* for the *continentum.*

254

The thigh of this leveret is good for those that have
the gout. To the purpose of the trowel,—what is
the reason that the thighs of a gentlewoman are
always fresh and cool? This problem, said Gargantua, is neither in Aristotle, in Alexander
Aphrodiseus, nor in Plutarch. There are three
causes, said the monk, by which that place is
naturally refreshed. *Primo*, because the water runs
all along it. *Secundo*, because it is a shady place,
obscure and dark, upon which the sun never shines.
And thirdly, because it is continually flabbelled,
blown upon and aired by the north winds of the hole
arstic, the fan of the smock, and flipflap of the codpiece. And lusty, my lads! Some bousing liquor,
page! So! Crack, Crack, Crack![4] O how good is
God, that gives us of this excellent juice! I call
him to witness, if I had been in the time of Jesus
Christ, I would have kept him from being taken by
the Jews in the garden of Olivet. And the devil
fail me, if I should have failed to cut off the hams of
those gentlemen Apostles, who ran away so basely
after they had well supped, and left their good
master in the lurch. I hate that man worse than
poison that offers to run away, when he should fight
and lay stoutly about him. Oh that I were but King
of France for fourscore or a hundred years! By
God! I should whip like curtail-dogs these runaways of Pavia. A plague take them, why did they
not choose rather to die there, than to leave their
good prince in that pinch and necessity! Is it not
better and more honourable to perish in fighting
valiantly than to live in disgrace by a cowardly
running away? We are like to eat no great store of

---

[4] *Crack, etc.*—Friar John expresses how quick he swallowed
that glass of wine.

goslings this year, therefore, friend, reach me some of that roasted pig there.

Diavolo, is there no more must? No more sweet wine? *Germinavit radix Jesse! Je renie ma vie, j'enrage de soif!* I renounce my life, I rage for thirst! This wine is none of the worst. What wine drink you at Paris? I give myself to the devil, if I did not once keep open house at Paris for all comers six months together. Do you know Friar Claud of the High Kilderkins? Oh the good fellow that he is! But I do not know what fly hath stung him of late, he is become so hard a student. For my part, I study not at all. In our abbey we never study for fear of the mumps,[5] which disease in horses is called the mourning in the chine. Our late abbot was wont to say, that it is a monstrous thing[6] to see a learned monk. By God! Master! my friend! *Magis magnos clericos non sunt magis magnos sapientes.* You never saw so many hares as there are this year. I could not anywhere come by a goss-hawk, nor tassel of falcon. My Lord Belloniere promised me a lanner, but he wrote to me not long ago, that he was become pursy. The partridges will so multiply henceforth, that they will go near to eat up our ears. I take no delight in the stalking-horse; for I catch

5 *Mumps.*—*Auripeaulx,* an Angevin word; as indeed Rabelais brings in all the various words of the several provinces of France, which makes his work the more humorous and diverting. It means the pain in the ears, orillons, as it is called at Paris. It is an imposthumous swelling in the parotid glands on the right and left side of the throat. Intense studying, Friar John insinuates, would so strain and affect these glands as to cause the ear-ache.

6 *Monstrous thing, etc.*—Guy Patin affirms in one of his letters, that formerly it was a proverb: Indoctus ut monachus, Ignorant or unlearned as a monk: and in our time there has appeared a famous abbot maintaining in print, that it were to be wished the same could be said now-a-days.

such cold, that I am like to founder myself at that sport. If I do not run, toil, travel, and trot about, I am not well at ease. True it is that in leaping over the hedges and bushes, my frock [7] leaves always some of its wool behind it. I have recovered a dainty greyhound; I give him to the devil, if he suffer a hare to escape him. A groom was leading him to my Lord Huntlittle, and I robbed him of him. Did I ill? No, Friar John, said Gymnast, no, by all the devils that are, no! So, said the monk, do I attest [8] these same devils so long as they last, or rather, virtue God! what could that gouty limpard have done with so fine a dog? By the body of God! he is better pleased when one presents him with a good yoke of oxen. How now! said Ponocrates, you swear, Friar John? It is only, said the monk, but to grace and adorn my speech.[9] They are colours of a Ciceronian rhetoric.

CHAPTER XL

WHY MONKS ARE THE OUTCASTS OF THE WORLD; AND WHEREFORE SOME HAVE BIGGER NOSES THAN OTHERS

By the faith of a Christian, said Eudemon, I do wonderfully dote, and enter in a great ecstasy, when

---

[7] *My frock, etc.*—It is true that this way of living, for one of my cloth, oftentimes brings upon me very mortifying rebukes from my superiors.

[8] *So——do I attest, etc.*—So may it happen to such sort of people as long as they live.

[9] *Adorn my speech.*—Menage has marked at this passage in his Rabelais, that Longinus, in his Discourse of the Sublime, sect. 14, actually says that swearing, now and then, on a proper occasion, does grandem efficere orationem.

I consider the honesty and good fellowship of this
monk; for he makes us here all merry. How is it,
then, that they exclude the monks from all good
companies, calling them feast-troublers, marrers of
mirth, and disturbers of all civil conversation, as the
bees drive away the drones from their hives? *Ig-
navum fucos pecus*, said Maro, *à præsepibus arcent.*
Hereunto, answered Gargantua, there is nothing so
true, as that the frock and cowl draw to them the
opprobries, injuries, and maledictions of the world,
just as the wind called Cecias [1] attracts the clouds.
The peremptory reason is, because they eat the
ordure and excrements of the world, that is to say,
the sins of the people, and, like dung-chewers, and
excrementitious eaters, they are cast into the privies
and secessive places, that is, the convents and abbeys,
separated from political conversation, as the jakes and
retreats of a house are. But if you conceive how an
ape in a family is always mocked, and provokingly
incensed, you shall easily apprehend how monks are
shunned of all men, both young and old. The ape [2]
keeps not the house as a dog doth; he draws not in
the plough as the ox; he yields neither milk nor
wool as the sheep; he carrieth no burthen as a horse
doth. That which he doth, is only to conskite,
spoil, and defile all, which is the cause wherefore he
hath of men mocks, frumperies and bastonadoes.

After the same manner a monk (I mean those
lither, idle, lazy monks) doth not labour [3] and work

[1] *Cecias.*—This is taken from Aristotle. 'Est etiam ventus
nomine Cecias, quem Aristoteles ita flare dicit, ut nubes non
procul propellat, sed ut ad sese vocet:' says Aulus Gellius,
l. 2, c. 22.
[2] *The ape, etc.*—Taken from Plutarch.
[3] *Doth not labour, etc.*—This reason of people's hating and
despising the monks so much, is expressed in the following
quatrain:

as do the peasant and artificer; doth not ward and
defend the country, as doth the man-of-war; cureth
not the sick and diseased, as the physician doth; doth
neither preach nor teach, as do the Evangelical
doctors and school-masters; doth not import com-
modities and things necessary for the commonwealth,
as the merchant doth.   Therefore is it, that by and
of all men they are hooted at, hated and abhorred.
Yea, but, said Grangousier, they pray to God for us.
Nothing less, answered Gargantua.   True it is, that
with a tingle tangle jangling of bells they trouble
and disquiet all their neighbours about them.   Right,
said the monk; a mass, a matin, a vesper well rung is
half said.[4]   They mumble out great store of legends
and psalms, by them not at all understood: they say
many pater-nosters, interlarded with Ave-Maries,
without thinking upon, or apprehending the meaning
of what it is they say, which truly I call mocking
of God, and not prayers.[5]   But so help them God,
as they pray for us, and not for being afraid to lose
their victuals, their manchets, and good fat pottage.
All true Christians, of all estates and conditions, in
all places, and at all times, send up their prayers to

> Of mouths above a million, we
>   Can furnish you each hour,
> Who, as the drone defrauds the bee,
>   Do other's gains devour.

A verse which is applicable to all monks, and all religions,
though particularly fitted to the Cordeliers. See the Jesuit's
Passe-par-tout in 1607.

[4] *A mass well rung is half said.*—In the same sense we say, A
beard well lathered is half shaved.

[5] *Mocking of God, and not prayers.*—Perhaps Rabelais, who
understood High Dutch, had the German proverb in view, 'Gotts
gespat, und nicht gotts gebet,' which, however, sounds better in
that tongue, because of the allusion from gespat, mocking, to
gebet, praying.

God, and the Mediator prayeth and intercedeth for them, and God is gracious to them. Now such a one is our good Friar John, therefore every man desireth to have him in his company. He is no bigot or hypocrite, he is not torn and divided betwixt reality and appearance, no wretch of a rugged and peevish disposition, but honest, jovial, resolute, and a good fellow. He travels, he labours, he defends the oppressed, comforts the afflicted, helps the needy, and keeps the close of the abbey. Nay, said the monk, I do a great deal more than that; for, whilst we are despatching our matins and anniversaries in the quire, I make withal some cross-bow strings, polish glass-bottles and bolts; I twist lines and weave purse nets,⁶ wherein to catch coneys. I am never idle. But now, hither come, some drink, some drink here! Bring the fruit. These chestnuts are of the wood of Estrox,⁷ and with good new wine are able to make you a fine cracker and composer of bum-sonnets. You are not as yet, it seems, well-moistened in this house with the sweet wine and must. By God, I drink to all men freely, and at all fords, like a proctor or promoter's horse. Friar John, said Gymnast, take away the snot that hangs at your nose. Ha, ha! said the monk, am not

⁶ *Weave purse nets, etc.*—'Facito aliquid operis: ut semper te diabolus inveniat occupatum——vel fiscellam texe junco: vel canistrum lentis plecte viminibus——Apum fabrica alvearia ——Texantur et lina capiendis piscibus,' says St Jerome to the monk Rusticus, in the canon nunquam, etc. The abuse of this canon was got to such a pitch at the time of the Concordat, that the monks and abbots, when their repasts, etc., were over, hardly minded anything else but these trifles, and whistling to canary birds and linnets. (See Brantôme Illus. Men.) Friar John, a downright rake, used to busy himself in these matters, during the time of divine service, and when he was at church at his prayers.
⁷ *Estrox.*—A certain tract in Lower Poitou, abounding with all manner of good fruit.

I in danger of drowning, seeing I am in water even
to the nose ? No, no—*Quare ?* *Quia*—though some
water come out from thence, there never goes in
any ;[8] for it is well antidoted with pot-proof armour,
and sirrup of the vine-leaf.

Oh my friend, he that hath winter-boots made of
such leather may boldly fish for oysters, for they will
never take water.   What is the cause, said Gargantua,
that Friar John hath such a fair nose ?[9] Because,
said Grangousier, that God would have it so,[10] who
frameth us in such form, and for such end, as is most
agreeable with his divine will, even as a potter
fashioneth his vessels.   Because, said Ponocrates, he
came with the first to the fair of noses, and therefore
made choice of the fairest and the greatest.   Pish !
said the monk, that is not the reason of it, but,

[8] *Never goes in any.*—He never drinks any water. Friar
John's thought answers to the ' vino suffocatus aquam in nullam
corporis partem admittit,' in Bebelius' facetious Tales, l. 3.   It
has been made into a song in a French play, where a tun-bellied
toper is made to say thus :

> ' Le jus de la treille
> Dans une bouteille
> Court trop de danger, etc.'

> *Anglicè.*
> The juice of the grape
> May make its escape,
> If you in a bottle do lodge it:
> But it's safe. let me tell ye,
> When stowed in my belly;
> Nought but water comes out of that budget.

[9] *Such a fair nose.*—Rabelais bringing in this question towards
the end of the repast, has a view to an ancient way of speaking
of those who, being quite unemployed, or out of discourse, look
at people's noses as they pass by, to see whose snout is hand-
somest.

[10] *Because that God would have it so.*—An answer like that
of Xanthus to his gardener in Æsop's life.

261

according to the true monastical philosophy, it is because my nurse had soft teats,[11] by virtue whereof, whilst she gave me suck, my nose did sink in as in so much butter. The hard breasts of nurses make children short-nosed. But hey, gay! *Ad formam nasi cognoscitur ad te levavi*,[12] I never eat any confections, page, whilst I am at the bibbery. *Item*, bring me rather some toasts.

―――

CHAPTER XLI

HOW THE MONK MADE GARGANTUA SLEEP, AND OF HIS HOURS AND BREVIARIES

SUPPER being ended, they consulted of the business in hand, and concluded that about midnight they should fall unawares upon the enemy, to know what manner of watch and ward they kept, and that in the mean while they should take a little rest, the better to refresh themselves. But Gargantua could not sleep by any means, on which side soever he turned himself. Whereupon the monk said to him, I never sleep soundly but when I am at sermon or

―――――――

[11] *Soft teats.*—Bouchet in his 24th Sereé (which I take to mean his Evenings' Conferences, for I never saw the book) says that Friar John's answer is not altogether a joke, for that famous surgeon, Ambrose Paræus, has maintained, that the hardness of a nurse's breast may make a child have a flat nose.

[12] *Ad te levavi.*—Bruscambille has repeated it in his prologue on large noses. And from thence a pleasant she-sinner, being deceived, cried out, 'Nase, me decepisti:' Nose, thou hast deceived me. (She would never judge a cock by his comb any more.) [The reader will find some admirable illustrations of this, and the preceding, note in Dr Ferriar's *Illustrations of Sterne*, I. chap. vi.]

prayers. Let us therefore begin, you and I, the
seven penitential psalms, to try whether you shall
not quickly fall asleep. The conceit pleased Gargantua very well, and beginning the first of these
psalms, as soon as they came to the words, Beati
quorum, they fell asleep, both the one and the other.
But the monk, for his being formerly accustomed to
the hour of claustral matins,[1] failed not to awake a
little before midnight, and being up himself, awaked
all the rest, in singing aloud, and with a full, clear
voice, the song,

> Awake, O Reinian, Ho, awake!
> Awake, O Reinian, Ho!
> Get up, you no more sleep must take,
> Get up, for we must go.

When they were all roused and up, he said, My
masters, it is a usual saying, that we begin matins
with coughing, and supper with drinking. Let us
now, in doing clean contrarily, begin our matins
with drinking, and at night before supper we shall
cough as hard as we can. What, said Gargantua,
to drink so soon after sleep? This is not to live
according to the diet and prescript rule of the physicians, for you ought first to scour and cleanse your
stomach of all its superfluities and excrements. O
well physicked, said the monk; a hundred devils
leap into my body, if there be not more old
drunkards than old physicians! I have made this
paction and covenant with my appetite, that it

---

[1] *To the hour of claustral matins.*—It is an observation of Sir
Edwin Sandys, that if the Pope should take a fancy to arm all
the monks of his empire, and make them turn soldiers, there
would be no resisting such men, who have been so long accustomed to obey orders, to live upon a little, to rise early, and
to sleep upon hard stones or bare boards. (I translate M. le
Duchat's words, not having Sir Edwin's book by me.)

always lieth down, and goes to bed with myself, for to that I every day give very good order, then the next morning it also riseth with me, and gets up when I am awake. Mind you your charges, gentlemen, or tend your cures[2] as much as you will. I will get me to my drawer, in terms of falconry, my tiring. What drawer or tiring do you mean? said Gargantua. My breviary, said the monk, for just as the falconers, before they feed their hawks, do make them draw at a hen's leg, to purge their brains of phlegm, and sharpen them to a good appetite, so, by taking this merry little breviary in the morning, I scour all my lungs, and am presently ready to drink.

After what manner, said Gargantua, do you say these fair hours and prayers of yours? After the manner of Whipfield,[3] said the monk, by three psalms, and three lessons,[4] or nothing at all, he that

[2] *Tend your cures, etc.*—Gargantua had said to Friar John, that he ought first to scour (écurer) his stomach, etc. The friar therefore answers in terms borrowed from falconry, wherein the word cures means the hawk's excrements.

[3] *After the manner of Whipfield.*—Read, *Secundùm usum Fecan.* Fecan is an abbey of regular canons, and was allowed the privilege of the Haute-Justice (see Cotgrave) by Richard III., Duke of Normandy, who likewise obtained from the Pope (John XVII.) that the said religious should be exempt from the Archbishop of Rouen's jurisdiction, and might take cognisance of all cases relating to their own men even in spirituals. (See Du Chesne.) What had turned into a proverb the recital of the prayers (heures) of Fecan, was an extreme relaxation of the rule, and remissness of discipline among the religious of that abbey, who extended their privileges even to a total, or at least partial omission of their prayers.

[4] *Three Psalms and three lessons.*—Cavalier-like. So the Draper in Patelin—

'Il est avocat potatif,
A trois leçons et à trois pseaumes.'

This way of speaking is borrowed from the breviary (mass or

will.   I never tie myself to hours, prayers, and sacraments: for they are made for the man, and not the
man for them.   Therefore is it, that I make my
prayers in fashion of stirrup-leathers; I shorten or
lengthen them when I think good.   *Brevis oratio
penetrat cælos, et longa potatio evacua tscyphos.*   Where
is that written?   By my faith, saith Ponocrates, I
cannot tell, my pillicock, but thou art more worth
than gold.   Therein, said the monk, I am like you:
but, *venite, apotemus.*[5]   Then made they ready store
of carbonadoes, or rashers on the coals, and good
fat soups, or brewis with sippets; and the monk
drank what he pleased.   Some kept him company,
and the rest did forbear, for their stomachs were
not as yet opened.   Afterwards every man began
to arm and befit himself for the field.   And
they armed the monk against his will; for he
desired no other armour for back and breast, but
his frock, nor any other weapon in his hand, but
the staff of the cross.   Yet at their pleasure was
he completely armed cap-à-pie, and mounted upon
one of the best horses in the kingdom,[6] with a good
slashing shable by his side, together with Gargantua, Ponocrates, Gymnast, Eudemon, and five
and twenty more of the most resolute and adven-

service books) where the office is fixed to more or fewer Psalms
and lessons, according as the day is more or less solemn.
    5 *Venite, apotemus.*—The monk alludes to the *venite adoremus*
of his breviary.
    6 *Upon one of the best horses in the kingdom.*—*Sus ung bon coursier
du royaulme.*   M. le Duchat will have it that Rabelais here
means a Neapolitan horse, and that he speaks after the way of
the Italians, who, by the bare word kingdom, commonly understand, and would have others also understand, the kingdom of
Naples.   Like our Irishmen, who when they mean such a one
is their countryman, instead of saying he is Irish, or of Ireland,
they say he is of the kingdom.   Is such a one of the kingdom ?
I have often heard them say so myself to one another.

265

turous of Grangousier's house, all armed at proof with
their lances in their hands, mounted like St George,
and every one of them having a harquebusier behind
him.

CHAPTER XLII

HOW THE MONK ENCOURAGED HIS FELLOW-CHAMPIONS, AND HOW HE HANGED UPON A TREE

THUS went out those valiant champions on their
adventure, in full resolution to know what enterprise they should undertake, and what to take heed
of, and look well to, in the day of the great and
horrible battle.   And the monk encouraged them,
saying, My children, do not fear nor doubt, I will
conduct you safely.   God and Sanct Benedict be
with us!   If I had strength answerable to my
courage, by's death, I would plume them for you
like ducks.[1]   I fear nothing but the great ordnance;
yet I know of a charm by way of prayer, which the
sub-sexton of our abbey taught me, that will preserve a man from the violence of guns, and all
manner of fire-weapons and engines; but it will
do me no good, because I do not believe it.   Nevertheless, I hope my staff of the cross shall this day
play devilish pranks amongst them.   By God! whoever of our party shall offer to play the duck,[2] and
shrink when blows are a dealing, I give myself to
the devil, if I do not make a monk of him in my

---

[1] *Like ducks.*—The contrary way against the grain, as they
pluck ducks.
[2] *Play the duck.*—*i.e.*, dip down the head, as ducks dive in the
water, when they are in fear.

266

stead, and hamper him within my frock, which is a
sovereign cure against cowardice. Did you never
hear of my Lord Meurles's[3] greyhound, which was
not worth a straw in the fields? He put a frock
about his neck: by the body of God! there was
neither hare nor fox that could escape him, and,
which is more, he lined all the bitches in the
country, though before that he was feeble-reined,
and *de frigidis et maleficiatis*.[4]

The monk uttering these words in choler, as he
passed under a walnut-tree, in his way towards the
causey, he broached the vizor of his helmet on the
stump of a great branch of the said tree. Nevertheless, he set his spurs so fiercely to the horse,
who was full of mettle, and quick on the spur, that
he bounded forwards, and the monk, going about to
ungrapple his vizor, let go his hold of the bridle,
and so hanged by his hand upon the bough, whilst
his horse stole away from under him. By this means
was the monk left, hanging on the walnut-tree, and
crying for help, murder, murder, swearing also that
he was betrayed. Eudemon perceived him first, and
calling Gargantua said, Sir, come and see Absalom
hanging. Gargantua being come, considered the
countenance of the monk, and in what posture he
hanged; wherefore he said to Eudemon, You were
mistaken in comparing him to Absalom; for Absalom
hung by his hair, but this shaveling monk hangeth
by the ears. Help me, said the monk, in the devil's
name! is this a time for you to prate? You seem to me
to be like the decretalist preachers,[5] who say, that who-

3 *Meurles.*—An ancient and honourable family at Montpelier,
where they still enjoy eminent posts both civil and military.
4 *Ex frigidis, etc.*—*Frigid et maleficiat* is properly said of a
man that is impotent, either by nature or by some witchery, such
as tying the codpiece point, which see explained elsewhere.
5 *You seem to me to be like the decretalist preachers.*—This answers

soever shall see his neighbour in the danger of death,
ought, upon pain of trisulk[6] excommunication, rather
choose to admonish him to make his confession to
a priest, and put his conscience in the state of peace,
than otherwise to help and relieve him.

And therefore when I shall see them fallen into
a river, and ready to be drowned, I shall make them
a fair long sermon, *De contemptu Mundi, et fuga
seculi;* and when they are stark dead, shall then go
to their aid and succour in fishing after them. Be
quiet, said Gymnast, and stir not, my minion. I
am now coming to unhang thee, and to set thee at
freedom, for thou art a pretty little gentle monachus.
*Monachus in claustro non valet ova duo; sed quando est
extra bene valet triginta.* I have seen above five
hundred hanged,[7] but I never saw any have a better
countenance in his dangling and pendilatory swag-
ging. Truly, if I had so good a one, I would willingly hang thus all my lifetime. What, said the
monk, have you almost done preaching? Help me,
in the name of God, seeing you will not in the name
of the other spirit,[8] or, by the habit which I wear,
you shall repent it, *tempore et loco prælibatis.*[9]

Then Gymnast alighted from his horse, and,
climbing up the walnut-tree, lifted up the monk

to that of St Austin, in reference to one who, rather than strive
to shake off his sins, is puzzling his brains about how it should
possibly be that original sin could descend from his parents
to him.

[6] *Trisulk.*—Three-pointed, like Jupiter's thunder.

[7] *I have seen above five hundred hanged.*—Gymnast speaks here
like the grand provost of Paris, or of the army.

[8] *The other spirit.*—This is, the devil, in whose name he had
at first cried out for help. This is the reverse of Virgil's
' Flectere si nequeo superos, acheronta movebo.'

[9] *Tempore et loco prælibatis.*—Rabelais' motto, says the author
of the judgment upon Rabelais. We might have believed him,
had he brought any proof of it.

with one hand by the gussets of his armour under
the arm-pits, and with the other undid his vizor
from the stump of the broken branch, which done,
he let him fall to the ground and himself after.   As
soon as the monk was down, he put off all his
armour,[10] and threw away one piece after another
about the field, and, taking to him again his staff of
the cross, remounted up to his horse, which Eudemon
had caught in his running away.   Then went they
on merrily, riding along on the high way.

CHAPTER XLIII

HOW THE SCOUTS AND FORE-PARTY OF PICROCHOLE WERE MET WITH BY GARGANTUA, AND HOW THE ·MONK SLEW CAPTAIN DRAWFORTH, AND THEN WAS TAKEN PRISONER BY HIS ENEMIES

PICROCHOLE, at the relation of those who had escaped
out of the broil and defeat, wherein Tripet[1] was
untriped, grew very angry that the devils should
have so run upon his men, and held all that night
a council of war, at which Rashcalf and Touchfaucet[2] concluded his power to be such, that he was

---

[10] *He put off all his armour.*—Like David, when he went
against Goliath.

[1] *Tripet.—Lors que Tripet feut estripé.*   Captain Tripet, of
whom before, in chap. 35, it is said, that Gymnast made him
disembogue his soul amidst the soups and broths which came
out of him through his guts.

[2] *Rashcalf and Touchfaucet.*—Hastiveau may be taken for
Rashcalf well enough, I confess; but strictly it means a sort of
grapes, so called, because it comes in haste, *i.e.*, it is sooner ripe
than other grapes, and, as C. Stephens in his Prædium Rusticum
observes, denotes a rash man, who is too hasty either to give or
take counsel.   Touquedillon, I own, may likewise be made to

able to defeat all the devils of hell, if they should
come to jostle with his forces. This Picrochole did
not fully believe, though he doubted not much of
it. Therefore sent he under the command and conduct of the Count Drawforth,[3] for discovering of
the country, the number of sixteen horsemen, all
well mounted upon light horses for skirmish, and
thoroughly besprinkled with holy water ; [4] and every
one for their field-mark or cognizance had the sign
of a star [5] in his scarf, to serve at all adventures, in
case they should happen to encounter with devils;
that by the virtue, as well of that Gregorian water,[6]

mean Touchfaucet; but it is a word properly of Languedoc,
where they call a Touquedillon a bully, *qui touche de loin*, who
touches at a distance, but whose heart fails him when he comes
to a ' close engagement. The artillery strikes de loin, at a
distance, and therefore we see in chap. 26, Touquedillon was
set over that of Picrochole.

3 *Drawforth.—Tiravant.* A partizan, whose business was
tirer avant, to advance before, to get intelligence, and discover
the enemy and the country round about.

4 *Thoroughly besprinkled with holy water.*—There is nothing in
all this that is not applicable to the ancient Burgundian men-at-
arms. The people of the two Burgundies were, and still are
(those of the Upper Burgundy especially), extremely superstitious,
and the bandoleer of those men-at-arms, with the Burgundy
cross on them, was very like that part of a priest's habiliment
called a stole.

5 *A star.*—Read a stole, not a star; *Une estolle*, Rabelais says,
not *une étoile.*—[*N.B.*—The passage is not correctly understood
by either the translator or commentator.]

6 *Gregorian water.*—Gregory I. was not the introducer of the
holy water, but he was a strong recommender of it, insomuch
that the very husbands who had conversed with their wives, or
as the play says, had *carnalitered* with them, were not to enter
the church till they had washed themselves with that water,
33, v. 4, c. Rabelais does not spell it Gregoriene, but Gringoriane,
which is a corruption of Gregoriene, as Brinborion comes from
Breviarium, corruptly, and indeed contemptuously used for the
Romish psalter.

as of the stars which they wore, they might make them disappear and vanish.[7]

In this equipage they made an excursion upon the country, till they came near to the Vauguyon, which is the valley of Guyon, and to the Hospital, but could never find anybody to speak unto; whereupon they returned a little back, and took occasion to pass above the aforesaid Hospital, to try what intelligence they could come by in those parts. In which resolution riding on, and by chance in a pastoral lodge, or shepherd's cottage near to Coudray, hitting upon the six pilgrims, they carried them way-bound and manacled, as if they had been spies, for all the exclamations, adjurations, and requests that they could make. Being come down from thence towards Sevillé, they were heard by Gargantua, who said then unto those that were with him, Comrades and fellow soldiers, we have here met with an encounter, and they are ten times in number more than we. Shall we charge them or no? What a devil, said the monk, shall we do else? Do you esteem men by their number, rather than by their valour and prowess? With this he cried out, Charge, devils, charge! Which when

---

[7] *Disappear and vanish.*

　　　‘ Les diables fuit et adversaires,
　　　　Et chasse fantasmes contraires.’

　　It drives away both carnal foes and devils,
　　And guards from sprights and all contrarient evils,

Says, in Peter Grosnet's collection, an ancient rhyme, speaking of the marvellous effects of holy water. Picrochole's people imagined they should, by virtue of this blessed water, put to flight every mother's son of the Gargantuists, whom they took for real devils from the time they beheld Gymnast's wonderful feats of activity, he having likewise told them he was a devil, though a poor one.

the enemies heard, they thought certainly that they had been very devils, and therefore even then began all of them to run away as hard as they could drive, Drawforth only excepted, who immediately settled his lance on its rest, and therewith hit the monk with all his force on the very middle of his breast, but, coming against his horrific frock, the point of the iron, being with the blow either broke off or blunted, it was, in matter of execution, as if you had struck against an anvil with a little wax-candle.

Then did the monk, with his staff of the cross, give him such a sturdy thump and whirret betwixt his neck and shoulders, upon the acromion bone, that he made him lose both sense and motion, and fall down stone dead at his horse's feet; and, seeing the sign of the star which he wore scarfwise, he said unto Gargantua, These men are but priests, which is but the beginning of a monk; by St John, I am a perfect monk, I will kill them to you like flies. Then ran he after them at a swift and full gallop, till he overtook the rear, and felled them down like tree-leaves,[8] striking athwart and along and every way. Gymnast presently asked Gargantua if they should pursue them ? To whom Gargantua answered, By no means ; for, according to right military discipline, you must never drive your enemy unto despair, for that such a strait doth multiply his force, and increase his courage, which was before broken and cast down; neither is there any better help, or outgate of relief for men that are amazed, out of

---

[8] *Like tree-leaves.*—Read, like rye, *seille* in French, an old word for *ségle*, and both from the Latin *secale.* Sir T. U. mistook this *seille* for *feuille.* Rye, says M. le Duchat, is cut in the beginning of the harvest, and doubtless, as the Germans mow it, so there are, or at least were, in France, provinces where they mowed it likewise. This makes Rabelais say, that Friar John felled down, like rye, such of the enemy as came first to hand.

heart, toiled, and spent, than to hope for no favour
at all. How many victories have been taken out of
the hands of the victors by the vanquished, when
they would not rest satisfied with reason, but
attempt to put all to the sword, and totally to
destroy their enemies, without leaving so much as
one to carry home news of the defeat of his fellows !
Open, therefore, unto your enemies all the gates and
ways, and make to them a bridge of silver rather
than fail, that you may be rid of them. Yea, but,
said Gymnast, they have the monk. Have they the
monk ? said Gargantua. Upon mine honour then it
will prove to their cost. But to prevent all dangers,
let us not yet retreat, but halt here quietly, as in an
ambush; for I think I do already understand the
policy and judgment of our enemies. They are
truly more directed by chance and mere fortune,
than by good advice and counsel. In the mean
while, whilst these made a stop under the walnut-
trees, the monk pursued on the chase, charging all
he overtook, and giving quarter to none, until he
met with a trooper, who carried behind him one of
the poor pilgrims, and there would have rifled him.
The pilgrim, in hope of relief at the sight of the
monk, cried out, Ha, my Lord Prior,[9] my good
friend, my Lord Prior, save me, I beseech you, save
me ! Which words being heard by those that rode
in the van, they instantly faced about, and seeing
there was nobody but the monk that made this great
havoc and slaughter among them, they loaded him
with blows as thick as they use to do an ass with
wood.[10] But of all this he felt nothing, especially

[9] *My Lord Prior.*—As yet Friar John was no more than the
Prior of Sermaise. See notes on chap. 27.
[10] *An ass with wood.*—Back and belly; for such is the loading

when they struck upon his frock, his skin was so
hard. Then they committed him to two of the
marshal's men to keep, and, looking about, saw nobody coming against them, whereupon they thought
that Gargantua and his party were fled. Then was
it that they rode as hard as they could towards the
walnut-trees to meet with them, and left the monk
there all alone, with his two foresaid men to guard
him. Gargantua heard the noise and neighing of
the horses, and said to his men, Comrades, I hear
the track and beating of the enemy's horse-feet, and
withal perceive that some of them come in a troop
and full body against us. Let us rally and close
here, then set forward in order, and by this means
we shall be able to receive their charge, to their loss
and our honour.

CHAPTER XLIV

HOW THE MONK RID HIMSELF OF HIS KEEPERS, AND HOW PICROCHOLE'S FORLORN HOPE WAS DEFEATED

THE monk, seeing them break off thus without
order, conjectured that they were to set upon Gargantua and those that were with him, and was
wonderfully grieved that he could not succour them.
Then considered he the countenance of the two
keepers in whose custody he was, who would have
willingly run after the troops to get some booty and
plunder, and were always looking towards the valley
unto which they were going. Farther, he syllogized,
saying, These men are but badly skilled in matters
of an ass carrying wood to market. He seems to be covered all
over with it.

The Monk rids himself of his keepers.

of war, for they have not required my parole, neither
have they taken my sword from me.   Suddenly hereupon he drew his brackmard or horseman's sword,
wherewith he gave the keeper which held him on
the right side, such a sound slash, that he cut clean
through the jugular veins, and the sphagitid or trans-
parent arteries of the neck, with the fore-part of
the throat called the gargareon, even unto the two
adenes, which are throat-kernels ; and, redoubling
the blow, he opened the spinal marrow betwixt the
second and third vertebræ.   There fell down that
keeper stark dead to the ground.   Then the monk,
reining his horse to the left, ran upon the other,
who, seeing his fellow dead, and the monk to have
the advantage of him, cried with a loud voice, Ha,
my Lord Prior, quarter ! I yield, my Lord Prior,
quarter, quarter, my good friend, my Lord Prior !
And the monk cried likewise, My Lord Posterior,
my friend, my Lord Posterior, you shall have it upon
your posteriorums !   Ha, said the keeper, my Lord
Prior, my minion, my gentle Lord Prior, I pray God
make you an Abbot !   By the habit, said the monk,
which I wear, I will here make you a cardinal.
What ! do you use to pay ransoms to religious men ?
You shall therefore have by and by a red hat of my
giving.[1]   And the fellow cried, Ha, my Lord Prior,

[1] *A red hat of my giving.*—That is, *I will cut off your head and
so give you a red hat.*   Thus a 'cardinal en Greve' (the place of
execution at Paris) is proverbially said of a criminal that is be-
headed, and upon this wretched proverb turns the sting of James
Spifame's epitaph.   Menot, who preached at the beginning of the
sixteenth century, once said, towards the close of a sermon of his,
in the Passion week, that though there were preachers who durst
carry truth with them into the pulpit, they were threatened to be
made cardinals without going to Rome, etc., and the authors of
the Catholicon d'Espagne, long after that preacher, made use of
the same expression in two places of that satire.

my Lord Prior, my Lord Abbot that shall be, my
Lord Cardinal, my Lord all! Ha, ha, hes! no my
Lord Prior! my good little Lord the Prior! I yield,
render and deliver myself up to you! And I
deliver thee, said the monk, to all the devils in
hell.—Then at one stroke he cut off his head,
cutting his scalp upon the temple-bones, and lifting
up in the upper part of the skull the two triangulary
bones called sincipital, or the two bones bregmatis,
together with the sagittal commissure or dart-like
seam which distinguisheth the right side of the head
from the left, as also a great part of the coronal or
fore-head bone, by which terrible blow likewise he
cut the two meninges or films which enwrap the
brain, and made a deep wound in the brain's two
posterior ventricles, and the cranium or skull abode
hanging upon his shoulders by the skin of the peri-
cranium behind, in form of a doctor's bonnet, black
without and red within. Thus fell he down also to
the ground stark dead.

And presently the monk gave his horse the spur,
and kept the way that the enemy held who had
met with Gargantua and his companions in the
broad highway, and were so diminished of their
number, for the enormous slaughter that Gargantua
had made with his great tree amongst them, as also
Gymnast, Ponocrates, Eudemon, and the rest, that
they began to retreat disorderly and in great haste,
as men altogether affrighted and troubled in both
sense and understanding, and as if they had seen
the very proper species and form of death before
their eyes ; or, rather, as when you see an ass with
a brizze or gad-bee under his tail, or fly that stings
him, run hither and thither without keeping any
path or way, throwing down his load to the ground,
breaking his bridle and reins, and taking no breath

nor rest, and no man can tell what ails him, for they
see not any thing touch him—so fled these people
destitute of wit, without knowing any cause of flying,
only pursued by a panic terror, which in their minds
they had conceived. The monk, perceiving that
their whole intent was to betake themselves to their
heels, alighted from his horse, and got upon a big
large rock, which was in the way, and with his great
brackmard sword laid such load upon those runaways, and with main strength fetching a compass
with his arm without feigning or sparring, slew and
overthrew so many, that his sword broke in two
pieces. Then thought he within himself that he
had slain and killed sufficiently, and that the rest
should escape to carry news. Therefore he took up
a battle-axe of those that lay there dead, and got
upon the rock again, passing his time to see the
enemy thus flying, and to tumble himself amongst
the dead bodies, only that he suffered none to carry
pike, sword, lance, nor gun with him, and those
who carried the pilgrims bound he made to alight,
and gave their horses unto the said pilgrims, keeping
them there with him under the hedge, and also
Touchfaucet, who was then his prisoner.

CHAPTER XLV

HOW THE MONK CARRIED ALONG WITH HIM THE
PILGRIMS, AND OF THE GOOD WORDS THAT
GRANGOUSIER GAVE THEM

This skirmish being ended, Gargantua retreated
with his men, excepting the monk, and about the
dawning of the day they came unto Grangousier,

who in his bed was praying unto God for their
safety and victory. And seeing them all safe and
sound, he embraced them lovingly, and asked what
was become of the monk? Gargantua answered
him, that without doubt the enemies had the monk.
Then have they mischief and ill luck, said Grangousier, which was very true. Therefore is it a
common proverb to this day, to give a man the
monk, or as in French, *luy bailler le moyne*, when
they would express the doing unto one a mischief.
Then commanded he a good breakfast to be provided
for their refreshment. When all was ready, they
called Gargantua, but he was so aggrieved that the
monk was not to be heard of, that he would neither
eat nor drink. In the meanwhile, the monk comes,
and from the gate of the outer court cries out aloud,
Fresh wine, fresh wine, Gymnast my friend!
Gymnast went out and saw that it was Friar John,
who brought along with him six pilgrims and
Touchfaucet prisoners; whereupon Gargantua likewise went forth to meet him, and all of them made
him the best welcome that possibly they could, and
brought him before Grangousier, who asked him of
all his adventures. The monk told him all, both
how he was taken, how he rid himself of his keepers,
of the slaughter he had made by the way, and how
he had rescued the pilgrims, and brought along with
him Captain Touchfaucet. Then did they altogether
fall to banqueting most merrily. In the meantime
Grangousier asked the pilgrims what countrymen
they were, whence they came, and whither they
went? Sweer-to-go in the name of the rest
answered, My sovereign lord, I am of Saint Genou
in Berry, this man is of Palau, this other is of Onzay,
this of Argy, this of St Nazarand, and this man of
Villebrenin. We come from St Sebastian near

Nantes,[1] and are now returning, as we best may, by easy journeys. Yea, but, said Grangousier, what went you to do at Saint Sebastian ? We went, said Swear-to-go, to offer up unto that Sanct our vows against the plague. Ah, poor men, said Grangousier, do you think that the plague comes from St Sebastian? Yes, truly, answered Swear-to-go, our preachers tell us so indeed. But is it so, said Grangousier, do the false prophets teach you such abuses ?[2] Do they thus blaspheme the Sancts and holy men of God, as to make them like unto the devils, who do nothing but hurt unto mankind,—as Homer writeth, that the plague was sent into the camp of the Greeks by Apollo, and as the poets feign a great rabble of Vejoves and mischievous gods ? So did a certain Cafard or dissembling religionary preach at Sinay, that Saint Anthony sent the fire into men's legs, that St Eutropius made men hydropic,[3] St Gildas, fools, and that St Genou made them goutish. But I punished him so exemplarily, though he called me heretic for it, that since that time no such

[1] *St Sebastian near Nantes, etc.*—It is at Peligny, near Nantes, where the body of St Sebastian is said to be kept; though the possession of it is likewise insisted upon by Rome, Soissons, and Narbonne.

[2] *Such abuses.*—Without offence to the well-meaning Grangousier, there's no such great hurt in it as he fancies. If some saints, when they are angered, send certain distempers, as is believed by the Romanists, they likewise cure them when they . please. This is what H. Stephens frankly confesses, in chap. 38 of his Apology for Herodotus.

[3] *St Eutropius made men hydropic, etc.*—See Agrippa, ch. 57, *De Vanitate Scientiarum*, and H. Stephens, chap. 38, of the Apology for Herodotus. 'Ridendi sunt,' says the former, 'qui à nominis similitudine et vocum confusione, et per similia futilia inventa sanctis quædam morborum genera adscribunt, ut Germani caducum morbum Valentino, quia hoc nomen (fallen) cadere significat, et Galli Eutropio addicant Hydropicos, ob consimilem sonum.'

279

hypocritical rogue durst set his foot within my
territories. And truly I wonder that your king
should suffer them in their sermons to publish such
scandalous doctrine in his dominions; for they deserve
to be chastised with greater severity than those who,
by magical art, or any other device, have brought the
pestilence into a country. The pest killeth but the
bodies, but such abominable impostors empoison our
very souls. As he spake these words, in came the
monk very resolute, and asked them, Whence are you,
you poor wretches? Of Saint Genou, said they.
And how, said the monk, does the Abbot Gulligut
the good drinker, and the monks, what cheer make
they? By God's body, they'll have a fling at your
wives, and breast them to some purpose, whilst you
are upon your roaming rant and gadding pilgrimage.[4]
Hin, hen, said Sweer-to-go, I am not afraid of mine,
for he that shall see her by day will never break his
neck to come to her in the night-time. Yea, marry,
said the monk, now you have hit it. Let her be as
ugly as ever was Proserpina, she will once, by the

[4] *Gadding Pilgrimage.*—Time was that these devout journey-
ings were in great vogue, but they never had so much success, as
when the pilgrim undertook them with a view to have children.
Toleno, in that epigram of Beza's Tollendæ cupidus Toleno
prolis, is a famous example of this. The good man was rich,
but had no children, though he had been married some years. In
full assurance that he should soon see himself a father, could he
but make heaven his friend, he courageously undertakes at once a
pilgrimage to Loretto, another to the Holy Sepulchre, and a third
to Mount Sinai. It is easy to imagine how great a fatigue he
underwent, during so long a peregrination. But how transported
was he, when, upon his return home, after a three years' voyage,
he found his family increased with three lovely boys, whom he
had not the trouble of getting? Certainly, the piety of our
ancestors was of great advantage in this respect; and since it has
insensibly grown cold, Mademoiselle Sevin had good reason to say
in Fenestæ, l. 3, 'The world was going to be no more, and mankind would soon be at an end, for want of pilgrimages.'

Lord God, be overturned, and get her skin-coat ·
shaken, if there dwell any monks near to her; for a
good carpenter will make use of any kind of timber.
Let me be peppered with the pox, if you find not
all your wives with child at your return; for the
very shadow of the steeple of an abbey is fruitful.
It is, said Gargantua, like the water of Nilus in
Egypt, if you believe Strabo and Pliny, lib. 7, cap. 3.
What virtue will there be, then, said the monk, in
their bullets of concupiscence, their habits, and their
bodies ?

Then said Grangousier, Go your ways, poor men,
in the name of God the Creator ! to whom I pray
to guide you perpetually, and henceforward be not
so ready to undertake these idle and unprofitable
journeys.   Look to your families, labour every man
in his vocation, instruct your children, and live as
the good Apostle St Paul directeth you: in doing
whereof, God, his angels and sancts, will guard and
protect you, and no evil or plague at any time shall
befal you.   Then Gargantua led them into the hall
to take their refection; but the pilgrims did nothing
but sigh, and said to Gargantua, O how happy is that
land which hath such a man for their lord !   We
have been more edified and instructed by the talk
which he had with us, than by all the sermons that
ever were preached in our town.   This is, said
Gargantua, that which Plato saith, lib. 5, de Republ.,
That those commonwealths are happy, whose rulers
philosophise, and whose philosophers rule.   Then
caused he their wallets to be filled with victuals, and
their bottles with wine, and gave unto each of them
a horse to ease them upon the way, together with
some pence [5] to live by.

[5] *Some pence.—Quelques Carolus:* some *Caroluses:* a *Carolus,* Cotgrave says, is a piece of white money, worth tenpence, Tour, *i.e.,*

CHAPTER XLVI

HOW GRANGOUSIER DID VERY KINDLY ENTERTAIN TOUCHFAUCET HIS PRISONER

TOUCHFAUCET was presented unto Grangousier, and by him examined upon the enterprise and attempt of Picrochole, what it was he could pretend to, or aim at, by the rustling stir and tumultuary coil of this his sudden invasion. Whereunto he answered, that his end and purpose was to conquer all the country, if he could, for the injury done to his cake-bakers. It is too great an undertaking, said Grangousier; and, as the proverb is, He that gripes too much, holds fast but little. The time is not now as formerly, to conquer the kingdoms of our neighbour princes, and to build up our own greatness upon the loss of our nearest Christian brother. This imitation of the ancient Herculeses, Alexanders, Hannibals, Scipios, Cæsars, and other such heroes, is quite contrary to the profession of the gospel of Christ, by which we are commanded to preserve, keep, rule and govern every man his own country and lands, and not in a hostile manner to invade others; and that which heretofore the Barbarians and Saracens called prowess and valour, we now call robbing, thievery, and wickedness. It would have been more

Tournois, or a just English penny. *Carolus de Bezançon,* a silver coin, worth about ninepence sterling; *Carolus de Flanders,* another, worth about three shillings sterling. I apprehend our author to mean the first, because M. le Duchat's note is, *Carolus,* a piece of money, worth ten deniers, stamped with a large K and a crown over it. King Charles VIII. was the first that caused this piece to be coined, and marked with the first letter of his name in Latin, viz., *Karolus.*

commendable in him to have contained himself
within the bounds of his own territories, royally
governing them, than to insult and domineer in
mine, pillaging and plundering everywhere like a
most unmerciful enemy; for, by ruling his own with
discretion, he might have increased his greatness, but
by robbing me, he cannot escape destruction. Go
your ways in the name of God, prosecute good
enterprises, show your king what is amiss, and never
counsel him with regard unto your own particular
profit, for the public loss will swallow up the private
benefit. As for your ransom, I do freely remit it to
you, and will that your arms and horse be restored
to you; so should good neighbours do, and ancient
friends, seeing this our difference is not properly
war. As Plato, lib. 5, de Repub., would not have it
called war but sedition, when the Greeks took up
arms against one another, and that, therefore, when
such combustions should arise amongst them, his
advice was to behave themselves in the managing of
them with all discretion and modesty. Although
you call it war, it is but superficial, it entereth not
into the closet and inmost cabinet of our hearts.
For neither of us hath been wronged in his honour,
nor is there any question betwixt us in the main,
but only how to redress, by the bye, some petty faults
committed by our men—I mean, both yours and
ours, which, although you knew, you ought to let
pass; for these quarrelsome persons deserve rather to
be contemned than mentioned, especially seeing I
offered them satisfaction according to the wrong.
God shall be the just judge of our variances, whom
I beseech, by death rather to take me out of this
life, and to permit my goods to perish and be
destroyed before mine eyes, than that by me or
mine he should in any sort be wronged. These

words uttered, he called the monk, and before them
all thus spoke unto him. Friar John, my good
friend, is it you that took prisoner the Captain
Touchfaucet here present? Sir, said the monk,
seeing himself is here, and that he is of the years of
discretion, I had rather you should know it by his
confession, than by any words of mine. Then said
Touchfaucet, My sovereign lord, it is he indeed
that took me, and I do therefore most freely yield
myself his prisoner. Have you put him to any
ransom? said Grangousier to the monk. No, said
the monk, of that I take no care. How much
would you have for having taken him? Nothing,
nothing, said the monk, I am not swayed by that,
nor do I regard it. Than Grangousier commanded
that, in presence of Touchfaucet, should be delivered
to the monk for taking him the sum of threescore
and two thousand saluts [1] (in English money, fifteen
thousand and five hundred pounds), which was done,
whilst they made a collation or little banquet to the
said Touchfaucet, of whom Grangousier asked, If he
would stay with him, or if he loved rather to return
to his king? Touchfaucet answered, that he was
content to take whatever course he would advise him

[1] *Saluts.*—Two things occur to my thoughts concerning this
species of money, which I do not think Rabelais here has employed
preferable to any other, without some reason. First, that Friar
John, having saved Touchfaucet's life, and contented himself with
only making him his prisoner, it was a very proper way of re-
warding him with *saluts* (*salut* signifying safety, preservation,
safe-guard, etc.). Secondly, that as this coin was called *salut*,
only because it had on one side the angelical salutation, represented
with the word *Ave*, God save you, by which our French ancestors
expressed *check*, at chess-play, and even *check-mate:* the *Ave* of the
saluts, paid to Friar John, might always put him in mind of that
gallant action of his, in giving *check* and *mate* to one of Picrochole's
generals. As to their value, Cotgrave says, ' *Saluts* were an old
French crown, worth about five shillings sterling.'

to. Then, said Grangousier, return unto your king, and God be with you.

Then he gave him an excellent sword of a Vienne blade,[2] with a golden scabbard wrought with vine branch-like flourishes, of fair goldsmith's work, and a collar or neck-chain of gold, weighing seven hundred and two thousand merks (at eight ounces each),, garnished with precious stones of the finest sort, esteemed at a hundred and sixty thousand ducats,, and ten thousand crowns more, as an honourable donative by way of present. After this talk Touch-faucet got to his horse, and Gargantua for his safety allowed him the guard of thirty men-at-arms, and six score archers[3] to attend him under the conduct

[2] *Vienne blade.*—At Vienne, in the lower Dauphiné, are made excellent sword-blades, by means of certain *martinets* (water-mills for an iron forge, says Cotgrave). These *martinets* (or hammers, as Bowyer calls them), rise and fall alternately, and with the greatest regularity possible, by the motion of the wheels, which are turned by the stream of a little river called Gere. [Tilt-hammers, in English.]

[3] *Thirty men-at-arms, and six score archers.*—The French *noblesse* (gentry) being grown plunderers and freebooters in the wars of the preceding reigns, they were reduced into a body of regular troops of horse, under Charles VII., consisting of fifteen hundred lancemen and archers, the companies whereof, more or less strong, were distributed to the princes, and most experienced captains of the kingdom. Each man-at-arms had in his train four horses, two of which were for the service of himself to ride on, and the other two were, one of them a sumpter-horse, and the other for a servant called *coûtillier,* either because he rode by his master's side (*côte*), or rather, I should think, because he was armed with a good cutlass. There were twice as many archers, obliged to have each two horses, one for himself, and the other for his baggage; but two archers had no more pay than one man-at-arms, that is, per day half-a-crown, value thirteen sous, six deniers;, both the man-at-arms and archer were to be gentlemen. See farther on this subject, the Life of Louis XII., by Seyssel, last chap., and Fauchet, l. 2, c. 1, of his 'Treatise of Warfare and Arms.'

285

of Gymnast, to bring him even unto the gate of the rock Clermond, if there were need. As soon as he was gone, the monk restored unto Grangousier the three-score and two thousand saluts, which he had received, saying, Sir, it is not as yet the time for you to give such gifts—stay till this war be at an end, for none can tell what accidents may occur, and war, begun without good provision of money before-hand for going through with it, is but as a breathing of strength, and blast that will quickly pass away. Coin is the sinews of war. Well then, said Grangousier, at the end I will content you by some honest recompense, as also all those who shall do me good service.

CHAPTER XLVII

HOW GRANGOUSIER SENT FOR HIS LEGIONS, AND HOW TOUCHFAUCET SLEW RASHCALF, AND WAS AFTER-WARDS EXECUTED BY THE COMMAND OF PICRO-CHOLE

ABOUT this same time those of Besse, of the Old Market, of St James' Bourg, of the Draggage,[1] of Parillé, of the Rivers,[2] of the rocks of St Pol,[3] of the Vaubreton, of Pautillé, of the Brehemont, of Clain-bridge, of Cravant, of Grandmont, of the town at the Badger-holes,[4] of Huymes, of Segré, of Husse, of

[1] *Draggage.*—Trainneau, a place so called.
[2] *Rivers.*—*Riviere.* Another place so called.
[3] *Rocks of St Pol.*—Parish in the diocese of Tours, in which there is a priory dependant on the abbey of St Paul de Comeri, of the Order of St Benet.
[4] *Badger-holes.*—*Des Bourdes.* I know not why the translator

St Lovant, of Panzoust, of the Coldraux, of Verron, of Coulaines, of Chose, of Varenes, of Bourgueil, of the Bouchard Island, of the Croullay, of Narsay, of Cande, of Montsoreau,[5] and other bordering places, sent ambassadors unto Grangousier, to tell him that they were advised of the great wrongs which Picrochole had done him, and in regard of their ancient confederacy, offered him what assistance they could afford, both in men, money, victuals, and ammunition, and other necessaries for war. The money, which by the joint agreement of them all was sent unto him, amounted to six score and fourteen millions two crowns and a half of pure gold. The forces wherewith they did assist him, did consist of fifteen thousand cuirassiers,[6] two and thirty thousand light horsemen, fourscore and nine thousand dragoons,[7] and a hundred and forty thousand volunteer adventurers. These had with them eleven thousand and two hundred cannons, double cannons, long pieces of artillery called basilisks, and smaller sized ones, known by the name of spirols, besides the mortar-pieces and granadoes. Of pioneers they had seven and forty thousand, all victualled and paid for six months and four days of advance. Which offer Gargantua did not altogether refuse, nor wholly accept of; but, giv-

calls this place the Badger-holes; nor why he omits the next in Rabelais' list, Villaumere.

5 *Cande, Montsoreau, etc.*— Cande is a borough of Touraine, and Montsoreau, another, very near Cande, where the Vienne enters the Loire. Parillé, or Parillai, is a village half a league from Chinon, just at the end of the Nun's-bridge (see Du Chesne's Antiquities of the Towns, etc., chap. of those of Chinon). The other places mentioned here by Rabelais, are of Anjou, Touraine, and the election of Chinon, for the most part. At Croulai, which is very near Chinon, there is a convent of Cordeliers.

6 *Cuirassiers.*—Called men-at-arms in the original.

7 *Dragoons.*—*Harquebusiers.*

ing them hearty thanks, said, that he would compose
and order the war by such a device, that there
should not be found great need to put so many honest
men to trouble in the managing of it; and therefore
was content at that time to give order only for bringing along the legions, which he maintained in his
ordinary garrison towns of the Deviniere, of Chavigny,
of Gravot, and of the Quinquenais, amounting to the
number of two thousand cuirassiers, three score and
six thousand foot soldiers, six and twenty thousand
dragoons, attended by two hundred pieces of great
ordnance, two and twenty thousand pioneers, and
six thousand light horsemen, all drawn up in troops,
so well befitted and accommodated with their commissaries, sutlers, farriers, harness-makers, and other
such like necessary members in a military camp; so
fully instructed in the art of warfare, so perfectly
knowing and following their colours, so ready to hear
and obey their captains, so nimble to run, so strong
at their charging, so prudent in their adventures, and
every day so well disciplined, that they seemed rather
to be a concert of organ-pipes, or mutual concord
of the wheels of a clock, than an infantry and
cavalry, or army of soldiers.

Touchfaucet immediately after his return presented himself before Picrochole, and related unto
him at large all that he had done and seen, and at
last endeavoured to persuade him with strong and
forcible arguments to capitulate and make an agreement with Grangousier, whom he found to be the
honestest man in the world; saying further, that it
was neither right nor reason thus to trouble his
neighbours, of whom they never received anything
but good. And in regard of the main point, that
they should never be able to go through stitch with
that war, but to their great damage and mischief:

for the forces of Picrochole were not so considerable
but that Grangousier could easily overthrow them.

He had not well done speaking, when Rashcalf
said out aloud, Unhappy is that prince, which is by
such men served, who are so easily corrupted, as I
know Touchfaucet is. For I see his courage so
changed, that he had willingly joined with our
enemies to fight against us and betray us, if they
would have received him; but, as virtue is of all,
both friends and foes, praised and esteemed, so is
wickedness soon known and suspected, and although
it happen the enemies do make use thereof for their
profit, yet have they always the wicked and the
traitors in abomination.

Touchfaucet, being at these words very impatient,
drew out his sword, and therewith ran Rashcalt
through the body, a little under the nipple of his left
side, whereof he died presently, and pulling back his
sword out of his body, said boldly, So let him perish,
that shall a faithful servant blame. Picrochole incontinently grew furious, and seeing Touchfaucet's
new sword[8] and his scabbard so richly diapered with
flourishes of most excellent workmanship, said, Did
they give thee this weapon so feloniously therewith
to kill before my face my so good friend Rashcalf?
Then immediately commanded he his guard to hew
him in pieces, which was instantly done, and that so
cruelly, that the chamber was all dyed with blood.
Afterwards he appointed the corpse of Rashcalf to be
honourably buried, and that of Touchfaucet to be
cast over the walls into the ditch.

The news of these excessive violences were
quickly spread through all the army; whereupon
many began to murmur against Picrochole, in so far

---

[8] *New sword*, *etc.*—The same which Grangousier had given
him.

that Pinchpenny[9] said to him, My sovereign lord, I know not what the issue of this enterprise will be. I see your men much dejected, and not well resolved in their minds, by considering that we are here very ill provided of victuals, and that our number is already much diminished by three or four sallies. Furthermore, great supplies and recruits come daily in to your enemies : but we so moulder away, that, if we be once besieged, I do not see how we can escape a total destruction. Tush, pish ! said Picrochole, you are like the Melun eels, you cry before they come to you.[10] Let them come ! let them come ! if they dare.

CHAPTER XLVIII

HOW GARGANTUA SET UPON PICROCHOLE WITHIN THE ROCK CLERMOND, AND UTTERLY DEFEATED THE ARMY OF THE SAID PICROCHOLE

GARGANTUA had the charge of the whole army, and his father Grangousier stayed in his castle, who, encouraging them with good words, promised great rewards unto those that should do any notable service. Having thus set forward, as soon as they had gained the pass at the ford of Vede, with boats and bridges speedily made, they passed over in a

9 *Pinchpenny.*—In the original it is, Grippe-pineau, Gripe-grape, not gripe, or pinchpenny. The pineau, says Cotgrave, is a kind of white and longish grape, whereof is made the vin pineau, excellent strong wine. M. le Duchat says, This person was, in all probability, one that distinguished himself at the sacking of the Abbey-close at Sevillé.

10 *Before the, come to you.*—Read, before they begin to skin you. Davant qu'on vous escorche.

trice. Then considering the situation of the town,
which was on a high and advantageous place, Gargantua thought fit to call his council and pass that
night in deliberation upon what was to be done.
But Gymnast said unto him, My sovereign lord, such
is the nature and complexion of the French, that
they are worth nothing but at the first push. Then
they are more fierce than devils. But if they linger
a little, and be wearied with delays, they will prove
more faint and remiss than women. My opinion is,
therefore, that now presently after your men have
taken breath, and some small refection, you give order
for a resolute assault, and that we storm them instantly.
His advice was found very good, and for effectuating
thereof he brought forth his army into the plain field,
and placed the receives [subsides] on the skirt
or rising of a little hill. The monk took along with
him six companies of foot, and two hundred horsemen well armed, and with great diligence crossed
the marsh, and valiantly got upon the top of the
green hillock even unto the highway which leads to
Loudun. Whilst the assault was thus begun, Picrochole's men could not tell what was best, to issue
out and receive the assailants, or keep within the
town and not to stir. Himself in the meantime,
without deliberation, sallied forth in a rage with the
cavalry of his guard, who were forthwith received
and royally entertained with great cannon-shot, that
fell upon them like hail from the high grounds, on
which the artillery was planted. For which purpose
the Gargantuists betook themselves unto the valleys,
to give the ordnance leave to play and range with
the larger scope.

Those of the town defended themselves as well as
they could, but their shot passed over without doing
any hurt at all. Some of Picrochole's men, that had

escaped our artillery, set most fiercely upon our
soldiers, but prevailed little; for they were all let in
betwixt the files, and there knocked down to the
ground, which their fellow-soldiers seeing, they
would have retreated, but the monk having seized
upon the pass, by which they were to return, they
ran away and fled in all the disorder and confusion
that could be imagined.

Some would have pursued after them, and followed
the chase, but the monk withheld them, apprehending that in their pursuit the pursuers might lose their
ranks, and so give occasion to the besieged to sally
out of the town upon them. Then staying there
some space, and none coming against him, he sent
the Duke Phrontist, to advise Gargantua to advance
towards the hill upon the left hand, to hinder
Picrochole's retreat at that gate; which Gargantua
did with all expedition, and sent thither four brigades
under the conduct of Sebast, which had no sooner
reached the top of the hill, but they met Picrochole
in the teeth, and those that were with him scattered.

Then charged they upon them stoutly, yet were
they much endamaged by those that were upon the
walls, who galled them with all manner of shot, both
from the great ordnance, small guns, and bows.
Which Gargantua perceiving, he went with a strong
party to their relief, and with his artillery began to
thunder so terribly upon that canton of the wall, and
so long, that all the strength within the town, to
maintain and fill up the breach, was drawn thither.
The monk, seeing that quarter which he kept besieged void of men and competent guards, and in a
manner altogether naked and abandoned, did most
magnanimously on a sudden lead up his men towards
the fort, and never left it till he had got up upon it,
knowing, that such as come to the reserve in a

conflict bring with them always more fear[1] and
terror, than those that deal about them with their
hands in the fight.

Nevertheless he gave no alarm till all his soldiers
had got within the wall, except the two hundred
horsemen, whom he left without to secure his entry.
Then did he give a most horrible shout, so did all
those who were with him, and immediately thereafter, without resistance, putting to the edge of the
sword the guard that was at that gate, they opened
it to the horsemen, with whom most furiously they
altogether ran towards the east gate, where all the
hurly-burly was, and coming close upon them in the
rear, overthrew all their forces.

The besieged, seeing that the Gargantuists had
won the town upon them, and that they were like to
be secure in no corner of it, submitted themselves
unto the mercy of the monk, and asked for quarter,
which the monk very nobly granted to them, yet
made them lay down their arms; then, shutting
them up within churches, gave order to seize upon
all the staves of the crosses, and placed men at the
doors to keep them from coming forth. Then,
opening the east gate, he issued out to succour
and assist Gargantua. But Picrochole, thinking it
had been some relief coming to him from the town,
adventured more forwardly than before, and was
upon the giving of a most desperate home-charge,
when Gargantua cried out, Ha! Friar John, my
friend! Friar John! you are come in a good hour.
Which unexpected accident so affrighted Picrochole
and his men, that, giving all for lost, they betook
themselves to their heels, and fled on all hands.

---

[1] *More fear*, *etc.*—This is almost word for word taken from
Thucydides, L 5, c. 2.

Gargantua chased them till they came near to Vaugaudry, killing and slaying all the way, and then
sounded the retreat.

CHAPTER XLIX

HOW PICROCHOLE IN HIS FLIGHT FELL INTO GREAT
MISFORTUNES, AND WHAT GARGANTUA DID AFTER
THE BATTLE

PICROCHOLE, thus in despair, fled towards the
Bouchard Island, and in the way to Rivière his horse
stumbled and fell down, whereat he on a sudden
was so incensed, that he with his sword without
more ado killed him in his choler; then, not finding
any that would remount him, he was about to have
taken an ass at the mill that was thereby; but the
miller's men did so baste his bones, and so soundly
bethwack him, that they made him both black and
blue with strokes; then, stripping him of all his
clothes, gave him a scurvy old canvas jacket wherewith to cover his nakedness. Thus went this poor
choleric wretch, who passing the water at Port-
Huaux, and relating his misadventurous disasters,
was foretold by an old Lourpidon hag,[1] that his
kingdom should be restored to him at the coming of
the Cocklicranes.[2] What is become of him since

[1] *Lourpidon hag.*—Dirty nasty hag. See M. le Duchat for the
etymon of that word.
[2] *At the coming of the Cocklicranes.*—That is, never. Rabelais, l.
4, c. 32, 'If he stepped back, it was sea-cockle-shells.' In the
original it is in both places cocquecigrües. The shells of sea-
hedgehogs are called cocquecigrües, and, according to this last
passage, M. Menage thought that the proverbial expression, hinted
at in the first, was occasioned by the sea-urchins, only turning

we cannot certainly tell, yet was I told that he is
now a porter at Lyons, as testy and pettish in humour
as ever he was before, and would be always, with
great lamentation, inquiring at all strangers of the
coming of the Cocklicranes, expecting assuredly,
according to the old woman's prophecy, that at their
coming he shall be re-established in his kingdom.
The first thing Gargantua did after his return into
the town was to call the muster-roll of his men,
which when he had done he found that there were
very few either killed or wounded, only some few
foot of Captain Tolmere's [3] company, and Ponocrates,
who was shot with a musket-ball through the
doublet. [4]   Then he caused them all at and in their
several posts and divisions to take a little refreshment, which was very plenteously provided for them
in the best drink and victuals that could be had for

themselves in their shells, without moving forward or backwards;
and he quotes Rondelet for this: but he mistook Rondelet's words,
l. 18, De piscibus. ' Omnibus (echinis) crusta est tenuis, undique
spinis sive aculeis armata quæ pro pedibus sunt.   Ingredi est his
in orbe volvi.'   This does not mean that the sea-hedgehogs,
instead of walking, only turn in their shells, but that the prickly
sharp points of their shells serve them for feet, and that they
walk, or have a progressive motion, by rolling.   As for the word
cocquecigruës, I am of opinion, that as the ancients had their
sphinxes and chimeras, we have our cocquecigruës, or creatures
made up of a cock, a cygnet (young swan) and a crane (grus), to
which sometimes is added the word sea, to make the thing more
extraordinary, and at the same time more ridiculous.

    [3] *Tolmere's.*—Τολμηρὸς, audacious, rash, one of Gargantua's
captains.

    [4] *Through the doublet.*—This does honour both to Gargantua
and Ponocrates, it being reasonable to believe that the preceptor,
who, it is plain, was a universalist, *i.e.*, an all-round sportsman,
as the saying is, did not thus expose himself without being
prompted thereto by a most commendable zeal to follow everywhere his princely pupil, whom a noble ardour had hurried into
the thickest of the fight.

money, and gave order to the treasurers and commissaries of the army, to pay for and defray that
repast, and that there should be no outrage at all,
nor abuse committed in the town, seeing it was his
own. And furthermore commanded, that immediately after the soldiers had done with eating and
drinking for that time sufficiently, and to their own
heart's desire, a gathering should be beaten, for
bringing them altogether, to be drawn upon the
piazza before the castle, there to receive six months'
pay completely. All which was done. After this,
by his direction, were brought before him in the said
place all those that remained of Picrochole's party,
unto whom, in the presence of the princes, nobles,
and officers of his court and army, he spoke as
followeth.

CHAPTER L

GARGANTUA'S SPEECH TO THE VANQUISHED

Our forefathers and ancestors of all times have been
of this nature and disposition, that, upon the winning
of a battle, they have chosen rather, for a sign and
memorial of their triumphs and victories, to erect
trophies and monuments in the hearts of the vanquished by clemency, than by architecture in the
lands which they had conquered. For they did hold
in greater estimation the lively remembrance of men,
purchased by liberality, than the dumb inscription of
arches, pillars, and pyramids, subject to the injury of
storms and tempests, and to the envy of every one.
You may very well remember of the courtesy, which
by them was used towards the Bretons, in the battle

of St Aubin of Cormier,[1] and at the demolishing of
Partenay. You have heard, and hearing admire,
their gentle comportment towards those at the
barriers[2] of Spaniola, who had plundered, wasted,
and ransacked the maritime borders of Olone and
Thalmondois. All this hemisphere of the world
was filled with the praises and congratulations which
yourselves and your fathers made, when Alpharbal
King of Canarre,[3] not satisfied with his own
fortunes, did most furiously invade the land of
Onyx, and with cruel piracies molest all the
Armorick Islands, and confine regions of Britany.
Yet was he in a set naval fight[4] justly taken and
vanquished by my father, whom God preserve and
protect. But what? Whereas other kings and
emperors, yea those who entitle themselves Catholics,
would have dealt roughly with him, kept him a close
prisoner, and put him to an extreme high ransom, he
entreated him very courteously,[5] lodged him kindly

[1] *Battle, etc.*—Near Dol, in Bretagne, the 28th of July, 1484,
between the Duc de Bretagne and Charles VIII.

[2] *Spaniola.*—Read, towards the barbarians (not barriers) of
Spain.

[3] *Alpharbal, King of Canarre.*—In ch. 13, there has been notice
taken of this war, and the defeat of the Canarines: but as in
several editions we read Ganarrians; and that in the prol. of l. 4
the author speaks of the Genoese as cheats (gannatori) and a
people whose sole view in everything is gain, I know not, but
that under the name of Canarre, we are to understand the city of
Genoa, there being, besides, a wondrous agreement between the
lenity which Grangousier is here said to have shown the
Ganarrians, whom he had subdued, and the clemency which the
good King Louis XII. manifested towards the Genoese in 1507,
when he forced that people to return to their obedience under
him.

[4] *In a set naval fight.*—Instead of naval fight read only a fight.
The word *navale* in some editions is wrong printed for *navré,*
which signifies wounded, and should precede taken and vanquished.

[5] *He entreated him very courteously, etc.*—Several things seem

with himself in his own palace, and out of his
incredible mildness and gentle disposition sent him
back with a safe conduct, laden with gifts, laden
with favours, laden with all offices of friendship.
What fell out upon it? Being returned into his
country, he called a parliament, where all the
princes and states of his kingdom being assembled,
he showed them the humanity which he had found
in us, and therefore wished them to take such course
by way of compensation therein, as that the whole
world might be edified by the example, as well of
their honest graciousness to us, as of our gracious
honesty towards them. The result hereof was, that
it was voted and decreed by an unanimous consent,
that they should offer up entirely their lands,
dominions, and kingdoms, to be disposed of by us
according to our pleasure.

Alpharbal in his own person presently returned
with nine thousand and thirty-eight great ships of
burden, bringing with him the treasures, not only of
his house and royal lineage, but almost of all the
country besides. For he embarking himself to set
sail with a west-north-east wind, every one in heaps
did cast into the ship gold, silver, rings, jewels,
spices, drugs, and aromatical perfumes, parrots,
pelicans, monkeys, civet-cats, black-spotted weasels,
porcupines, etc. He was accounted no good
mother's son, that did not cast in all the rare and
precious things he had.

Being safely arrived, he came to my said father,
and would have kissed his feet. That action was

here to agree with Louis XII. who when he became King of
France, disdained to revenge himself on his enemies, whose
caballings had before occasioned his being clapped up in the
strong tower of Bourges, after he had lost the battle of St Aubin
du Cormier.

found too submissively low, and therefore was not
permitted, but in exchange he was most cordially
embraced. He offered his presents; they were not
received, because they were too excessive: he
yielded himself voluntarily a servant and vassal, and
was content his whole posterity should be liable to
the same bondage; this was not accepted of, because
it seemed not equitable: he surrendered, by virtue
of the decree of his great parliamentary council, his
whole countries and kingdoms to him, offering the
deed and conveyance, signed, sealed, and ratified by
those that were concerned in it; this was altogether
refused, and the parchments cast into the fire. In
end, this free good will and simple meaning of the
Canarrines wrought such tenderness in my father's
heart, that he could not abstain from shedding tears,
and wept most profusely; then, by choice words
very congruously adapted, strove in what he could to
diminish the estimation of the good offices which he
had done them, saying, that any courtesy he had
conferred upon them was not worth a rush, and
what favour soever he had showed them, he was
bound to do it. But so much the more did
Alpharbal augment the repute thereof. What was
the issue? Whereas for his ransom in the greatest
extremity of rigour, and most tyrannical dealing,
could not have been exacted above twenty times a
hundred thousand crowns, and his eldest sons detained as hostages, till that sum had been paid, they
made themselves perpetual tributaries, and obliged
to give us every year two millions of gold at four
and twenty carats fine. The first year we received
the whole sum of two millions; the second year of
their own accord they paid freely to us three and
twenty hundred thousand crowns; the third year,
six and twenty hundred thousand; the fourth year,

three millions, and do so increase it always out of
their own good will, that we shall be constrained to
forbid them to bring us any more. This is the
nature of gratitude and true thankfulness. For
time, which gnaws and diminisheth all things else,
augments and increaseth benefits; because a noble
action of liberality, done to a man of reason, doth
grow continually, by his generous thinking of it, and
remembering it.

Being unwilling therefore any way to degenerate
from the hereditary mildness and clemency of my
parents, I do now forgive you, deliver you from all
fines and imprisonments, fully release you, set you at
liberty, and every way make you as frank and free as
ever you were before. Moreover, at your going out
of the gate, you shall have every one of you three
months' pay [6] to bring you home into your houses
and families, and shall have a safe convoy of six
hundred cuirassiers and eight thousand foot under
the conduct of Alexander, esquire of my body, that
the clubmen of the country may not do you any
injury. God be with you! I am sorry from my
heart that Picrochole is not here; for I would have
given him to understand, that this war was undertaken against my will, and without any hope to
increase either my goods or renown. But seeing he
is lost, and that no man can tell where, nor how he
went away, it is my will that this kingdom remain
entire to his son; who, because he is too young, he
not being yet full five years old, shall be brought up
and instructed by the ancient princes, and learned
men of the kingdom. And because a realm, thus
desolate, may easily come to ruin, if the covetousness

---

[6] *Three months' pay.*—At 105 sous a month, which was the pay
of the French infantry at that time. See Cenault de Mensur., etc.,
edition of 1547.

and avarice of those, who by their places are obliged
to administer justice in it, be not curbed and re-
strained, I ordain and will have it so, that Ponocrates
be overseer and superintendent above all his governors, with whatever power and authority is requisite
thereto, and that he be continually with the child,
until he find him able and capable to rule and
govern by himself.

Now I must tell you, that you are to understand
how a too feeble and dissolute facility in pardoning
evil-doers giveth them occasion to commit wickedness afterwards more readily, upon this pernicious
confidence of receiving favour. I consider, that
Moses, the meekest man that was in his time upon
the earth, did severely punish the mutinous and
seditious people of Israel. I consider likewise, that
Julius Cæsar, who was so gracious an emperor, that
Cicero said of him, that his fortune [7] had nothing
more excellent than that he could, and his virtue
nothing better ·than that he would, always save and
pardon every man; he, notwithstanding all this, did
in certain places most rigorously punish the authors
of rebellion. After the example of these good men,
it is my will and pleasure, that you deliver over unto
me, before you depart hence, first, that fine fellow
Marquet, who was the prime cause, origin, and
ground-work of this war, by his vain presumption
and overweening: secondly, his fellow cake-bakers,
who were neglective in checking and reprehending
his idle hair-brained humour in the instant time:
and lastly, all the counsellors, captains, officers, and
domestics of Picrochole, who have been incendiaries

[7] *That his fortune*, etc.—'Nihil habet nec fortuna tua majus,
quàm ut possis, nec natura tua melius, quàm ut velis conservare
quàm plurimos,' says Cicero to Cæsar in his Oration for Qu
Ligarius.

or fomenters of the war, by provoking, praising, or counselling him to come out of his limits thus to trouble us.

CHAPTER LI

HOW THE VICTORIOUS GARGANTUISTS WERE RECOMPENSED AFTER THE BATTLE

WHEN Gargantua had finished his speech, the seditious men whom he required were delivered up unto him, except Swashbuckler, Durtaille, and Smalltrash, who ran away six hours before the battle —one of them as far as to Lainielneck at one course, another to the valley of Vire, and the third even unto Logroine, without looking back, or taking breath by the way—and two of the cake-bakers who were slain in the fight. Gargantua did them no other hurt, but that he appointed them to pull at the presses of his printing-house, which he had newly set up. Then those who died there he caused to be honourably buried in Blacksoille valley,[1] and Burn-hag-field,[2] and gave order that the wounded should be dressed and had care of in his great hospital or nosocome. After this, considering the great prejudice done to the town and its inhabitants

---

[1] *Blacksoille valley.—La vallee des noirettes.* Noir does indeed signify black; but here *noirettes* means *nucetum*, a plantation of walnut or other nut-trees; and is the same as noisette. The common people of Tours, as well as those of Bourges, Orleans, Paris, and elsewhere, often pronounce R for S, and S for R. True it is, that it was more customary for them to do so formerly than now-a-days. They were wont to say Jerus Maria, for Jesus Maria, and of consequence noirettes for noisettes.

[2] *Burn-hag-field.—*Camp de Brusle-vieille.

Dividing the spoil.

he re-imbursed their charges, and repaired all the
losses that by their confession upon oath could
appear they had sustained; and, for their better
defence and security in times coming against all
sudden uproars and invasions, commanded a strong
citadel to be built there with a competent garrison
to maintain it. At his departure he did very
graciously thank all the soldiers of the brigades that
had been at this overthrow, and sent them back to
their winter-quarters in their several stations, and
garrisons; the decumane legion [3] only excepted, whom
in the field on that day he saw do some great exploit,
and their captains also, whom he brought along with
himself unto Grangousier.

At the sight and coming of them, the good man
was so joyful, that it is not possible fully to describe
it. He made them a feast the most magnificent,
plentiful, and delicious that ever was seen since the
time of the King Ahasuerus. At the taking up of
the table he distributed amongst them his whole cupboard of plate, which weighed eight hundred thousand and fourteen besants of gold, in great antique
vessels, huge pots, large basins, big tasses, cups,
goblets, candlesticks, comfit-boxes, and other such
plate, all of pure massy gold besides the precious
stones, enamelling, and workmanship, which by all
men's estimation was more worth than the matter of
the gold. Then unto every one of them out of his
coffers caused he to be given the sum of twelve
hundred thousand crowns ready money. And,
further, he gave to each of them for ever and in

---

[3] *The decumane legion.*—After the example of the tenth legion
in Julius Cæsar's army. It is manifest from Cæsar's own
account of the Gallic wars, l. 1, from Dion. n. 38, and Frontinus'
Stratag. xi. that that legion always performed better than any
other of the same army.

perpetuity, unless he should happen to decease without heirs, such castles and neighbouring lands of his as were most commodious for them. To Ponocrates he gave the rock Clermond; to Gymnast, the Coudray; to Eudemon, Monpensier; Rivau, to Tolmere; to Ithibolle, Montsaureau; to Acamus, Cande; Varenes, to Chironacte; Gravot, to Sebaste; Quinquenais, to Alexander; Ligre, to Sophrone; and so of his other places.

CHAPTER LII

HOW GARGANTUA CAUSED TO BE BUILT FOR THE MONK THE ABBEY OF THELEME

THERE was left only the monk to provide for, whom Gargantua would have made Abbot of Sevillé, but he refused it. He would have given him the Abbey of Bourgueil, or of Sanct Florent, which was better, or both, if it pleased him; but the monk gave him a very peremptory answer, that he would never take upon him the charge nor government of monks. For how shall I be able, said he, to rule over others, that have not full power and command of myself?[1] If

[1] *That have not full power and command of myself.*—Carried away by the evil customs of the times, Gargantua was going to commit two very considerable faults in offering two rich abbeys to Friar John, who was not of an age nor of morals regular enough to be fit for, or deserve either of them, much less both. But to excuse his not accepting his prince's offer, the monk, who prefers his liberty to all advantages whatever, represents to him, that, not knowing how to govern himself, he was much less able to govern others, which answers to the sense of the law, 'absurdum quippe est, ut alios regat, qui se ipsum regere nescit,' quoted on this very subject by John, bishop of Chiemsée, suffragan of Saltzburg, in ch. 27, n. 7, of his Onus Ecclesiæ.

you think I have done you, or may hereafter do you
any acceptable service, give me leave to found an
abbey after my own mind and fancy. The motion
pleased Gargantua very well, who thereupon offered
him all the country of Theleme by the river of Loire,
till within two leagues of the great forest of Port-
Huaut. The monk then requested Gargantua to
institute his religious order contrary to all others.
First then, said Gargantua, you must not build a wall
about your convent, for all our abbeys are strongly
walled and mured about. See, said the monk, and
not without cause,[2] where there is mur before and
mur behind, there is store of murmur, envy, and
mutual conspiracy. Moreover, seeing there are
certain convents in the world,[3] whereof the custom
is, if any women come in, I mean chaste and honest
women, they immediately sweep the ground which
they have trod upon; therefore was it ordained, that
if any man or woman, entered into religious orders,
should by chance come within this new abbey,
all the rooms should be thoroughly washed and
cleansed through which they had passed. And
because in all other monasteries and nunneries all is
compassed, limited, and regulated by hours, it was
decreed that in this new structure there should be
neither clock nor dial, but that according to the
opportunities, and incident occasions, all their hours [4]

[2] *See, said the monk, and not without cause.*—Very true, said the
monk, and not without cause, for (speaking of abbeys being always
well walled) where there is mur (a wall) before, and mur behind,
there is store of murmur (murmuring), etc. Which last is as
true as the first; the more shame for those that live in them, and
are so well provided for, as they generally are.

[3] *Certain convents in the world.*—The Carthusians. Peter Viret,
Of True and False Religion, l. 6, c. 6.

[4] *All their hours, etc.*—What's the meaning of this ? It should
be all their works, not all their hours; 'Toutes les œuvres,' not
' toutes les heures.'

should be disposed of; for, said Gargantua, the greatest loss of time that I know, is to count the hours.[5] What good comes of it? Nor can there be any greater dotage in the world than for one to guide and direct his courses by the sound of a bell, and not by his own judgment and discretion.

Item, Because at that time they put no women into nunneries, but such as were either purblind, blinkards, lame, crooked, ill-favoured, mis-shapen, fools, senseless, spoiled, or corrupt;[6] nor encloistered any men, but those that were either sickly, subject to defluxions, ill-bred[7] louts, simple sots, or peevish trouble-houses. But to the purpose, said the monk. A woman that is neither fair nor good, to what use serves she? To make a nun of, said Gargantua. Yea, said the monk, to make shirts and smocks. Therefore was it ordained, that into this religious order should be admitted no women that were not fair, well-featured, and of a sweet disposition; nor men that were not comely, personable, and well-conditioned.[8]

Item, Because in the convents of women, men come not but underhand, privily, and by stealth; it was therefore enacted, that in this house there shall be no

[5] *To count the hours.*—Pantagruel lays down the same principle, l. 4, ch. 64, and proves it by several very pleasant arguments. I know a tradesman in London, a great economist, that curses the clocks, for making his apprentices lose so much time in counting the hours.

[6] *Purblind, blinkards, lame, crooked, etc.*—This was one of the abuses of those times, if we believe the author of the Onus Ecclesiæ, in ch. 22, art. 8.

[7] *Ill-bred.*—*Mal-nez,* which I take to mean ill-conditioned, of an ungentle nature, or perverse disposition. See next note.

[8] *Well-conditioned.*—Or of a sweet disposition; *bien naturez,* i.e., as M. le Duchat observes, *benè nati, d'un beau naturel.* The reverse of the *mal-nez,* mentioned in the last note.

women in case there be not men, nor men in case there be not women.

Item, Because both men and women, that are received into religious orders, after the expiring of their noviciat or probation year were constrained and forced perpetually to stay there all the days of their life; it was therefore ordered, that all whatever, men or women, admitted within this abbey, should have full leave to depart with peace and contentment, whensoever it should seem good to them so to do.

Item, For that the religious men and women did ordinarily make three vows, to wit, those of chastity, poverty, and obedience; it was therefore constituted and appointed, that in this convent they might be honourably married, that they might be rich, and live at liberty. In regard of the legitimate time of the persons to be initiated, and years under and above which they were not capable of reception, the women were to be admitted from ten till fifteen, and the men from twelve till eighteen.

CHAPTER LIII

HOW THE ABBEY OF THE THELEMITES WAS BUILT AND ENDOWED

For the fabric and furniture of the abbey, Gargantua caused to be delivered out in ready money seven and twenty hundred thousand, eight hundred and one and thirty of those golden rams of Berry,[1] which have a

---

[1] *Golden rams, etc.*—Rabelais says, 'Moutons à la grande laine,' long-woolled sheep; a gold coin so called because of a lamb engraved on it, with these words round it, 'Agnus Dei qui tollis,' etc. They afterwards coined demi-moutons, which, being no

sheep stamped on the one side, and a flowered cross
on the other; and for every year until the whole
work were completed, he allotted threescore nine
thousand crowns of the sun, and as many of the
seven stars, to be charged all upon the receipt of the
custom.[2] For the foundation and maintenance
thereof for ever, he settled a perpetual fee-farm-rent
of three and twenty hundred, threescore and nine
thousand, five hundred and fourteen rose nobles,
exempted from all homage, fealty, service, or burden
whatsoever, and payable every year at the gate of the
abbey; and of this, by letters patent passed a very
good grant. The architecture was in a figure
hexagonal, and in such a fashion, that in every one
of the six corners there was built a great round tower
of threescore feet in diameter, and were all of a like
form and bigness. Upon the north side ran along

more than half the value of the other, were for that reason called
'Moutons à la petite laine,' short-woolled sheep.
   [2] *Upon the receipt of the custom.*—Here Sir T. U. and, which is
more surprising, M. Motteux, mistakes the word *dive* to mean
douanne; a river called Dive for a custom-house. Rabelais says,
'Sus la recepte de la Dive,' *i.e.*, upon the receipt of the Dive;
which I confess I did not readily take for a river, till I looked
into Moreri's Dictionary (for neither Duchat nor the Dutch
scholiast take the least notice of the word *dive*). That Dictionary, under the word *la dive*, gives an account of two rivers of
that name, in Latin Diva et Deva; one in Normandy, the other,
which I take to be that here meant, is in Poitou. Moreri gives a
pretty curious account of it, and of the Huguenots being defeated
in an engagement on the banks of it, in 1569, and other particulars too long to be taken notice of here. But after all, the
English reader will ask what Rabelais can mean by charging a
rent upon the receipt of a Dive; in answer to which I may say,
perhaps there are duties payable for goods passing to and fro on
that river: but M. le Duchat resolves it into a joke, by saying,
that it is a common thing in France, by way of banter, to assign
a rent-charge upon the vapours or fogs of the rivers Seine, Loire,
etc. Effects, add they, very liquid, but not over clear.

the river of Loire, on the bank whereof was situated
the tower called Arctic. Going towards the east,
there was another called Calaer,—the next following
Anatole,—the next Mesembrine,—the next Hesperia,
and the last Criere. Every tower was distant from
the other the space of three hundred and twelve
paces. The whole edifice was everywhere six
storeys high, reckoning the cellars under ground for
one. The second was arched after the fashion of a
basket-handle, the rest were ceiled with pure wains-
cot, flourished with Flanders fretwork, in the form of
the foot of a lamp, and covered above with fine
slates, with an indorsement of lead, carrying the
antique figures of little puppets,[3] and animals of all
sorts, notably well suited to one another, and gilt,
together with the gutters, which jetting without the
walls from betwixt the cross-bars in a diagonal
figure, painted with gold and azure, reached to the
very ground, where they ended into great conduit-
pipes, which carried all away into the river from
under the house.

This same building was a hundred times more
sumptuous and magnificent than ever was Bonnivet,
Chambourg, or Chantilly;[4] for there were in it nine

[3] *Figures of little puppets.*—*Manequins* in the original. It means,
says Duchat, in this place, not puppets, but a certain very common
and pretty ornament in architecture, viz., osier or other baskets
filled with flowers and fruits. Manequin comes from mane,
because such a basket is easy to carry in the hand (manus).
From whence our English word maund, among the market people,
which means a large basket for apples, greens, or the like.
Manequin, says Du Cange, 'arca penaria quæ manu gestatur.'
The latter Greeks call this manequin Μανίσκιον. The word
manequin is now extended to all sorts of baskets.

[4] *Bonnivet, Chambourg, or Chantilly.*—The edition of 1535, and
that of Dolet, speak only of Bonnivet, a castle or palace begun on
a magnificent plan in sight of Chatteleraut, by Admiral Bonnivet,
who did not live to finish it, being killed at the battle of Pavia.

thousand three hundred and two and thirty chambers, every one whereof had a withdrawing room, a handsome closet, a wardrobe, an oratory, and neat passage, leading into a great and spacious hall. Between every tower, in the midst of the said body of building, there was a pair of winding, such as we now call lanthorn stairs, whereof the steps were part of porphyry, which is a dark red marble, spotted with white, part of Numidian stone, which is a kind of yellowishly-streaked marble upon various colours, and part of serpentine marble, with light spots on a dark green ground, each of those steps being two and twenty feet in length, and three fingers thick, and the just number of twelve betwixt every rest, or, as we now term it, landing-place. In every resting-place were two fair antique arches where the light came in: and by those they went into a cabinet, made even with, and of the breadth of the said winding, and the re-ascending above the roofs of the house ending conically in a pavilion. By that vize or winding, they entered on every side into a great hall, and from the halls into the chambers. From the Arctic tower unto the Criere, were the fair great libraries in Greek, Latin, Hebrew, French, Italian, and Spanish, respectively distributed in their several cantons, according to the diversity of these languages. In the midst there was a wonderful scalier or winding-stair, the entry whereof was without the house, in a vault or arch, six fathoms broad. It was made in such symmetry and largeness, that six men at arms with their lances in their rests might together in a breast ride all up to

See Brantôme, tome i., p. 203. As for Chambourg, or rather Chambort (where King Stanislaus lately resided), which is likewise unfinished, it was begun by Francis I. in 1536. See Brantôme, p. 275 of tome i.

the very top of all the palace. From ·the tower Anatole to the Mesembrine were fair spacious galleries, all covered over and painted with the ancient prowesses, histories, and descriptions of the world. In the midst thereof there was likewise such another ascent and gate, as we said there was on the river-ride. Upon that gate was written in great antique letters that which followeth.

CHAPTER LIV

THE INSCRIPTION SET UPON THE GREAT GATE OF THELEME

Here enter not vile bigots, hypocrites,
Externally devoted apes, base snites,
Puft-up, wry-necked beasts, worse than the Huns,
Or Ostrogots, fore-runners of baboons:[1]

[1] *Fore-runners of baboons.*—I know not what Sir T. U. means by fore-runners of baboons. It should be Ye wrinkled old baboons, *Vieulx matagotz.* M. le Duchat observes, that in this strophe (or stanza) in which the author's satire falls particularly on all sorts of religions, viz., monks, and others, given up to what they call a contemplative life, under the name of matagots, which is but magots lengthened out, and which means a sort of very large monkey, Rabelais points at the oldest among the monks. Before in chap. 40, with respect to the idle, slothful life of the monks, he compares them to monkeys; and lower, in chap. 60, l. 4, he actually calls them matagots, when like so many noddies (Μάταιος, *ineptus*) he sends them to consider of, philosophise upon, and to contemplate the close-stool-pan of Gaster, Greek for belly, whom he supposes to be the idol of monks, and other slow-bellies. [Ozell's difficulty may be surmounted without much trouble. The original verses are as follow :—

'Cy n'entrez pas, hypocrites, bigotz,
Vieux matagotz, marmiteux boursouflés,
Torcoulx, badaulx, plus que n'estoyent les Gotz,
Ny Ostrogotz, precurseurs des magotz,' etc.

311

Cursed snakes, dissembling varlets,[2] seeming sancts,
Slipshop caffards, beggars pretending wants,
Fat chuffcats, smell-feast knockers, doltish gulls,
Out-strouting cluster-fists, contentious bulls,
Fomenters of divisions and debates,
Elsewhere, not here, make sale of your deceits.
    Your filthy trumperies
    Stuffed with pernicious lies
      (Not worth a bubble),
      Would only trouble
    Our earthly paradise,
    Your filthy trumperies.

Here enter not attorneys, barristers,
Nor bridle-champing law-practitioners;
Clerks, commissaries, scribes, nor pharisees,
Wilful disturbers of the people's ease:
Judges, destroyers, with an unjust breath,
Of honest men, like dogs ev'n unto death.
Your salary is at the gibbet-foot:
Go drink there! for we do not here fly out
On these excessive courses, which may draw
A waiting on your courts by suits in law.

Rabelais calls the monks 'old apes' (*Vieux matagotz*, or *magotz*, an epithet which Leroux defines as *Mot injurieux qu'on dit à quelqu'un qu'on querelle*), and goes on, in a strain of grotesque exaggeration, to say that they possess more evil qualities than distinguished even the Goths and Ostrogoths, who were their forerunners as scourges of the human race. An ape has ever been the symbol of malicious mischief, and an old ape is its quintessence.]

    [2] *Dissembling varlets.*—This should be varlets with mittens, *gueux mitouflez*. Mendicants, who, though not allowed to wear gloves at any time of the year, may, in the depth of a rigorous winter, wear mittens of black cloth, or at least of a smoke-dried colour.

Law-suits, debates, and wrangling
Hence are exil'd, and jangling.
  Here we are very
  Frolic and merry,
And free from all entangling,
Law-suits, debates, and wrangling.

Here enter not base pinching usurers,
Pelf-lickers, everlasting gatherers,
Gold-graspers, coin-gripers, gulpers of mists,
With harpy-griping claws, who, though your chests
Vast sums of money should to you afford,
Would ne'ertheless add more unto that hoard,
And yet not be content,—you clunchfists dastards,
Insatiable fiends, and Pluto's bastards,
Greedy devourers, chichy sneakbill rogues,
Hell-mastiffs gnaw your bones, your rav'nous dogs.
  You beastly-looking fellows,
  Reason doth plainly tell us,
    That we should not
    To you allot
  Room here, but at the gallows,
  You beastly-looking fellows.

Here enter not fond makers of demurs
In love adventures, peevish jealous curs,
Sad pensive dotards, raisers of garboyles,
Hags, goblins, ghosts, firebrands of household broils,
Nor drunkards, liars, cowards, cheaters, clowns,
Thieves, cannibals, faces o'ercast with frowns,
Nor lazy slugs, envious, covetous,
Nor blockish, cruel, nor too credulous,—
Here mangy, pocky folks shall have no place,
No ugly lusks, nor persons of disgrace.
  Grace, honour, praise, delight,
  Here sojourn day and night.

Sound bodies lin'd
With a good mind,
Do here pursue with might
Grace, honour, praise, delight.

Here enter you, and welcome from our hearts,
All noble sparks, endow'd with gallant parts.
This is the glorious place which bravely shall
Afford wherewith to entertain you all.
Were you a thousand, here you shall not want
For any thing: for what you'll ask we'll grant.
Stay here you, lively, jovial, handsome, brisk,
Gay, witty, frolic, cheerful, merry, frisk,
Spruce, jocund, courteous, furtherers of trades,
And in a word, all worthy, gentle blades.
  Blades of heroic breasts
  Shall taste here of the feasts,
   Both privily
   And civilly,
  Of the celestial guests,
  Blades of heroic breasts.

Here enter you, pure, honest, faithful, true,
Expounders of the Scriptures old and new.
Whose glosses do not blind our reason, but
Make it to see the clearer, and who shut
Its passages from hatred, avarice,
Pride, factions, covenants, and all sort of vice.
Come, settle here a charitable faith,
Which neighbourly affection nourisheth.
And whose light chaseth all corrupters hence,
Of the blest word, from the aforesaid sense.
  The Holy Sacred Word,
  May it always afford
   T' us all in common,
   Both man and woman,

A spiritual shield and sword,
The Holy Sacred Word.

Here enter you all ladies of high birth,
Delicious, stately, charming, full of mirth,
Ingenious, lovely, miniard, proper, fair,
Magnetic, graceful, splendid, pleasant, rare,
Obliging, sprightly, virtuous, young, solacious,
Kind, neat, quick, feat, bright, compt, ripe, choice,
    dear, precious,
Alluring, courtly, comely, fine, complete,
Wise, personable, ravishing and sweet,
Come joys enjoy. The Lord celestial
Hath given enough, wherewith to please us all.
    Gold give us, God forgive us,
    And from all woes relieve us;
        That we the treasure
        May reap of pleasure,
    And shun whate'er is grievous,
    Gold give us, God forgive us.

CHAPTER LV

WHAT MANNER OF DWELLING THE THELEMITES HAD

In the middle of the lower court there was a stately
fountain of fair alabaster. Upon the top thereof
stood the three Graces, with their cornucopias, or
horns of abundance, and did jet out the water at
their breasts, mouth, ears, eyes, and other open
passages of the body. The inside of the buildings
in this lower court stood upon great pillars of Cassy-
dony stone, and Porphyry marble, made archwise
after a goodly antique fashion. Within those were
spacious galleries, long and large, adorned with

315

curious pictures, the horns of bucks and unicorns; with rhinoceroses, water-horses, called hippopotames; the teeth and tusks of elephants, and other things well worth the beholding. The lodging of the ladies, for so we may call those gallant women, took up all from the tower Arctic unto the gate Mesembrine. The men possessed the rest. Before the said lodging of the ladies, that they might have their recreation, between the two first towers, on the outside, were placed the tilt-yard, the barriers or lists for tournaments, the hippodrome or riding court, the theatre or public play-house, and natatory or place to swim in, with most admirable baths in three stages,[1] situated above one another, well furnished with all necessary accommodation, and store of myrtle-water. By the river-side was the fair garden of pleasure, and in the midst of that the glorious labyrinth. Between the two other towers were the courts for the tennis and the baloon.[2] Towards the tower Criere stood the orchard full of all fruit trees, set and ranged in a quincuncial order. At the end of that was the great park, abounding with all sort of venison. Betwixt the third couple of towers were the butts and marks for shooting with a snap-work gun, an ordinary bow for common archery, or with a cross-bow. The office-houses were without the tower Hesperia, of one story high. The stables were beyond the offices, and before them stood the falconry, managed by ostrich-keepers and falconers, very expert in the art, and it was yearly supplied and furnished by the

---

[1] *In three stages.*—That is in three stories: on one was a hot bath; on another, a lukewarm bath; and on the third, one quite cold, into each of which, by means of pipes, the water was distributed just as they would have it.
[2] *Baloon.*—A game played with a large hand-ball filled with air, derived from the Romans.

Candians, Venetians, Sarmates, now called Mos-
coviters, with all sorts of most excellent hawks, eagles,
gerfalcons, goshawks, sacres, lanners, falcons, spar-
hawks, marlins, and other kinds of them, so gentle
and perfectly well-manned, that, flying of themselves
sometimes from the castle for their own disport, they
would not fail to catch whatever they encountered.
The venery, where the beagles and hounds were
kept, was a little farther off, drawing towards the
park.

All the halls, chambers, and closets or cabinets were
richly hung with tapestry, and hangings of divers
sorts, according to the variety of the seasons of the
year. All the pavements and floors were covered
with green cloth. The beds are all embroidered.
In every back-chamber or withdrawing room there
was a looking-glass of pure crystal set in a frame of
fine gold, garnished all about with pearls, and was of
such greatness, that it would represent to the full
the whole lineaments and proportion of the person
that stood before it. At the going out of the halls,
which belong to the ladies' lodging, were the per-
fumers and trimmers, through whose hands the
gallants past when they were to visit the ladies.
Those sweet artificers did every morning furnish the
ladies' chambers with the spirit of roses, orange
flower water,[3] and angelica; and to each of them
gave a little precious casket vapouring forth the
most odoriferous exhalations of the choicest aromatical scents.

[3] *Orange flower water.*—It is in the original *eau de naphe*, on
which M. le Duchat observes, that Franciosini, at the word *nanfa*,
confounds the *eau de naphe* with orange flower water. But
Boccace, in Journ. 8, Nov. 10, of his Decameron, makes two
different sorts of them, on which see Ruscelli in his edition of the
Decameron. Torriano says, *nanfa* is a mixture of musk and
orange flowers.

CHAPTER LVI

HOW THE MEN AND WOMEN OF THE RELIGIOUS ORDER OF THELEME WERE APPARELLED

THE ladies of the foundation of this order were apparelled after their own pleasure and liking. But, since that of their own accord and free will they have reformed themselves, their accoutrement is in manner as followeth. They wore stockings of scarlet crimson, or ingrained purple dye, which reached just three inches above the knee, having a list beautified with exquisite embroideries, and rare incisions of the cutter's art. Their garters were of the colour of their bracelets, and circled the knee a little both over and under. Their shoes, pumps, and slippers were either of red, violet, or crimson velvet, pinked and jagged like lobster wadles.

Next to their smock they put on the pretty kirtle or vasquin of pure silk camblet : above that went the taffaty or tabby vardingale, of white, red, tawny, grey, or of any other colour. Above this taffaty petti-coat they had another of cloth of tissue, or brocade, embroidered with fine gold, and interlaced with needlework, or as they thought good, and according to the temperature and disposition of the weather, had their upper coats of satin, damask, or velvet, and those either orange, tawny, green, ash-coloured, blue, yellow, bright red, crimson, or white, and so forth; or had them of cloth of gold, cloth of silver, or some other choice stuff, enriched with purple, or embroidered according to the dignity of the festival days and times wherein they wore them.

Their gowns, being still correspondent to the season, were either of cloth of gold frizzled with a

318

silver-raised work; of red satin, covered with gold
purl; of tabby, or taffaty, white, blue, black, tawny,
etc., of silk serge, silk camblet, velvet, cloth of silver,
silver tissue, cloth of gold, gold wire, figured velvet,
or figured satin, tinselled and overcast with golden
threads, in divers variously purfled draughts.

In the summer, some days, instead of gowns, they
wore light handsome mantles, made either of the
stuff of the aforesaid attire, or like Moresco rugs,
of violet velvet frizzled, with a raised work of
gold upon silver purl, or with a knotted cord-work
of gold embroidery, everywhere garnished with little
Indian pearls. They always carried a fair panache,
or plume of feathers, of the colour of their muff,
bravely adorned and tricked out with glistering
spangles of gold. In the winter time they had their
taffaty gowns of all colours, as above named, and
those lined with the rich furrings of hind-wolves, or
speckled linxes, black spotted weasels, martlet skins
of Calabria, sables, and other costly furs of an inestimable value. Their beads, rings, bracelets,
collars, carcanets, and neck-chains were all of
precious stones, such as carbuncles, rubies, baleus,
diamonds, sapphires, emeralds, turquoises, garnets,
agates, beryles, and excellent margarites. Their
head-dressing also varied with the season of the year,
according to which they decked themselves. In
winter it was of the French fashion; in the spring,
of the Spanish; in summer, of the fashion of Tus-
cany, except only upon the holy days and Sundays,
at which times they were accoutred in the French
mode, because they accounted it more honourable
and better befitting the garb of a matronal pudicity.

The men were apparelled after their fashion.
Their stockings were of tamine or of cloth-serge, of
white, black, scarlet, or some other ingrained colour.

Their breeches were of velvet, of the same colour
with their stockings, or very near, embroidered and
cut according to their fancy. Their doublet was of
cloth of gold, of cloth of silver, of velvet, satin,
damask, taffaties, etc., of the same colours, cut, embroidered, and suitably trimmed up in perfection.
The points were of silk of the same colours, the tags
were of gold well enamelled. Their coats and
jerkins were of cloth of gold, cloth of silver, gold
tissue or velvet embroidered, as they thought fit. ·
Their gowns were every whit as costly as those of
the ladies. Their girdles were of silk, of the colour
of their doublets. Every one had a gallant sword by
his side, the hilt and handle whereof were gilt, and
the scabbard of velvet, of the colour of his breeches,
with a chape of gold, and pure goldsmith's work.
The dagger of the same. Their caps or bonnets
of black velvet, adorned with jewels and buttons of
gold. Upon that they wore a white plume, most
prettily and minion-like parted by so many rows of
gold spangles, at the end whereof hung dangling in
a more sparkling resplendency fair rubies, emeralds,
diamonds, etc.; but there was such a sympathy
betwixt the gallants and the ladies, that every day
they were apparelled in the same livery. And that
they might not miss, there were certain gentlemen
appointed to tell the youths every morning what
vestments the ladies would on that day wear; for all
was done according to the pleasure of the ladies. In
these so handsome clothes, and habiliments so rich,
think not that either one or other of either sex did
waste any time at all; for the masters of the ward-
robes had all their raiments and apparel so ready for
every morning, and the chamber-ladies were so well
skilled, that in a trice they would be dressed, and
completely in their clothes from head to foot. And,

to have those accoutrements with the more con-
veniency, there was about the wood of Theleme, a
row of houses of the extent of half a league, very
neat and cleanly, wherein dwelt the goldsmiths,
lapidaries, jewellers, embroiderers, tailors, gold-
drawers, velvet-weavers, tapestry-makers, and upholsterers, who wrought there every one in his own
trade, and all for the aforesaid jolly friars and nuns
of the new stamp. They were furnished with matter
and stuff from the hands of the Lord Nausiclete,[1]
who every year brought them seven ships from the
Perlas and Cannibal Islands, laden with ingots of
gold, with raw silk, with pearls and precious stones.
And if any margarites, called unions [pearls], began
to grow old, and lose somewhat of their natural
whiteness and lustre, those by their art they did
renew,[2] by tendering them to eat to some pretty
cocks, as they use to give casting unto hawks.

[1] *Lord Nausiclete.*—Seigneur Nausiclete. Seigneur means only
Sire, which in French is the general appellation of a rich
merchant, or a great wholesale dealer. As for the word
Nausiclete, the old Dutch scholiast says, Nausiclete comes from
Ναυσίκλυτος, which, adds he, signifies one that is renowned for
having a multitude of ships.

[2] *Those by their art they did renew, etc.*—We see here that even
in Rabelais' time, the art of re-blanching, or making tarnished
pearls look white, was no secret in France; and yet in Henry the
Great's time an Italian, one Tontuchio, who likewise made
counterfeit pearls to a great degree of perfection, was accounted
the inventor of the secret of whitening again the true pearls when
they began to turn yellow.

CHAPTER LVII

HOW THE THELEMITES WERE GOVERNED, AND OF THEIR MANNER OF LIVING

ALL their life was spent not in laws, statutes, or rules, but according to their own free will and pleasure. They rose out of their beds when they thought good: they did eat, drink, labour, sleep, when they had a mind to it, and were disposed for it. None did awake them, none did offer to constrain them to eat, drink, nor to do any other thing; for so had Gargantua established it. In all their rule, and strictest tie of their order, there was but this one clause to be observed,

DO WHAT THOU WILT.

Because men that are free, well-born, well-bred, and conversant in honest companies, have naturally an instinct and spur that prompteth them unto virtuous actions, and withdraws them from vice, which is called honour. Those same men, when by base subjection and constraint they are brought under and kept down, turn aside from that noble disposition, by which they formerly were inclined to virtue, to shake off and break that bond of servitude, wherein they are so tyrannously enslaved; for it is agreeable with the nature of man to long after things forbidden, and to desire what is denied us.

By this liberty they entered into a very laudable emulation, to do all of them what they saw did please one. If any of the gallants or ladies should say, Let us drink, they would all drink. If any one of them said, Let us play, they all played. If one said, Let us go a-walking into the fields, they went

all. If it were to go a-hawking or a-hunting, the
ladies mounted upon dainty well-paced nags, seated
in a stately palfrey saddle,[1] carried on their lovely
fists,[2] miniardly begloved every one of them, either
a sparhawk, or a laneret, or a merlin, and the young
gallants carried the other kinds of hawks. So nobly
were they taught, that there was neither he nor she
amongst them, but could read, write, sing, play upon
several musical instruments, speak five or six several
languages, and compose in them all very quaintly,
both in verse and prose. Never were seen so valiant
knights, so noble and worthy, so dextrous and skilful
both on foot and a-horseback, more brisk and lively,
more nimble and quick, or better handling all
manner of weapons than were there. Never were
seen ladies so proper and handsome, so miniard and
dainty, less forward, or more ready with their hand,
and with their needle, in every honest and free
action belonging to that sex, than were there. For
this reason, when the time came, that any man of
the said abbey, either at the request of his parents,
or for some other cause, had a mind to go out of it,
he carried along with him one of the ladies, namely
her whom he had before that chosen for his mistress,[3]
and they were married together. And if they had

---

[1] *Seated in a stately palfrey saddle.*—This is not the meaning of
'avecques leur palefroy guorrior;' it means followed by horses of
parade, their stately palfreys.

[2] *Their lovely fists.*—Rabelais says, only fists, without any
epithet; sur le poing. The ladies' lovely fists put me in mind of
the addresses from Corporations in Queen Anne's time, 'Madam,
we kiss your great hand.'

[3] *Namely her whom he had before that chosen for his mistress.*—
Quite contrary. Read, namely her who had before that chosen
him for her humble servant: '*Celle laquelle l'auroy prins pour son
devot, i.e.,* Her who had consented that he should devote himself to her service on the footing of a declared lover.

formerly in Theleme lived in good devotion and amity, they did continue therein and increase it to a greater height in their state of matrimony: and did entertain that mutual love till the very last day of their life, in no less vigour and fervency, than at the very day of their wedding.[4]

Here must not I forget to set down unto you a riddle, which was found under the ground, as they were laying the foundation of the abbey, engraven in a copper plate, and it was thus as followeth.

CHAPTER LVIII

A PROPHETICAL RIDDLE

POOR mortals, who wait for a happy day,
Cheer up your hearts, and hear what I shall say:
If it be lawful firmly to believe
That the celestial bodies can us give

[4] The Abbé de Marsy conjectures, that Rabelais, under the pretext of this foundation, attacks indirectly the three vows which constituted the essence of every monastic society. This institution, founded on the principles of reason and natural religion, is in effect a censure on monastic vows. The modern editors of Rabelais conceive such an establishment especially worthy of Friar John, in whose actions they continually recognise Cardinal Jean du Bellay, who setting aside his poetical and martial talents, was like most other men of his robe in that age, a gourmand, a lover of wine, of pleasure, and above all of women, and who at the same time was secretly married. It appears evident to them that this famous convent represents the *maison de plaisance* built by the Cardinal, on the neck of land connecting la Marne to Saint-Maur-des-Fosses; Rabelais lived at St Maur, previous to his nomination to the cure of Meudon.

Wisdom to judge of things that are not yet;
Or if from heaven such wisdom we may get,
As may with confidence make us discourse
Of years to come, their destiny and course;
I to my hearers give to understand,
That this next winter, though it be at hand,
Yea and before, there shall appear a race
Of men, who, loth to sit still in one place,
Shall boldly go before all people's eyes,
Suborning men of divers qualities,
To draw them unto covenants and sides,
In such a manner, that whate'er betides,
They'll move you, if you give them ear, no doubt,
With both your friends and kindred to fall out.
They'll make a vassal to gain-stand his lord,
And children their own parents; in a word,
All reverence shall then be banished,
No true respect to other shall be had.
They'll say that every man should have his turn,
Both in his going forth and his return;
And hereupon there shall arise such woes,
Such jarrings, and confused to's and fro's,
That never was in history such coils
Set down as yet, such tumults and garboyles.
Then shall you many gallant men see by
Valour stirr'd up, and youthful fervency,
Who, trusting too much in their hopeful time,
Live but a while, and perish in their prime.
Neither shall any, who this course shall run,
Leave off the race which he hath once begun,
Till they the heavens with noise by their conten-
   tion
Have fill'd, and with their steps the earth's dimen-
   sion.
Then those shall have no less authority,
That have no faith, than those that will not lie;

For all [men] shall be governed by a rude,
Base, ignorant, and foolish multitude;
The veriest lout of all shall be their judge,
O horrible and dangerous deluge!
Deluge I call it, and that for good reason,
For this shall be omitted in no season;
Nor shall the earth of this foul stir be free,
Till suddenly you in great store shall see
The waters issue out, with whose streams the
Most moderate of all shall moisten'd be,
And justly too; because they did not spare
The flocks of beasts that innocentest are,
But did their sinews, and their bowels take,
Not to the gods a sacrifice to make,
But usually to serve themselves for sport.
And now consider, I do you exhort,
In such commotions so continual,
What rest can take the globe terrestrial?
Most happy then are they, that can it hold,
And use it carefully as precious gold,
By keeping it in gaol, whence it shall have
No help but him, who being to it gave.
And to increase his mournful accident,
The sun, before it set in th' occident,
Shall cease to dart upon it any light,
More than in an eclipse, or in the night,—
So that at once its favour shall be gone
And liberty with it be left alone.
And yet, before it come to ruin thus,
Its quaking shall be as impetuous
As Ætna's was, when Titan's sons lay under,
And yield, when lost, a fearful sound like thunder.
Inarimé did not more quickly move,
When Typheus did the vast huge hills remove,
And for despite into the sea them threw.
    Thus shall it then be lost by ways not few,

And changed suddenly, when those that have it
To other men that after come shall leave it.
Then shall it be high time to cease from this
So long, so great, so tedious exercise;
For the great waters told you now by me,
Will make each think where his retreat shall be;
And yet, before that they be clean disperst,
You may behold in th' air, where nought was erst,
The burning heat of a great flame to rise,
Lick up the water, and the enterprise.
    It resteth after those things to declare,
That those shall sit content, who chosen are,
With all good things, and with celestial manne,
And richly recompensed every man:
The others at the last all stripp'd shall be,
That after this great work all men may see
How each shall have his due.   This is their lot;
O he is worthy praise that shrinketh not.

No sooner was this enigmatical monument read
over, but Gargantua, fetching a very deep sigh, said
unto those that stood by, It is not now only, I
perceive, that people called to the faith of the
gospel, and convinced with the certainty of evangelical truths, are persecuted.   But happy is that
man that shall not be scandalized, but shall always
continue to the end, in aiming at that mark, which
God by his dear Son hath set before us, without
being distracted or diverted by his carnal affections
and depraved nature.
    The monk then said, What do you think in your
conscience is meant and signified by this riddle?
What? said Gargantua,—the progress and carrying
on of the divine truth.   By St Goderan,[1] said the

---

[1] *St Goderan.*—There is a St Goderanc, Bishop of Seez,

monk, that is not my exposition. It is the style of
the prophet Merlin.² Make upon it as many grave
allegories and glosses as you will, and dote upon it
you and the rest of the world as long as you please;
for my part, I can conceive no other meaning in it,
but a description of a set at tennis in dark and
obscure terms. The suborners of men are the
makers of matches, which are commonly friends.
After the two chases are made, he that was in the
upper end of the tennis-court goeth out, and the
other cometh in. They believe the first, that saith
the ball was over or under the line. The waters
are the heats that the players take till they sweat
again. The cords of the rackets are made of the

brother of St Opportunus, massacred by an emissary of Chrode-
bert, who had invaded the possessions of the church.
    ² *It is the style of the prophet Merlin.*—Rabelais means Merlin
de Saint Gelais, who died in 1555, sixty-seven years old. This
poet's Christian name was generally written Melin; many have
writ it Mellin, in imitation of those who in Latin have it
Mellinus: yet there is no such saint as either Melin or Mellin.
Longueil is perhaps the first that, by allusion to Merlin, has
called St Gelais, Merlinus Gelasianus : Marot afterwards called
him Merlin, in his Eclogue to the king, and in a translation
(which he addresses to him) of Martial's 9th epigram, l. 3.
John Bouchet also calls him Merlin, in the 100th epistle,
written to the Abbot Ardillon in October, 1536.
    Under a supposition that these verses are a sort of prophecy,
one would be apt to think Friar John meant to ascribe it
to the English Merlin, famous about the year 500, for prophecies printed in folio, at Paris, in 1498; but that is far from
being the case, except as to the style of the enigma, which is
indeed mysterious; for as to the piece itself the monk was the
better able to give the explanation of, as he had met with it in
the works of the poet Melin de St Gelais, his contemporary ; it
was actually that poet who wrote it, except the two first, and
the last ten verses, which are Rabelais' own; and that's the
reason why they are diversely read, according as the author
thought fit to alter them in the different editions that were
made of the first book of his romance.

guts of sheep or goats. The globe terrestrial is the tennis-ball. After playing when the game is done, they refresh themselves before a clear fire, and change their shirts; and very willingly they make all good cheer, but most merrily those that have gained. And so, farewell.[3]

[3] *And so, farewell.*—The conclusion of the first Book is a chef-d'œuvre still more ingenious than the masterpiece of subterfuge at the commencement. In an age when men were sent to the stake for an unguarded expression, Rabelais dared not only to publish this enigma, but also to make Gargantua exclaim, after it had been read, fetching a very deep sigh, 'It is not now only, I perceive, that people called to the faith of the gospel, and convinced with the certainty of evangelical truths, are persecuted.' The monk then demands from him what he thinks is meant by the enigma, and Gargantua makes answer, 'The progress and carrying on of the divine truth.' See how grave he is, when he smells the fire; but here one must needs admire the wit of the author in enveloping with ingenious badinage the most hardy verities. Friar John cries out àpropos; 'By Sanct Goderan, that is not my exposition. Make upon it as many grave allegories and glosses as you will; for my part, I can conceive no other meaning in it, but a description of a set at tennis, couched in dark and obscure terms;' and proceeds to develop this idea, in a manner as innocuous as it is amusing. This finishes the chapter and the Book; in such wise that Rabelais adding no comments thereto, seems to insinuate to all ill-disposed readers, that by giving similar explanations of his enigmatical romance throughout, they should discover nothing therein save bagatelles, or joyous folastreries.

.

END OF BOOK I.

.

Colston & Coy. Limited. Printers, Edinburgh.

www.ingramcontent.com/pod-product-compliance
Lightning Source LLC
Chambersburg PA
CBHW030912270326
41929CB00008B/673